10

Powerful Love Spells That Work

A Spell Book to Attract Love, Passion and Romance with Witchcraft Magic, Spells and Rituals

BY HAZEL EVERMORE

The Lost Book Project

Published by The Lost Book Project
124 City Road
London, EC1V 2NX. United Kingdom
www.TheLostBookProject.com

ISBN: 978-1-7384637-0-1

Library of Congress Cataloging-in-Publication Data

Names: Evermore, Hazel, author.
Title: 101 Powerful Spells for Baby Witches / Hazel Evermore.
Description: London: The Lost Book Project, 2023
Identifiers: ISBN 978-1-7384637-0-1
Subjects: LCSH Witchcraft. | Magic. | Wicca.
Classification: LCC BF1566 .E96 2023 | DDC 133.4/3—dc23

Cover Design: Luisa

Printed in United Kingdom

First Edition

TABLE OF CONTENTS

CHAPTER 1.

INTRODUCTION

Welcome, dear reader, to a journey of empowerment and enchantment through the mastery of love magic. Whether you're brand new to the world of witchcraft or a seasoned practitioner, this book is an invitation to explore the transformative power of love spells. Within these pages lies a pathway to deepening connections, healing hearts, and discovering the profound magic of love through the use of highly potent, powerful and easy to follow love spells.

Love, in all its forms, is a universal and timeless force that connects us all. It is the heartbeat of our lives, the pulse of our emotions, and the fabric of our relationships. Yet, love can also be complex, challenging, and mystifying. This is where the beauty of love magic comes into play. Love magic is not about manipulation or coercion; instead, it's about aligning with the natural, vibrant energies of love to bring more joy, harmony, and passion into our lives.

In "101 Powerful Love Spells That Work," we delve deep into the world of love magic. This book is created to be your guide and companion in learning how to cast love spells that are not only effective but also ethical and empowering. From the foundational practices of setting intentions and choosing the right ingredients to the art of crafting and casting spells that resonate with your heart's deepest desires, this book covers it all.

As a practitioner of many years, I have accumulated vast knowledge and experience in many forms of magick, and these spells have been crafted from the best. My aim has been to provide you with a comprehensive guide that will walk you through various aspects of love magic.

You'll discover spells that help mend a broken heart, rituals that spark a new romance, and incantations that strengthen the love you already have. We'll also explore the crucial role of self-love and confidence in making any love spell work effectively.

This book is more than just a collection of spells; it's a journey into the heart of what it means to wield the incredible power of love magic responsibly. Together, let us embark on this magical journey, with open hearts and a courageous spirit, we will discover the transformative and universal power of love.

What to Expect?

As you turn each page of "101 Powerful Love Spells That Work," you're embarking on an enlightening path that includes a diverse range of love spells and rituals. This book is designed to be a comprehensive guide, offering you insights into the art of love magic. You'll learn about various types of spells, including those for attracting new love, deepening existing relationships, and enhancing self-love. Alongside these, you'll find rituals that aid in healing from heartbreak, managing unrequited love, and even rekindling lost passion.

This book serves as both an introduction to newcomers and a deepening of knowledge for seasoned practitioners. It is crafted for everyone with an interest in love magic. Whether you are a beginner curious about your first spell or an experienced witch looking to deepen your practice, there's something here for you.

These spells and rituals in this book are from ancient practices, found in various forms across cultures and eras. They are a means of aligning your energy with your intentions in matters of the heart. However, contrary to some common misconceptions, love spells are not about controlling or manipulating others. They are about working with the natural energies of love, attraction, and emotional connection. Ethics and respect for free will are paramount in love magic, and this book is dedicated to upholding these values in every spell and ritual shared.

Ethical considerations are at the heart of this book. We firmly believe that love magic, when practiced with respect and integrity, can be a force for positive change. Therefore, we emphasize the importance of ethical practices in every spell and ritual. Additionally, this book isn't just about casting spells; it's also about personal growth and empowerment. Love magic is a journey of self-discovery, helping you understand your desires, heal past wounds, and embrace a future filled with love and positivity.

Personal Journey

Embarking on my own journey into love magic was a path filled with discovery, introspection, and, most importantly, profound transformation. Like many who find their way to these enchanting practices, my initial curiosity was sparked by a desire to understand the deeper connections in my own life. What started as a tentative exploration soon blossomed into a passionate pursuit of knowledge and skill in the art of love magic. Along the way, I learned that the true essence of this craft lies not in wielding power over others, but in fostering a deeper understanding and harmony within ourselves and our relationships.

Through my journey, I've encountered countless stories of transformation and positivity, a testament to the responsible practice of love magic. I've seen individuals who, through the thoughtful application of love spells, have not only mended strained relationships but also discovered a newfound confidence and self-love. Others have found that these practices opened doors to meaningful connections they had long yearned for. Each story is a unique tapestry woven with threads of hope, resilience, and the power of intention.

In sharing my journey and these spells, my aim is to bridge the gap between the mystical world of love magic and your personal experiences. Whether you seek to heal, to love, or to grow, the pages of this book are an invitation to you to embark on your own magical journey, guided by wisdom, ethics, and a deep respect for the universal force that is love.

How to Use This Book

Navigating through "101 Powerful Love Spells That Work" is an adventure in itself, one where you'll discover a spell or a piece of wisdom on every page that will resonate with your own journey in love and magic. To make the most of this book, here's a little guide on how to approach it, whether you're just beginning your journey or are an experienced practitioner looking to deepen your practice.

For Beginners: If you're new to the world of love magic, I recommend starting at the very beginning. The initial chapters lay the groundwork, offering essential insights into the nature of love spells, ethical considerations, and basic practices. Take your time to understand these foundations, as they will greatly enhance your practice and understanding of the spells that follow. Don't hesitate to revisit these sections as you progress; they are designed to be a continuous source of guidance and inspiration.

For Advanced Practitioners: If you're already experienced in the craft, you might choose to dive straight into the specific spells or sections that pique your interest. However, I encourage you to also explore the chapter on ethical considerations as it provides deeper insights and reflections that should enrich your existing practice. The chapters following the 101 spells may be particularly appealing, offering new perspectives and methods to incorporate into your rituals.

Exploring the Spells: The heart of this book lies in its collection of 101 love spells. Each spell is detailed with clear instructions, intended outcomes, and necessary tools. They range from simple candle spells to more elaborate rituals, allowing you to choose according to your comfort level and needs. For those who wish to deepen their practice, there are also chapters on creating love potions, chants, and advanced techniques, perfect for expanding your magical repertoire.

Personalization: The most powerful magic comes from personal connection and intuition. Feel free to adapt and personalize the spells to suit your journey. Your energy and intention are key to making these spells work for you. As you try out different spells, I encourage you to keep a journal of your experiences. Note down the spells you perform, your feelings before and after, and any changes or outcomes you observe. This reflective practice will not only enhance your understanding of love magic but also serve as a personal record of your magical journey.

Use this book as a map for your exploration of love magic. Let it guide you, inspire you, and occasionally challenge you, as you discover the transformative power of love spells in your life.

CHAPTER 2.

THE FOUNDATIONS OF LOVE MAGIC

Love magic is a specialized branch of magical practices focused on matters of the heart. It encompasses various spells, rituals, and techniques aimed at enhancing, attracting, nurturing, and healing love in all its forms. Unlike other types of magic that might concentrate on fortune, protection, or spiritual growth, love magic is intimately tied to the emotions and relationships that form the core of our human experience. It's about creating balance and harmony in our romantic lives, fostering connections, and addressing the complex emotional landscapes we navigate in love. Love magic operates on the principle of aligning one's personal energy with the energies of love and desire, working in harmony with the universe to manifest one's love-related goals and intentions.

Historical Overview

The practice of love magic is as old as human civilization itself, with its roots deeply embedded in ancient cultures and traditions across the globe. In ancient Egypt, spells and amulets were used to ensure harmony and passion in marriages, while in Greece, rituals were performed in honor of Aphrodite, the goddess of love. The Romans, too, had their love spells, often seeking the guidance of Venus, their own goddess of love.

In medieval Europe, love potions and amulets became popular, with many seeking the services of wise women and men to solve matters of the heart. The Renaissance period saw a flowering of occult knowledge and practices related to love magic, blending pagan traditions with new insights.

Moving across the world, love magic was also a significant part of African, Asian, and Native American spiritual practices. African traditions, for instance, have a rich history of using herbs, roots, and rituals to attract love or secure a partner's affection. In Asian cultures, astrology and numerology have played pivotal roles in matters of love, determining auspicious times for marriages and love ceremonies.

The evolution of love magic over the centuries has been influenced by social, cultural, and religious changes. Today, it continues to thrive, blending ancient wisdom with contemporary practices, reflecting the timeless human quest for love and connection. This historical tapestry of love magic not only enriches our understanding of the craft but also connects us to the countless hearts and souls who have sought love's magic across ages and civilizations.

The Law of Attraction

The Law of Attraction is a fundamental principle in love magic, revolving around the idea that like attracts like. In the context of love magic, this means that the energy you put out into the universe—through your thoughts, emotions, and intentions—directly influences what you attract in your love life. When you focus your energy and attention on positive outcomes and emotions, you are more likely to draw those experiences and people into your life.

Understanding and utilizing the Law of Attraction in love magic begins with clarity of intention. Be clear about what you desire in your love life, whether it's attracting a new partner, enhancing an existing relationship, or cultivating more self-love. Your intentions should be specific and positive. Instead of focusing on what you don't want, center your energy on what you wish to bring into your life.

Your emotional state plays a crucial role in the Law of Attraction. Emotions like joy, passion, and gratitude are powerful attractors. When performing love spells or rituals, it's important to cultivate and embody these positive emotions, as they amplify the energy of your intentions and increase the likelihood of manifesting your desires.

Energy and Vibrations

Energy and vibrations are the essence of magic. Every thought, emotion, and intention emits a specific energetic vibration that interacts with the universe. Love spells and rituals are practices that intentionally align and manipulate these vibrations to manifest love-related goals.

To effectively work with energy and vibrations in love magic, it's essential to be mindful of your own energy field. Regular practices such as meditation, grounding, and energy cleansing can help you maintain a balanced and clear energy state, which is crucial for effective spellcasting.

When casting love spells, the energy you put into the preparation and execution of the spell is as important as the spell itself. This includes choosing the right time, setting, and materials that resonate with your intention. For instance, using rose quartz in a love spell amplifies vibrations of love and compassion, while casting a spell under a full moon can enhance its emotional potency.

The power of visualization cannot be overstated in working with energy and vibrations. Visualizing your desired outcome in vivid detail during a spell or ritual sends powerful vibrations into the universe. This practice harnesses your personal energy, aligning it with your intentions and amplifying the spell's effectiveness.

Understanding and harnessing the principles of the Law of Attraction and energy vibrations can transform your witchcraft practice, leading to more meaningful and successful outcomes in your love life. As you delve deeper into these principles, you'll discover a world where your intentions, emotions, and energies shape your experiences, bringing the magic of love into your reality.

Common Tools

In the practice of love magic, certain tools are commonly used for their symbolic meanings and the energies they possess. These tools serve as focal points for your intentions and enhance the effectiveness of your spells and rituals.

1. **Candles**: Candles are a staple in love magic. Different colors have specific associations—pink for romantic love, red for passion, and white for purity and new beginnings. The act of lighting a candle symbolizes igniting your intentions and sending them out into the universe.
2. **Crystals**: Crystals are powerful tools due to their natural energies and vibrations. Rose quartz is renowned for attracting love and healing heartache, while amethyst can help deepen emotional understanding. Carrying or placing these crystals around your space can amplify your love spells.
3. **Herbs**: Herbs have been used in love magic for centuries. Lavender can be used for calming and peaceful love spells, while basil is known for its properties in attracting love and enhancing sexual desire. Incorporating herbs into your spells can be done through infusions, anointings, or as part of a ritual setup.

4. **Tarot Cards and Runes**: These tools are often used for divination in love matters but can also be incorporated into spells. Specific cards or runes can be selected to represent the desired outcome or to guide the spell's direction.
5. **Personal Items**: Items that hold personal significance, like photographs or a piece of jewelry, can also be powerful in love magic. They act as physical representations of the person or relationship you are focusing on.

The Power of Intention

As with all magic and witchcraft, the power of intention is paramount. It's the driving force behind every spell and ritual, acting as the compass that guides magical energies towards your desired outcome. Setting clear, focused intentions is not just the first step; it's a critical component that determines the direction and effectiveness of your spellwork.

1. **Clarifying Your Desires**: Before casting any spell, take time to clarify exactly what you desire. Whether it's attracting a new love, deepening an existing relationship, or healing from heartache, your intention must be specific and unambiguous.
2. **Visualizing the Outcome**: Visualization is a potent tool in setting intentions. Imagine the outcome of your spell in as much detail as possible. Feel the emotions associated with achieving this outcome, as this emotional charge adds power to your intent.
3. **Affirming Your Intentions**: Use affirmations to reinforce your intentions. An affirmation is a positive, present-tense statement that anchors your intention and strengthens your resolve. For example, "I attract a loving, harmonious

relationship" or "I heal from past love wounds and open my heart to new love."

4. **Writing Down Your Intentions**: Putting your intentions into writing can make them more tangible and focused. Write down your intention on a piece of paper and either keep it on your altar during your spell or incorporate it into the spell itself.

Basic Spellcasting Techniques

Spellcasting, at its core, is about harnessing and directing energies to bring about desired changes in one's life or environment. Whether you're drawn to the art of magic for personal transformation, to connect with natural forces, or to manifest specific outcomes, understanding and mastering the basics is crucial.

1. **The Role of Intention**: Every spell begins with an intention. It's the focused desire or outcome you wish to achieve. Clarity of intention is fundamental. Before casting any spell, take the time to clarify exactly what you want to achieve. Write it down, speak it aloud, or meditate on it. Your intention should be concise and precise.
2. **Creating Sacred Space**: Spellcasting often involves creating a sacred or protected space. This can be as simple as setting up a small altar, lighting a candle, or casting a circle. The purpose is to create a boundary between the everyday world and the magical world, providing you with a focused environment for your work.
3. **Connecting with Elements**: Traditional spellcasting often involves calling upon the elements (earth, air, fire, water, and spirit) for their symbolic qualities and energies. Understanding

these elements and learning to incorporate them into your spells can enrich your practice. For example, using a bowl of water for purification, lighting a candle for transformation, or burning incense to symbolize air and thought.

4. **Visualization and Meditation**: Visualization is a powerful tool in spellcasting. It involves picturing your desired outcome in your mind's eye, as vividly as possible. Coupled with meditation, visualization helps in aligning your personal energy with your intention. Regular practice improves your focus and the effectiveness of your spells.
5. **Using Magical Tools**: While not mandatory, many spellcasters use tools like wands, athames (ritual knives), chalices, and pentacles. These tools can help direct energy and represent various aspects of the natural world. Remember, the power doesn't reside in the tools themselves, but in how they help you focus your intent and energies.
6. **Chanting and Incantations**: Words, especially when spoken with emotion and intent, carry energy. Chants or incantations can be used to raise and direct energy during spellcasting. These can be traditional chants passed down through generations or ones you create yourself. The rhythm and rhyme in chants can help to elevate energy and focus your intention.
7. **Timing and Phases**: In spellcasting, timing can be an important factor. Many practitioners consider the phases of the moon, days of the week, and even astrological alignments. For instance, a new moon is often seen as a time for new beginnings, while a full moon is for realization and completion.

8. **Closing and Grounding**: After casting a spell, it's important to close your sacred space, thank the elements or any deities you invoked, and ground yourself. This involves releasing any excess energy and reconnecting with the physical world, ensuring you don't carry the heightened energy of spellcasting into your everyday activities.
9. **Reflect and Record**: Keeping a record of your spells, the process, and the outcomes in a grimoire or book of shadows is invaluable. It not only serves as a reference but also helps you track your growth and learn from your experiences.

By learning basic spellcasting techniques and creating personalized rituals, you empower yourself in the practice of love magic. These techniques not only enhance your magical skills but also deepen your connection to your intentions, paving the way for more profound and meaningful outcomes in your journey of love magic.

Cleansing and Consecrating

Before diving into the heart of spellcasting, preparing your space and tools is essential. This preparation involves cleansing and consecrating – steps that purify your environment and tools, setting the stage for effective and focused magic.

1. **Cleansing Your Space**: Begin by physically cleaning your space to remove clutter and distractions. Then, perform an energetic cleansing to clear away any lingering negative energies. This can be done by burning sage, palo santo, or using sound vibrations like bells or singing bowls. As you cleanse, visualize the space being filled with clear, bright energy.

2. **Consecrating Your Tools**: Consecration is the act of blessing and dedicating your tools (candles, crystals, herbs, etc.) for your magical work. This can be done by passing them through the smoke of incense, visualizing them being imbued with light, or anointing them with oils. As you consecrate each tool, set the intention that it will be used for love and positive outcomes.
3. **Cleansing Yourself**: It's also important to cleanse your own energy. Take a ritual bath with salts, or simply spend a few moments in meditation, focusing on releasing any negativity and aligning yourself with your spell's purpose.

Creating a Sacred Space

Creating a sacred space is a deeply personal process that involves setting up an environment where you feel connected, peaceful, and empowered. This space becomes your magical sanctuary for spellcasting.

1. **Choosing Your Space**: Select a quiet, comfortable area where you won't be disturbed. This could be a corner of your bedroom, a dedicated altar space, or even a spot in nature.
2. **Decorating Your Space**: Decorate your space with items that resonate with love and harmony. This could include pink or red candles, rose quartz crystals, images of deities or symbols of love, and fresh flowers.
3. **Altar Setup**: If you're using an altar, arrange it in a way that feels harmonious and meaningful to you. Place your tools in an accessible manner, and consider including representations of the four elements (earth, air, fire, and water) to balance the energies.

4. **Creating a Peaceful Atmosphere**: Use soft lighting, gentle music, or scents like rose or jasmine to create a calming and inviting atmosphere. The sensory elements of your space should align with the feeling of love and warmth.
5. **Setting Boundaries**: If you're in a shared space, setting physical or energetic boundaries is important. This can be done by casting a circle or setting a clear intention that your sacred space is for love magic work only.

By cleansing and consecrating your space and tools, and creating a sacred environment, you lay the groundwork for successful and focused spellcasting. This preparatory work not only enhances the effectiveness of your spells but also aligns your own energy with the vibrations of love and magic you wish to attract.

Realistic Expectations

Setting realistic expectations is a crucial aspect of practicing love magic. While spells can be powerful tools in manifesting your desires, it's important to approach them with a balanced perspective.

1. **Patience is Key**: Understand that spells may not manifest instantaneously. Love magic often requires time to align circumstances and energies. Patience is not just waiting; it's maintaining a positive and hopeful mindset while the magic unfolds.
2. **Belief in the Process**: Having faith in the process is essential. Doubt can hinder the effectiveness of your spells. Trust in your abilities, your tools, and the energy you have put into your spellwork.

3. **Understanding Limitations**: Recognize that love magic has its limitations. It cannot force emotions or outcomes that are not meant to be.
4. **Being Open to Various Outcomes**: Be open to different forms of manifestation. Sometimes, the universe delivers outcomes in unexpected ways – perhaps not exactly what you asked for, but what you truly need.

Dealing with Outcomes

Handling the outcomes of love spells, whether they align with your expectations or not, is an integral part of your magical practice.

1. **Embracing Success**: If a spell works as intended, acknowledge and celebrate your success. Reflect on what elements of the spell contributed to its effectiveness and how you can apply these learnings to future spellwork.
2. **Learning from the Experience**: If a spell doesn't manifest as expected, take it as a learning opportunity. Reflect on the spellcasting process, your intentions, and the possible reasons why it didn't work. This reflection can provide valuable insights for future spells.
3. **Emotional Management**: Managing your emotions, especially if a spell doesn't yield the desired outcome, is crucial. Practice self-care and remember that one spell's outcome does not define your worth or your magical abilities.
4. **Adapting Your Practice**: Use the outcomes of your spells to adapt and evolve your practice. If certain approaches or tools seem more effective, consider incorporating them more into your routine.

5. **Seeking Guidance**: If you're consistently not seeing the results you desire, consider seeking guidance from more experienced practitioners. Sometimes, an external perspective can provide clarity and direction.

Setting realistic expectations and learning how to handle various outcomes are vital skills in the practice of love magic. They allow you to approach spellcasting with a grounded and open mindset, ready to embrace the magic and its results in all their forms.

CHAPTER 3.

ETHICAL BOUNDARIES IN LOVE MAGIC

As practitioners, we wield the power to influence not just our own emotional landscapes but potentially those of others. With this power comes a significant responsibility: to practice love magic in a way that is respectful, compassionate, and mindful of the impact it can have.

Ethics in magical workings are not just guidelines; they are the bedrock upon which effective and positive magical practices are built. They ensure that our actions align with the greater good and do not infringe upon the free will or well-being of others. When we manipulate emotional energies, we tread into sensitive areas of human experience. It is our duty to approach this with the utmost care and respect.

The Golden Rule of Love Magic: "Do No Harm"

At the heart of ethical love magic is a simple yet profound principle: "Do no harm." This golden rule is the guiding light for all practices in the field of love magic. It reminds us that our spells and rituals should bring positivity, harmony, and love into the world, not pain, manipulation, or control.

Adhering to this principle means that we:

1. **Respect Free Will**: Never cast a spell that aims to control, manipulate, or change the free will of another person. Love spells should focus on attracting and nurturing positive energies, not binding or coercing someone against their natural inclinations.
2. **Seek Positive Outcomes**: Our intentions and actions should always aim for outcomes that bring happiness, health, and harmony, both for ourselves and others. The best love

magic promotes mutual respect, understanding, and genuine connection.

3. **Avoid Negative Spells**: Spells that aim to break up relationships, cause discord, or bring harm to others, no matter how justified it might feel, go against the principle of "do no harm" and can have unforeseen negative consequences.
4. **Practice Self-Reflection**: Regularly reflect on your motivations and the potential impact of your spells. Ethical practice in love magic requires an honest assessment of whether your actions are for the highest good.

We must ensure that our workings in magic are not only fulfilling but also respectful and kind. As we delve deeper into the world of love spells and rituals, keeping this ethical foundation in mind will guide us towards practices that honor the sacredness of love and the dignity of all involved.

Respecting Free Will

In the practice of love magic, the concept of free will holds a place of utmost importance. Free will, the ability for each individual to make their own choices and decisions, is a fundamental aspect of human dignity and autonomy. In the context of love magic, respecting free will means acknowledging and honoring the right of each person to choose their own emotional and romantic paths without undue influence or manipulation.

Respecting free will in spellcasting is not just an ethical mandate; it is a recognition of the sacredness of love itself. True love cannot be forced or fabricated through magical means. It thrives on genuine feelings, mutual respect, and a natural connection. Therefore, spells aimed at creating love should focus on attracting love into your life in a way that allows others to respond based on their true feelings, free from external manipulation.

Consequences of Manipulating Free Will

Casting spells that manipulate or attempt to override someone's free will can have serious ethical and practical consequences. Ethically, such actions violate the personal autonomy and dignity of the individual, undermining the very essence of love, which is built on respect and mutual consent. From a practical standpoint, spells that interfere with free will can lead to outcomes that are inauthentic and fraught with problems.

1. **Karmic Repercussions**: In many spiritual traditions, it's believed that actions that harm or manipulate others can come back to affect the practitioner negatively. This concept, often known as the Law of Threefold Return in Wiccan traditions, suggests that whatever energy you put out into the world will return to you threefold.
2. **Unintended Outcomes**: Spells that tamper with free will often lead to unintended consequences. Forcing a connection or altering someone's feelings can create situations that are complicated, unfulfilling, and ultimately unsustainable.
3. **Emotional and Spiritual Imbalance**: Engaging in practices that manipulate free will can lead to an imbalance in your own emotional and spiritual wellbeing. It can create a disconnection from your true self and your natural path in love.
4. **Ethical Dilemmas**: Continually engaging in manipulative practices can lead to complex ethical dilemmas and a

damaged reputation in the magical community. It can also lead to a loss of trust in yourself and your abilities as a practitioner of love magic.

Respecting free will in love magic is not only a matter of ethical practice but also a recognition of the natural laws that govern genuine love and connection. By focusing your magical practice on enhancing your own attractiveness, fostering self-love, and creating opportunities for natural connections to flourish, you align with the true spirit of love magic. This approach ensures that the love you attract is real, fulfilling, and harmonious, both for yourself and for others involved.

Karmic Considerations

As with all magical practices, the concept of karma plays a significant role. Karma, in simple terms, refers to the idea that our actions and intentions have consequences, creating a cycle of cause and effect. In the context of love magic, this means being mindful of how your spells and intentions might impact not only your life but also the lives of others.

1. **Mindful Spellcasting**: It's crucial to approach love spells with a mindset that considers the long-term effects of your actions. Karma in love magic emphasizes the importance of positive, ethical practices. Spells cast with pure intentions and respect for free will are less likely to result in negative karmic repercussions.
2. **Avoiding Harmful Spells**: To minimize negative karma, avoid spells that aim to manipulate, control, or cause harm. Not only do these go against the ethical principles of love magic,

but they also risk creating adverse karmic effects that could manifest in various areas of your life.

3. **Intention for the Greater Good**: Focus your magical practice on intentions that contribute to the greater good. Love spells that foster understanding, healing, and genuine connection contribute to positive karmic outcomes.

Understanding Backlash

The concept of magical backlash, or the "threefold return," is particularly prevalent in Wiccan and other Neopagan traditions. It suggests that whatever energy you put out into the world, particularly in a magical context, will return to you three times over. In love magic, this principle underscores the importance of ethical practice.

1. **Consequences of Negative Magic**: Casting a love spell with negative or harmful intentions might result in the spell's energy coming back to you with greater intensity, causing emotional, spiritual, or even physical repercussions.
2. **Positive Energy Multiplies**: Conversely, love spells cast with positive, loving intentions can bring about beneficial outcomes, magnified in their return to you. This reinforces the idea of using love magic to enhance positive connections and self-growth.
3. **Balancing Actions**: If you find yourself having cast a spell that might have negative implications, it's important to take steps to balance the action. This could involve performing a ritual of release, focusing on healing and forgiveness, or redirecting your energies towards positive acts.

Understanding the role of karma and the concept of magical backlash is vital in practicing responsible and ethical love magic. By being mindful of these principles, you can guide your practice towards not only effective but also harmonious outcomes, aligning your magical journey with the universal laws of cause and effect.

Developing Your Own Personal Ethical Code

In the practice of love magic, crafting a personal ethical code is a vital step towards responsible and mindful spellcasting. This code acts as a moral compass, guiding your actions and decisions. Here's how you can develop your own set of ethical guidelines:

1. **Reflect on Your Values**: Consider what values are most important to you in your magical practice. Is it honesty, consent, non-manipulation, or harmlessness? Your ethical code should reflect these core values.
2. **Learn from Others**: Explore the ethical codes of experienced practitioners and magical traditions. While your code should be personal, understanding others' perspectives can provide valuable insights.
3. **Set Clear Boundaries**: Define what you are and are not willing to do in your love magic practice. These boundaries will help you navigate complex situations and make decisions that align with your ethical beliefs.
4. **Consider the Impact**: Think about the potential impact of your spells not just on yourself and the target, but also on others indirectly involved. Your ethical code should take into account the broader consequences of your magical work.

5. **Write It Down**: Once you've reflected on these points, write down your ethical code. This can be a simple list of principles or a more elaborate set of guidelines. Having it in writing makes it more concrete and easier to adhere to.

Checking Motives

Regularly checking your motives and intentions is crucial in adhering to your personal ethical code. This introspection ensures your spellcasting remains aligned with your moral principles.

1. **Before Casting a Spell**: Before performing any love spell, take a moment to reflect on your motives. Ask yourself why you are doing this spell and what you hope to achieve. Ensure that your intentions align with your ethical code.
2. **Seeking Clarity**: If you're unsure about the ethics of a spell, seek clarity. This could involve meditating on your intentions, consulting your written ethical code, or seeking advice from trusted fellow practitioners.
3. **Avoiding Impulsive Spellcasting**: Love magic should never be done on impulse. Give yourself time to consider all aspects of the spell and its potential impact. This deliberation can prevent ethical missteps.
4. **Periodic Review**: Set aside time regularly to review and possibly revise your ethical code. As you grow in your practice, your understanding of ethics might evolve, and your code should reflect this growth.
5. **Accountability**: Hold yourself accountable for your actions in your magical practice. If you realize you've acted against your ethical code, take steps to rectify the situation and learn from the experience.

Developing and adhering to a personal ethical code in love magic is not a one-time task but an ongoing process of reflection and growth. It's a commitment to practicing love magic in a way that honors the integrity of the craft and the wellbeing of all involved. By regularly checking your motives and aligning them with your ethical code, you ensure that your practice remains respectful, responsible, and true to the heart of love magic.

The Path Ahead

As we conclude our exploration of ethical boundaries in love magic, it's worth reflecting on the deeper implications of adhering to these principles. Ethical practice when practicing love spells is far more than a set of rules; it's a pathway to healthier relationships, personal growth, and a harmonious alignment with the universal energies of love.

When we respect ethical boundaries, we cultivate relationships that are grounded in authenticity and mutual respect. These bonds, formed without manipulation or coercion, are more likely to be fulfilling and enduring. They are based on true affinity and genuine connection, allowing for deeper, more meaningful interactions.

Ethical practice in magic also promotes introspection and self-awareness. It challenges us to examine our deepest desires and intentions, leading to significant personal growth. This journey of self-discovery helps us understand our emotional needs, desires, and the true essence of what we seek in relationships. It's a process that enhances our understanding of ourselves and our place in the tapestry of love and magic.

Moreover, adhering to ethical principles in our magical practice contributes to a broader positive impact. It radiates kindness, understanding, and genuine affection, influencing not just our romantic pursuits but our interactions with the world. This approach builds a foundation of trust in the craft, both within ourselves and in the wider community, enhancing the integrity and reputation of magical practices.

By following an ethical path in love magic, we open ourselves to the possibility of true love. This is a love that arises naturally, without force or manipulation, aligned with the universal energies of harmony and affection. It's a pathway that leads us not just to successful spellcasting but to a life enriched with deep, meaningful connections, and a profound sense of personal fulfillment. In this way, ethical love magic becomes a transformative journey, one that enriches our lives with love, understanding, and a deep connection to the magical world around us.

CHAPTER 4.

101 LOVE SPELLS

Welcome to the heart of our journey, and likely the reason you picked up this book. I present to you, 101 Love Spells. This comprehensive collection of potent love spells has been meticulously crafted to enrich your journey in the mystical world of love and attraction. Here, you will find spells of varying complexity and intensity, designed to cater to a wide spectrum of desires and needs in relation to love, attraction and commitment.

You will discover spells that range from simple incantations and candle rituals to more intricate ceremonies and potion-making. Each spell is presented with detailed instructions, guiding you step by step through the magical process. You'll find spells to attract love, enhance an existing relationship, heal from heartache, and even foster self-love and inner harmony.

This collection has been curated with both beginners and experienced practitioners in mind. For those new to love magic, the spells begin with simpler techniques, gradually building in complexity. This progression allows you to develop your skills and confidence as you explore deeper into the craft. Experienced practitioners will find advanced spells that offer new challenges and deeper insights into the art of love magic.

These spells have been carefully preserved and passed down through the ages, steeped in wisdom and enriched by the experiences of countless practitioners who have wielded them before. They are not mere words and rituals, but keys to unlocking mysteries and energies that have been tapped into and revered since time immemorial.

It's important to approach these spells with respect, mindfulness, and an open heart. Remember the ethical considerations discussed in the previous chapters, and always cast your spells with the highest intentions and respect for free will and harmlessness. Love magic, when practiced with care and respect, can be a beautiful and transformative experience, bringing joy, healing, and harmony into your life.

As you embark on this magical journey through the spells, allow yourself to be guided by your intuition and the desires of your heart. Whether you are seeking new love, nurturing an existing bond, healing from past hurts, or cultivating self-love, these spells are a gateway to a deeper understanding and experience of love in all its forms. Let these spells be your guide and companion as you explore the potent and transformative power of love magic.

1. Heart's Whisper Candle Spell

The Heart's Whisper Candle Spell is a gentle yet powerful ritual designed to awaken feelings of love and affection. Ideal for those seeking to foster or deepen a romantic connection, this spell combines the energies of intention and visualization to invoke love's tender aspects.

Purpose: To kindle and enhance feelings of love and affection.

Timing: Best performed on a Friday, Venus's day, or during a waxing moon phase to grow affection.

Materials:

1. Pink candle (symbolizing affection)
2. Rose oil (for enhancing love energies)
3. Paper and pen (for intentions)
4. Rose petals (symbol of love)
5. Personal item of affection (such as a photograph)

Preparation:

1. Cleanse your space with sage or visualization for purity.
2. Arrange the pink candle on a flat surface, surrounded by a circle of rose petals.

The Spell:

1. **Anointing the Candle**: Take the rose oil and anoint the pink candle, moving from the base to the wick, focusing on your intent of love and affection.
2. **Writing Your Intentions**: On the piece of paper, write down your feelings or wishes towards the person of your affection.

Be honest and direct, expressing your deepest desires for love.

3. **Placing the Personal Item**: If you have a personal item of the person, like a photograph, place it in front of the candle. This helps to direct your energy and intent more specifically.
4. **Lighting the Candle**: Light the pink candle while focusing on your intentions. Visualize the person being surrounded by love and affection.
5. **Chanting the Spell**: As the candle burns, chant softly: "Heart's whisper, clear and true, bring affection both fresh and new. By this candle's loving light, awaken feelings pure and bright."
6. **Meditation**: Spend a few minutes meditating on the candle flame. Imagine a soft, warm light enveloping both you and the person in the photograph, connecting your hearts.
7. **Concluding the Spell**: Once you feel your intentions have been set, allow the candle to burn out safely on its own. Keep the piece of paper with your intentions somewhere safe, like under your pillow or in a special box.

After the Spell:

- **Disposal of Materials**: Dispose of the rose petals in a natural way, like burying them or leaving them in a body of water.
- **Patience and Trust**: Have patience and trust that the universe will work to bring your intentions to fruition in a way that's best for everyone involved.

Note: Remember, this spell, like all spells intended to influence another's feelings, should be cast with the utmost respect for the free will of the other person. It's about awakening existing feelings, not manipulating or coercing someone against their will.

2. Rose Petal Attraction Charm

The Rose Petal Attraction Charm is a spell steeped in the time-honored tradition of using the natural magic of roses to attract love and affection. This spell utilizes the innate properties of rose petals, known for their strong connection to the heart and love, to draw romantic energy toward you.

Purpose: To attract love and affection into your life.

Timing: Perform this spell on a Friday, under the waxing moon, to harness Venus's energy and the moon's growing power.

Materials:

1. Fresh rose petals (preferably red or pink for love)
2. A small charm or locket
3. Rose oil or essence
4. A red or pink cloth
5. A small piece of paper and a pen

Preparation:

1. Begin by cleansing your space, perhaps with soothing music or incense, to create a harmonious environment.
2. Lay out the red or pink cloth as the base for your spell work.

The Spell:

1. **Infusing the Petals**: Take the rose petals and gently rub them with a few drops of rose oil, infusing them with your intent to attract love.

2. **Writing Your Intentions**: On a small piece of paper, write your desires for love and romance. Be specific about the qualities you seek in a partner or the feeling you wish to experience.
3. **Creating the Charm**: Open the locket or charm and place the infused petals and your written intentions inside. As you do this, visualize your life filled with the love you desire.
4. **Sealing the Charm**: Close the locket or charm, sealing your intentions within. Hold it in your hands and focus on sending your desires into the charm with warm, loving energy.
5. **Concluding the Ritual**: Wrap the charm in the red or pink cloth and keep it in a safe place, such as your bedroom or a personal altar, where it can continue to attract love energies to you.

After the Spell:

- **Carrying the Charm**: Carry the charm with you, especially in social situations, to enhance your allure and to draw love toward you.
- **Regular Recharging**: Periodically, open the charm to renew the rose petals and restate your intentions, keeping the energy fresh and potent.

This spell operates on the principle of like attracts like; by focusing your energy and intent through the charm, you align yourself with the energies of love and affection. The Rose Petal Attraction Charm is a gentle yet effective way to open your heart and life to the joys and wonders of love. Remember, the most powerful component of any spell is your intention and belief in the magic you are creating.

3. Simple Honey Jar Love Spell

The Simple Honey Jar Love Spell is a traditional and widely used spell in folk magic, renowned for its ability to sweeten relationships and attract love. This spell employs the natural sweetness of honey to draw affection and loving energies, making it an excellent choice for those seeking to enhance existing relationships or attract new love.

Purpose: To sweeten romantic feelings and attract loving, harmonious relationships.

Timing: Ideal to perform on a Friday to align with Venus, the planet of love, or during a waxing moon phase to grow affection.

Materials:

1. A small glass jar with a lid (like a mason jar)
2. Natural honey
3. Red or pink candles
4. Rose petals (red or pink for love)
5. A piece of paper and a pen
6. Optional: Personal items or photos of the person involved

Preparation:

1. Cleanse your space and your materials, ensuring a positive and pure environment for your spell.
2. Write down the names of those involved in the relationship, or your wishes for a future relationship, on the piece of paper.

The Spell:

1. **Filling the Jar**: Fill the jar halfway with honey while visualizing your relationship or desired relationship being filled with sweetness and love.
2. **Adding Your Intentions**: Place the piece of paper with the names or wishes into the jar, submerging it in the honey.
3. **Adding Rose Petals**: Gently add rose petals to the jar, each petal symbolizing a trait or aspect of the relationship you wish to enhance or attract.
4. **Sealing the Jar**: Once all items are in the jar, fill it up with more honey, covering everything completely. As you do this, visualize the sweetness of the honey enveloping your relationship with warmth and affection.
5. **Candle Ritual**: Seal the jar and light the red or pink candles around it. Focus on the flame and envision the warmth of the candles amplifying the sweet energy in the jar.
6. **Affirmation**: Chant or silently affirm your intentions for love and harmony. For example, "With this honey, sweet and pure, may love in my life be secure."
7. **Concluding the Spell**: Let the candles burn down safely while the jar sits between them, absorbing the energy.

After the Spell:

- **Placement of the Jar**: Place the honey jar in a special place in your home, like your altar or a place where you can see it daily, as a constant reminder of your intentions.
- **Regular Activation**: Occasionally, shake the jar gently to reactivate its energies, reaffirming your intentions for love and harmony.

The Simple Honey Jar Love Spell is a spell of gentle persuasion, working to sweeten the energies around you and attract positive, loving relationships. It is a reminder that, like honey, love is sweet, nurturing, and worth cherishing. Remember, the key to effective spellwork lies in your focus, intention, and belief in the magic you are creating.

4. Lavender Dreams Sachet

The Lavender Dreams Sachet spell combines the calming properties of lavender with the intention of bringing loving and peaceful dreams about a current or future love. Lavender, known for its soothing and harmonious qualities, is a perfect herb for spells focusing on emotional tranquility and romantic insights in dreams.

Purpose: To induce dreams of love and harmony, and to gain insight into your romantic life through your dreams.

Timing: Perform this spell on a Thursday night, as Thursday is associated with Jupiter and growth, or during a waxing moon for increasing emotional understanding.

Materials:

1. Dried lavender buds
2. Small fabric sachet or a piece of cloth and ribbon
3. Optional: Amethyst crystal (for peaceful sleep and psychic insight)
4. Optional: Rose petals (for added romantic energy)
5. A piece of paper and a pen

Preparation:

1. Cleanse your space, the materials, and especially the amethyst crystal if you are using one.
2. Write down on the paper what you wish to dream about or gain insight into regarding your love life.

The Spell:

1. **Filling the Sachet**: Open your sachet or lay out your cloth. Begin to fill it with dried lavender buds while focusing on your intention for loving and insightful dreams.
2. **Adding the Written Intentions**: Place the piece of paper with your written intentions into the sachet among the lavender buds.
3. **Adding Optional Items**: If using, add the amethyst crystal for psychic insight and peaceful sleep, and rose petals for additional romantic energy.
4. **Sealing the Sachet**: Tie the sachet with the ribbon or draw the strings closed. As you do this, visualize sealing your intention within.
5. **Activating the Sachet**: Hold the sachet in your hands and gently shake it as you affirm your intentions, saying something like, "Lavender sweet, dreams reveal, love's insights now unveil."
6. **Placing the Sachet for Sleep**: Place the sachet under your pillow or near your bed where you can smell the soothing scent as you sleep.

After the Spell:

- **Dream Journaling**: Upon waking, immediately record any dreams or feelings in a journal. Look for patterns, symbols, or messages about your romantic life.
- **Refreshing the Sachet**: Periodically, refresh the sachet with new lavender buds and reaffirm your intentions.

The Lavender Dreams Sachet is a gentle way to invite love into your dreams, offering insights and emotional balance. This spell helps you tap into your subconscious mind, allowing for a deeper understanding of your heart's desires and the path of your romantic life. Remember, the power of this spell lies in your intent and the natural properties of lavender to soothe, calm, and open the pathways to intuitive dreaming.

5. Pink Candle Affection Ritual

The Pink Candle Affection Ritual is a heartfelt and straightforward spell that harnesses the gentle energy of pink candles to foster affection and warmth in a relationship. Pink, the color of emotional love and harmony, is central to this ritual, making it perfect for deepening existing relationships or attracting tender affection.

Purpose: To enhance affection and emotional warmth in a current relationship or to attract a new, affectionate relationship.

Timing: Ideal to perform on a Friday, a day associated with Venus, the planet of love, or during a waxing or full moon to amplify emotional connection.

Materials:

1. A pink candle (representing affection and emotional love)
2. Rose oil or rose petals (for love and harmony)
3. Matches or a lighter
4. A piece of paper and a pen
5. A small dish or holder for the candle

Preparation:

1. Begin by cleansing your space with incense, sage, or visualization.
2. Write your intentions for affection on the piece of paper. These could be qualities you wish to attract in a relationship or affirmations of love for your current partner.

The Ritual:

1. **Anointing the Candle**: If using rose oil, anoint the pink candle from base to wick. If using rose petals, place them around the candle in the holder or dish.
2. **Placing Your Intentions**: Fold the paper with your intentions and place it under the candle holder or dish.
3. **Lighting the Candle**: Light the pink candle while focusing on your intentions for affection. Visualize a soft, nurturing light emanating from the candle, enveloping you and your current or future partner in warmth and affection.
4. **Affirmation or Chant**: As the candle burns, either say aloud or meditate on an affirmation related to love and affection. For instance: "With this flame, affection grows, warmth and love around it glows."
5. **Meditation and Visualization**: Spend a few minutes meditating on the flame, visualizing your relationship (current or future) blossoming with mutual affection, understanding, and emotional warmth.
6. **Concluding the Ritual**: Allow the candle to burn down safely. If you must extinguish it, do so with gratitude and the intent to resume the ritual later.

After the Ritual:

- **Disposal of Materials**: Once the candle has completely burned out, respectfully dispose of the wax and, if used, the rose petals.
- **Reflecting on Intentions**: Revisit the piece of paper with your intentions. You may choose to keep it in a special place, like your altar, or carry it with you as a reminder of your desire for affection.

The Pink Candle Affection Ritual is a simple yet powerful way to open your heart and life to the energies of affection and emotional warmth. By combining the symbolism of the pink candle, the scent of the rose, and the power of your intentions, you create a harmonious space for love to flourish. Remember, the effectiveness of this ritual lies in your sincerity, the purity of your intentions, and your belief in the power of love.

6. Love Drawing Bath Ritual

The Love Drawing Bath Ritual is a soothing and enchanting practice that uses the transformative power of water combined with specific love-enhancing ingredients. This ritual is designed to draw love towards you, whether it's nurturing self-love, rekindling the flame in a current relationship, or attracting a new romantic partner.

Purpose: To attract love, enhance romantic energy, and promote self-love.

Timing: Perform this ritual on a Friday to align with Venus, the planet of love, ideally during a waxing moon to draw in love.

Materials:

1. A bathtub filled with warm water
2. Rose petals (preferably red or pink)
3. Lavender buds (for relaxation and love)
4. Epsom salt or sea salt (for purification)
5. A few drops of rose or ylang-ylang essential oil (for love and attraction)
6. Pink or red candles (to symbolize love and passion)
7. Amethyst or rose quartz crystals (for love and emotional healing)

Preparation:

1. Cleanse your bathroom to create a sacred space, using incense, sage, or visualization.
2. Begin filling your bathtub with warm water, and as it fills, set your intention for love and romance.

The Ritual:

1. **Adding Ingredients**: Once the bath is drawn, add Epsom or sea salt to purify and prepare the water. Scatter the rose petals and lavender buds into the bath, releasing their essence.
2. **Oil and Crystal Placement**: Add a few drops of the chosen essential oil to the water. Place the amethyst or rose quartz crystals around the tub or carefully into the water if they are water-safe.
3. **Lighting Candles**: Place and light the pink or red candles around the bathtub, creating a circle of warm, loving light.
4. **Entering the Bath**: Slowly enter the bath, immersing yourself in the water. Feel the warmth enveloping you, symbolizing love's embrace.
5. **Meditation and Visualization**: While in the bath, close your eyes and visualize your life filled with the love you desire. Imagine the energy of the water infused with the petals and oils, drawing love into your life.
6. **Affirmations**: You may recite love affirmations or simply soak in the sensations, letting the water's energy work its magic.

After the Ritual:

- **Concluding the Bath**: Once you feel the ritual is complete, stand up and let the water drain. Visualize any negativity or blocks to love flowing away with the water.
- **Disposal of Petals**: Collect the rose petals and lavender buds. These can be returned to nature, perhaps in a garden or natural body of water, as a gesture of releasing your intentions to the universe.

- **Extinguish Candles**: Safely extinguish the candles, thanking them for their light and energy.

This Love Drawing Bath Ritual is a deeply personal experience, allowing you to connect with the elemental power of water and the loving energies of the Universe. It's an act of self-care and an expression of your readiness to welcome love into your life. Embrace the ritual as a sacred time for yourself, a moment to focus solely on your heart's desires and the love that awaits you.

7. Rose Quartz Harmony Amulet

The Rose Quartz Harmony Amulet ritual focuses on creating a powerful talisman for love and harmony using the natural properties of rose quartz. Known as the stone of universal love, rose quartz enhances love in virtually any situation and promotes emotional healing.

Purpose: To create an amulet that radiates harmonious love energy, helping to attract love, heal emotional wounds, and bring peace and harmony to relationships.

Timing: Conduct this ritual during a waxing moon to attract love, or on a Friday to align with Venus's energies.

Materials:

1. A piece of rose quartz
2. A small cloth pouch or a piece of jewelry to hold the rose quartz
3. Lavender or rose petals
4. A white or pink candle
5. Rose oil or lavender oil

Preparation:

1. Begin by cleansing the rose quartz in moonlight, sunlight, or with sage smoke.
2. Set up a small altar or sacred space where you can perform the ritual undisturbed.

The Ritual:

1. **Anointing the Candle**: Light the candle to start the ritual. Anoint it with a few drops of rose or lavender oil to enhance its love-drawing properties.
2. **Cleansing the Stone**: Hold the rose quartz in your hands and visualize it being bathed in a cleansing light. This process clears any previous energies and prepares it for your intentions.
3. **Infusing the Stone with Intentions**: While holding the stone, focus on your intentions for love, peace, and harmony. You might visualize a loving, peaceful energy surrounding you or emanating from the stone.
4. **Creating the Amulet**: Place the rose quartz in the cloth pouch. If you're using a piece of jewelry, you can set the stone in it now. Surround the amulet with lavender or rose petals.
5. **Finalizing the Amulet**: As the candle burns, let the stone absorb the energies of the surrounding elements. Recite an affirmation or chant, such as, "With love and harmony, I charge this amulet, to bring peace and love into my life."
6. **Concluding the Ritual**: Allow the candle to burn down safely. Store the amulet in a safe place overnight, preferably under your pillow or near your bed.

After the Ritual:

- **Carrying the Amulet**: Carry the amulet with you, especially in situations where you want to attract love or need emotional harmony. The amulet serves as a reminder of your intentions and a focal point for harmonious energies.

- **Recharging the Amulet**: Regularly recharge your amulet under moonlight and reaffirm your intentions to keep it potent.

The Rose Quartz Harmony Amulet is a powerful tool in love magic. It serves not just as a charm for attracting love but also as a personal talisman for emotional healing and harmony. The ritual of creating and carrying this amulet can be a deeply personal and empowering act, symbolizing your commitment to nurturing love and harmony in your life.

8. Sweetening Love Tea Spell

The Sweetening Love Tea Spell is a delightful and aromatic ritual that uses the power of herbs and intention to sweeten your romantic life. This spell is perfect for enhancing the sweetness in an existing relationship or attracting sweet, loving energies for those seeking new love.

Purpose: To enhance the sweetness in romantic relationships and attract loving energy.

Timing: Best performed on a Friday, the day of Venus, or during a waxing moon to increase love and affection.

Materials:

1. A teapot or cup for brewing
2. Herbal tea ingredients (such as rose petals, jasmine, lavender, or chamomile for love and relaxation)
3. Honey (for sweetness in love)
4. A pink or red candle (for love and affection)
5. A spoon (preferably silver for lunar energy)
6. Boiling water

Preparation:

1. Cleanse your tea-making space and materials with gentle music or incense to set a loving mood.
2. Light the pink or red candle to invite the energies of love.

The Spell:

1. **Blending the Herbs:** In your teapot or cup, mix the herbal tea ingredients. Each herb chosen should represent an aspect of love you wish to enhance or attract.
2. **Brewing the Tea:** Pour boiling water over the herbs, infusing them with your intention for sweet love. As the water turns color, visualize your romantic life blossoming with affection, understanding, and joy.
3. **Sweetening the Tea:** Stir in honey while chanting softly, "With this sweetness, I invite love, tender and bright, into my life."
4. **Sipping with Intention:** Lightly blow on the tea to cool it, then take a sip. Imagine drinking in the sweet energy of love. Savor each sip, allowing the warmth and sweetness to fill you.
5. **Meditating on Love:** As you drink your tea, meditate on the qualities you desire in a relationship. Picture a harmonious and loving partnership, or envision yourself radiating love and attracting the right person into your life.

After the Spell:

- **Extinguishing the Candle:** Once you've finished your tea, thank the universe for its blessings and gently extinguish the candle.
- **Disposal of Tea Leaves:** Dispose of the used tea leaves by returning them to the earth or composting them, symbolizing the planting of your intentions.
- **Reflecting on the Spell:** Spend a moment in quiet reflection, feeling the loving energy you've created and trusting the universe to bring love into your life.

The Sweetening Love Tea Spell is a simple yet effective way to infuse your life with the energy of love. Whether you're nurturing an existing relationship or preparing for a new one, this spell helps to set your intentions and align your energies with those of love and harmony. Remember, the magic is not just in the ingredients, but in your intentions and the love you pour into the ritual.

9. Moonlit Love Letter Ritual

The Moonlit Love Letter Ritual is a romantic and introspective practice, utilizing the reflective energy of the moon to reveal and amplify heartfelt desires. This ritual is particularly effective for expressing deep emotions and setting intentions for love, whether you are reaching out to a specific person or manifesting a new romantic connection.

Purpose: To articulate and manifest your deepest romantic desires and intentions.

Timing: Best performed during a full moon for maximum emotional and intuitive clarity, harnessing the moon's power to bring desires to light.

Materials:

1. A piece of high-quality paper or stationery
2. A pen with ink that feels special (possibly in red or pink)
3. A white or silver candle (to represent lunar energy)
4. An envelope
5. Rose petals or lavender (for love and clarity)
6. A moonstone or clear quartz crystal (for emotional clarity and connection to the moon)

Preparation:

1. Find a quiet, comfortable space where you can see the moon or feel its presence.
2. Cleanse your space and writing materials with sage, incense, or moonlight.

The Ritual:

1. **Candle Lighting**: Begin by lighting your white or silver candle, focusing on the moon's energy and inviting clarity and emotional truth into your space.
2. **Writing the Letter**: Sit down with your paper and pen. Reflect on your feelings and deepest desires for love. Write a letter to a specific person, the universe, or even yourself, expressing these desires openly and honestly. Pour your heart into the words, unfiltered and sincere.
3. **Crystal for Clarity**: Hold the moonstone or clear quartz in your hand as you write to strengthen your emotional connection to the moon and enhance clarity in your intentions.
4. **Sealing with Petals**: Once the letter is complete, sprinkle some rose petals or lavender inside, fold the letter, and place it in the envelope. These herbs add an extra layer of love energy and clarity to your intentions.
5. **Moonlight Charging**: Place the sealed envelope under the moonlight, either outdoors or on a windowsill where the moon's rays can reach it. Leave it there for the duration of the night to absorb the moon's powerful energy.
6. **Final Affirmation**: As you place the envelope under the moonlight, say a final affirmation or prayer, focusing on sending your desires into the universe, trusting that your emotional sincerity will guide them to fruition.

After the Ritual:

- **Disposing of the Letter**: If the letter was addressed to the universe or not meant for a specific person, you can burn it the next day, letting the smoke carry your intentions out into the world. Alternatively, you could bury it, symbolizing the planting of your desires.

- **Reflecting on Your Feelings**: Spend some time over the next few days reflecting on your feelings and watching for any signs or changes in your romantic life. Trust that your intentions have been heard and are in the process of manifesting.

The Moonlit Love Letter Ritual is a powerful tool for clarity and expression in the realm of love. It allows you to connect deeply with your innermost feelings and desires, offering them up to the universe or a specific individual in a way that is both symbolic and tangible. This ritual is a beautiful blend of introspection, lunar magic, and romantic intention, ideal for those ready to open their hearts and embrace love in its purest form.

10. Cherished Memories Photo Spell

The Cherished Memories Photo Spell is a tender and nostalgic ritual designed to strengthen the bonds of love by focusing on happy, shared memories. This spell is particularly effective for couples wishing to rekindle their affection and for individuals looking to draw in a love that echoes past joyful experiences.

Purpose: To enhance and deepen the emotional connection in a relationship by focusing on cherished memories, or to attract a new relationship that brings similar joy and happiness.

Timing: Ideal to perform during a waxing moon to grow the feelings of love and affection, or on a night with clear, starry skies to evoke the vastness of shared experiences.

Materials:

1. A photograph of a happy moment with your partner or a representation of your desired love
2. A small frame for the photograph
3. Blue or silver candles (symbolizing calm, trust, and emotional depth)
4. Lavender or chamomile (for peace and loving communication)
5. A piece of paper and a pen
6. A small dish or tray

Preparation:

1. Set up a quiet, intimate space for the ritual, ensuring privacy and a calm atmosphere.

2. Cleanse the area and materials with the soothing aroma of lavender or chamomile.

The Ritual:

1. **Framing the Photo**: Begin by placing the photograph in the frame. As you do this, reflect on the moment captured in the picture, recalling the feelings of joy, love, and connection.
2. **Candle Lighting**: Light the blue or silver candles, positioning them on either side of the framed photograph. These candles represent the depth and trust in your relationship.
3. **Writing Your Intentions**: On the piece of paper, write down your intentions for your relationship. Focus on the qualities and feelings you wish to enhance or attract, such as joy, understanding, and shared happiness.
4. **Creating the Sacred Space**: Place the framed photograph in the center of your dish or tray. Surround it with lavender or chamomile to foster peaceful and loving communication.
5. **Chanting Your Intentions**: Hold the paper with your written intentions and softly chant or whisper your desires to the universe, asking to strengthen your emotional bond or attract a love filled with joy.
6. **Sealing the Spell**: Place the paper with your intentions under the tray or dish. Let the candles burn down safely while you meditate on the photograph, reinforcing your connection to those cherished memories or your future love.

After the Ritual:

- **Keeping the Photograph Displayed**: Keep the framed photograph in a place where you can see it daily, such as a bedroom or personal space, to continually remind you of the love you share or seek.

- **Reflecting on Memories**: Regularly take time to reflect on the positive aspects of your relationship or past joyful experiences in love, reinforcing the spell's energy.

The Cherished Memories Photo Spell is a heartfelt way to connect with the fundamental joys of a relationship. It serves as a reminder of the happy moments that form the foundation of love and a beacon for future happiness in love. This spell weaves together the magic of memory, intention, and imagery to create a powerful catalyst for ongoing affection and emotional connection.

11. Gentle Embrace Incense Blend

The Gentle Embrace Incense Blend is a soothing and aromatic spell that harnesses the power of scents to create an atmosphere of love and gentle affection. This spell is ideal for setting the mood for a romantic evening, healing after arguments, or simply infusing your living space with loving energy.

Purpose: To foster a loving and gentle environment, encouraging affection and understanding in relationships.

Timing: Best crafted on a Friday, the day of Venus, or during a new moon for beginnings in love and harmony.

Materials:

1. Dried lavender (for peace and tranquility)
2. Dried rose petals (symbolizing love and affection)
3. Dried chamomile (for relaxation and harmony)
4. A mortar and pestle (for blending herbs)
5. Charcoal disc and a fireproof incense burner
6. Optional: A few drops of vanilla or jasmine essential oil (for sweetness and attraction)

Preparation:

1. Create a calm and clean space where you can blend your incense without distractions.
2. If you have a specific intention or person in mind, hold that thought as you prepare your materials.

The Spell:

1. **Blending the Incense**: Begin by placing equal parts of lavender, rose petals, and chamomile in your mortar. As you mix them, focus on your intentions for love and harmony.
2. **Adding Essential Oils**: If using, add a few drops of vanilla or jasmine essential oil to the blend. These scents add an extra layer of sweetness and attraction to the incense.
3. **Grinding the Blend**: Gently grind the herbs and petals together with the pestle. While doing so, chant softly or meditate on your desire for a gentle, loving atmosphere.
4. **Burning the Incense**: Light the charcoal disc in your fireproof burner and wait for it to turn gray. Then carefully sprinkle some of your incense blend on top of the charcoal.
5. **Spreading the Scent**: As the incense begins to smoke, waft the smoke gently around your room or space with a feather or your hand. Visualize the smoke carrying your intentions throughout the space, creating a bubble of gentle love and tranquility.

After the Spell:

- **Storing the Incense**: Keep any remaining blend in a sealed jar or container. You can use it again whenever you wish to recreate a loving and harmonious atmosphere.
- **Reflection and Integration**: Spend some time in the incensed space, absorbing the harmonious energies you've created. This can be an excellent opportunity for quiet reflection, meditation, or spending time with a loved one.

The Gentle Embrace Incense Blend spell is a beautiful way to use the natural energies of herbs and the transformative power of scent to create a nurturing environment conducive to love. It's a subtle yet powerful way to shift energies, promote understanding, and open the heart to the joys of affection and connection.

12. Harmonious Relationship Jar

The Harmonious Relationship Jar is a spell crafted to foster peace, understanding, and harmony in a romantic relationship. This spell is particularly effective for couples seeking to strengthen their bond and resolve conflicts, creating a lasting foundation of mutual respect and love.

Purpose: To promote harmony, understanding, and lasting peace in a relationship.

Timing: Ideal to perform on a Friday, aligning with Venus, the planet of love, or during a waxing moon to enhance growth and harmony in the relationship.

Materials:

1. A small glass jar with a lid
2. Honey or sugar (to sweeten the relationship)
3. Lavender buds (for calm and peace)
4. Rose petals (for love and affection)
5. Small amethyst or rose quartz crystals (for love and harmony)
6. A piece of paper and a pen
7. Red or pink ribbon

Preparation:

1. Cleanse your space and materials with calming incense or sage, setting a peaceful tone for the ritual.
2. Write both partners' names on the piece of paper, along with a positive affirmation about your relationship.

The Spell:

1. **Filling the Jar**: Begin by placing the names written on the paper at the bottom of the jar. Over it, layer the honey or sugar, envisioning it sweetening and nurturing your relationship.
2. **Adding Herbs and Petals**: Add lavender buds for calm and peace, followed by rose petals to symbolize the love you share.
3. **Placing the Crystals**: Gently place the amethyst or rose quartz crystals in the jar. These stones are known for their ability to promote emotional balance and harmony.
4. **Sealing the Jar**: Once all the elements are in place, seal the jar tightly. As you do this, visualize your relationship being protected and nurtured by the jar's contents.
5. **Binding the Jar**: Tie the red or pink ribbon around the jar while chanting or affirming your intentions for a harmonious and loving relationship.
6. **Finalizing the Spell**: Place the jar in a special place in your home, such as your bedroom or on a shared altar, where it can continuously emit harmonious energies.

After the Spell:

- **Regular Activation**: Occasionally shake the jar gently to reactivate its energies, reaffirming your commitment to a peaceful and loving relationship.
- **Maintenance of the Jar**: Over time, you may wish to open the jar to add new affirmations or refresh the contents, keeping the spell active and aligned with your growing relationship.

The Harmonious Relationship Jar serves as a physical representation of your commitment to maintaining peace and love in your partnership. It's a reminder of the sweetness, calm, and affection you strive for in your relationship, acting as a talisman to continually attract these qualities. This spell is a beautiful way to proactively nurture and cherish the bond you share with your partner.

13. Attraction Sigil Creation

The Attraction Sigil Creation spell is a powerful and personalized magical practice that involves designing a unique sigil to attract love and romantic attention. This spell is ideal for those who wish to draw a new love into their lives or enhance the attraction within an existing relationship.

Purpose: To create a personalized symbol that actively attracts love and romantic attention.

Timing: Best performed during a waxing moon to draw in love, or on a Friday for Venusian influences.

Materials:

1. A piece of paper
2. A pen or marker
3. Your imagination and focused intent
4. Optional: Red or pink candles (for love energy)
5. Optional: Rose oil or petals (to enhance attraction)

Preparation:

1. Find a quiet space where you can concentrate without interruptions.
2. If using candles, light them to set the mood and invite love energy into your space.

The Spell:

1. **Setting Your Intention**: Begin by clearly defining your intention for attraction. This could be something like "Attracting a loving partner" or "Enhancing love in my life."
2. **Creating the Sigil**: Write down your intention, then remove all vowels and duplicate letters, leaving you with a string of unique consonants. Using these letters, start to creatively combine them into a symbol or design. This is your sigil – a unique representation of your desire for love.
3. **Charging the Sigil**: Once you are satisfied with your sigil, focus on it intently. Visualize your desire for love and how this sigil will help bring that into your life. Imagine the sigil glowing with energy, charged with your intention.
4. **Activating the Sigil**: There are many ways to activate a sigil. You might choose to meditate on it, burn it (safely) and scatter the ashes to the wind, paint it on a rock and leave it in a special place, or keep it somewhere important to you. The key is the act of releasing the sigil and its intention into the universe.
5. **Closing the Spell**: If you lit candles, now is the time to extinguish them, thanking the universe for assisting in your magical work.

After the Spell:

- **Living with Your Sigil**: Keep the sigil in a place where you can see it regularly, but without actively focusing on it. This allows its magic to work in the background of your daily life.
- **Reflecting on Love**: Spend some time each day reflecting on the qualities of love you wish to attract, reinforcing the energy of your sigil.

Attraction Sigil Creation is a deeply personal magical act that combines creativity with focused intent. By designing and activating your own sigil, you are putting a piece of your energy and desire into the universe, asking it to respond with love. This spell is a powerful tool for those who wish to take an active role in attracting love into their lives.

14. Lovebird Feather Talisman

The Lovebird Feather Talisman is a charming and symbolic spell that utilizes the natural energy of a bird's feather to attract and nurture love. This spell is particularly effective for those seeking to draw in a romantic partner with similar qualities or to reinforce the bonds of love in an existing relationship.

Purpose: To attract a compatible romantic partner or to enhance the existing love in a relationship.

Timing: Ideal to perform on a Friday, the day of Venus, or during the waxing phase of the moon to attract new love or grow existing love.

Materials:

1. A feather (preferably naturally found, symbolizing a love that is free and true)
2. Red or pink thread
3. Rose oil or essential oil of your choice (for love and attraction)
4. Small beads or charms (to represent aspects of the love you seek or cherish)
5. A small pouch or piece of cloth

Preparation:

1. Cleanse your space and materials, creating a serene environment for your ritual.
2. If possible, find a feather during a walk or in a place that holds special meaning to you, as this adds personal significance to your talisman.

The Spell:

1. **Anointing the Feather**: Begin by anointing the feather with rose oil, infusing it with the energy of love and attraction.
2. **Attaching Beads and Charms**: Thread your beads or charms onto the red or pink thread, each one representing a quality you desire in your relationship or partner.
3. **Binding the Feather**: Carefully tie the threaded beads and charms to the feather, securing them in place. As you do this, focus on your intention for love and harmony.
4. **Chanting Your Intentions**: While tying the beads, softly chant or affirm your desires for love. For example, "Feathers light, love take flight, bring to me my heart's delight."
5. **Creating the Talisman**: Once the feather is adorned, place it in the small pouch or wrap it in a piece of cloth, creating a portable talisman.
6. **Finalizing the Spell**: Hold the talisman in your hands, close your eyes, and visualize your life enriched with the love you seek. Feel the feather talisman becoming a beacon for love.

After the Spell:

- **Carrying the Talisman**: Keep the feather talisman with you, especially when going to social events or in situations where you wish to attract or celebrate love.
- **Regular Recharging**: Periodically, take the talisman out and hold it while reaffirming your intentions for love. This keeps the energy of the talisman fresh and aligned with your heart's desires.

The Lovebird Feather Talisman is a beautiful and natural way to invite love into your life. It serves as a reminder of your desires and intentions for romance, acting as a magnet for love. Whether you're looking for a new partner or wishing to deepen the love in your current relationship, this talisman helps to focus and amplify your romantic aspirations.

15. Cinnamon Stick Charm for Passion

The Cinnamon Stick Charm for Passion is a spell that harnesses the fiery and stimulating energy of cinnamon to ignite or rekindle passion in a relationship. This spell is perfect for those seeking to enhance the physical and emotional passion in their love life, making it more vibrant and intense.

Purpose: To increase passion and desire in a romantic relationship or to attract a passionate love.

Timing: Best performed on a Tuesday for Mars's fiery energy, or during a waxing to full moon to amplify desire and attraction.

Materials:

1. A cinnamon stick (symbolizes fire and passion)
2. Red ribbon or thread (represents love and desire)
3. A small red candle (to invoke passion)
4. Essential oil of cinnamon or ginger (for added heat and intensity)
5. A piece of paper and a pen

Preparation:

1. Create a passionate and warm atmosphere in your space, perhaps with some romantic music or dim lighting.
2. Write your specific intentions for passion on the paper.

The Spell:

1. **Anointing the Cinnamon Stick**: Begin by anointing the cinnamon stick with the cinnamon or ginger oil, infusing it with your intentions for heightened passion and desire.

2. **Writing Your Intentions**: On the paper, write down your desires for passion in your relationship or future relationship. Be clear and specific about what you wish to manifest.
3. **Lighting the Candle**: Light the red candle to start the ritual, focusing on the flame as a symbol of the passion you wish to attract or enhance.
4. **Binding the Charm**: Wrap the cinnamon stick with the red ribbon or thread while focusing on your intentions. As you do this, you may choose to chant or say affirmations about the passion you are invoking.
5. **Sealing the Intentions**: Place the paper with your written intentions under the candle (ensure it's safe and won't catch fire). Let the candle's warmth symbolize the growing heat and intensity of your desires.
6. **Activating the Charm**: Hold the wrapped cinnamon stick over the flame (be careful not to burn it), allowing it to absorb the candle's energy. Visualize your relationship (current or future) becoming more passionate, exciting, and fulfilling.

After the Spell:

- **Carrying the Charm**: Keep the cinnamon stick charm with you, especially when you are with your partner or when you are open to attracting new love.
- **Rekindling the Flame**: Occasionally, light the red candle again and hold the charm near the flame to reaffirm and strengthen your intentions.

The Cinnamon Stick Charm for Passion is a potent way to bring a spark of excitement and fervor to your romantic life. It's an invocation for passion, reminding you and the universe of your desire for a deeply fulfilling and passionate relationship. Remember, the key to this spell is not just the ingredients but also the fiery energy and intention you infuse into the charm.

16. Stardust Love Wish Ritual

The Stardust Love Wish Ritual is a magical and imaginative spell that taps into the celestial energy of the stars to make a wish for love. This ritual is perfect for those who dream of a love that is as deep and vast as the night sky, inviting the universe to help manifest this desire.

Purpose: To make a heartfelt wish for love, using the symbolic power of the stars to carry your desires into the universe.

Timing: Ideally performed on a clear night where stars are visible, or during a new moon to symbolize new beginnings in love.

Materials:

1. A quiet outdoor space with a clear view of the stars
2. A piece of paper and a pen
3. A small fire-safe container or a fire pit
4. Matches or a lighter
5. Glitter or confetti (to represent stardust)

Preparation:

1. Find a comfortable and quiet spot where you can see the stars without distractions.
2. Meditate for a few moments under the night sky, attuning your energy to the vastness above.

The Ritual:

1. **Writing Your Love Wish**: On the piece of paper, write down your wish for love. These could be qualities you seek in a partner, the type of relationship you desire, or a message to the universe about your readiness for love.

2. **Adding Stardust**: Sprinkle glitter or confetti on your written wish, symbolizing the stardust that makes up the universe and us.
3. **Igniting Your Wish**: Safely light the paper on fire in your fire-safe container or fire pit, watching as your wish transforms into smoke and ascends towards the stars.
4. **Visualizing Your Wish Ascending**: As the paper burns, imagine your wish rising up to the stars, becoming one with the celestial energies. Visualize the stars receiving your wish and beginning the process of manifesting it into reality.
5. **Contemplating Under the Stars**: Spend some time looking at the stars, feeling connected to the universe and open to the love it has to offer. Feel the peace and trust in knowing that your wish is now part of the cosmic energy.

After the Ritual:

- **Reflecting on the Experience**: After completing the ritual, journal about your feelings and any insights that came to you while watching the stars.
- **Regular Star Gazing**: Whenever you gaze at the stars in the future, remember your wish and reaffirm your openness to love.

The Stardust Love Wish Ritual is a deeply spiritual and poetic way to express your desires for love. It connects you to the greater universe, reminding you that love is vast, mysterious, and as attainable as the stars in the sky. This ritual is a beautiful blend of hope, intention, and cosmic connection, ideal for anyone who believes in the power of love and the magic of the stars.

17. Companion Catnip Pouch

The Companion Catnip Pouch is a unique and playful love spell that draws upon the allure and charm of catnip to attract a companion who shares similar qualities of affection, playfulness, and warmth. This spell is ideal for those seeking a light-hearted and joyful approach to finding love.

Purpose: To attract a loving and playful romantic partner or to bring a sense of joy and playfulness into an existing relationship.

Timing: Best performed on a Friday, Venus's day, for love attraction, or during a waxing moon to grow the playful energy in your love life.

Materials:

1. Dried catnip (known for its attractive and joyful qualities)
2. A small cloth pouch or a square of fabric and ribbon
3. Rose quartz (for love and emotional connection)
4. Lavender (for peace and harmony)
5. A small personal item or written intention
6. Optional: A few drops of an essential oil like rose or jasmine for added attraction

Preparation:

1. Choose a relaxed and comfortable setting where you can focus on your intentions.
2. If using essential oil, add a few drops to the catnip to enhance its attraction properties.

The Spell:

1. **Filling the Pouch**: Begin by placing the dried catnip inside the cloth pouch. As you do so, focus on the qualities you seek in a partner or wish to enhance in your relationship - playfulness, affection, joy.
2. **Adding Crystals and Lavender**: Add a small rose quartz crystal to the pouch for love and emotional connection, along with a sprinkle of lavender for peace and harmony in your relationship.
3. **Incorporating Personal Energy**: If you have a small personal item or a piece of paper with your written intention, add this to the pouch. This infuses the spell with your personal energy and specific intentions.
4. **Sealing the Pouch**: Tie the pouch closed with the ribbon, or if using a pre-made pouch, pull the strings tight. As you seal the pouch, visualize your love life filled with the playful and affectionate energy of catnip.
5. **Activating the Pouch**: Hold the pouch in your hands, gently shake it to mix the contents, and speak your intentions aloud or in your heart. Affirm that the energies within are working to attract the companion you desire.

After the Spell:

- **Carrying the Pouch**: Keep the catnip pouch with you, especially in social situations, to attract a partner or to infuse your current relationship with joy and playfulness.
- **Refreshing the Pouch**: Periodically, open the pouch to renew the catnip and restate your intentions, keeping the energy fresh and aligned with your desires.

The Companion Catnip Pouch spell is a fun and light-hearted way to approach love magic. It reminds us that love can be joyful, playful, and deeply satisfying. This spell encourages you not only to seek love but to enjoy the process, staying open to the delightful surprises that relationships can bring.

18. Heartbeat Synchronization Spell

The Heartbeat Synchronization Spell is a deeply intimate and powerful ritual designed to align and synchronize the heartbeats of two individuals, symbolizing a profound emotional and spiritual connection. This spell is ideal for couples seeking to deepen their bond and understanding or for those who wish to attract a partner with whom they can share a deeply harmonized relationship.

Purpose: To deepen the emotional and spiritual connection in a relationship, creating a harmonious and synchronized bond between partners.

Timing: Best performed during a full moon to harness its energy for emotional connection and completion, or on a Friday to align with Venus, the planet of love and relationships.

Materials:

1. Two small red candles (representing each partner's heart)
2. A piece of string or ribbon, preferably red (symbolizing the connection between hearts)
3. A personal item from each partner (such as a small photo, a piece of jewelry, or a written note)
4. A quiet space where you can focus on the ritual undisturbed

Preparation:

1. Set up a sacred space, ensuring it's peaceful and free from distractions.
2. Place the personal items of each partner beside each candle.

The Spell:

1. **Lighting the Candles**: Begin by lighting the two red candles, representing the hearts of each partner. As you light them, focus on the intention of syncing your heartbeats and deepening your connection.
2. **Connecting the Candles**: Tie the piece of string or ribbon around both candles, symbolizing the linking of your hearts. As you tie the string, envision your heartbeats aligning and synchronizing.
3. **Meditation and Visualization**: Sit quietly in front of the candles. Close your eyes and take deep, slow breaths. Visualize your heartbeat and your partner's heartbeat. Imagine them slowly coming into a harmonious rhythm, beating together in perfect synchronization.
4. **Affirmation of Connection**: Chant or affirm your desire for a harmonized connection. You might say something like, "With every beat of our hearts, our love grows stronger, our bond deeper, our connection unbreakable."
5. **Focusing on the Personal Items**: Hold or focus on the personal items. Feel the presence and essence of each partner, bringing a sense of closeness and unity.
6. **Concluding the Ritual**: Allow the candles to burn down safely. As they burn, visualize the strengthening bond and synchronized heartbeats becoming a reality in your relationship.

After the Spell:

- **Reflecting on the Connection:** Spend time with your partner, if possible, after the ritual. Engage in activities that promote closeness and understanding.
- **Revisiting the Intentions:** Regularly revisit the intentions set during this spell, especially during moments of togetherness, to keep the energy alive and potent.

The Heartbeat Synchronization Spell is a powerful way to celebrate and strengthen the spiritual and emotional bond in a relationship. It serves as a reminder of the deep connections we share with our partners and the harmonious rhythms that can exist within a loving relationship.

19. Vanilla Bean Love Enhancer

The Vanilla Bean Love Enhancer is a sweet and sensual spell that utilizes the alluring and comforting properties of vanilla to enhance love and attraction in a relationship. This spell is perfect for those looking to add a spark of romance and deepen the emotional connection with their partner.

Purpose: To enhance romantic feelings, deepen emotional connections, and add a touch of sweetness to a relationship.

Timing: Ideal to perform on a Friday, associated with Venus, the planet of love, or during a waxing moon to increase romantic feelings.

Materials:

1. A vanilla bean (a symbol of warmth, attraction, and comfort)
2. A small jar or container
3. Honey (to sweeten the relationship)
4. Red or pink candles (for love and passion)
5. Rose petals (for romance and affection)
6. A piece of paper and a pen
7. Optional: A few drops of vanilla essential oil for enhanced effect

Preparation:

1. Create a loving and serene atmosphere, perhaps with soft lighting or romantic music.
2. Write down your desires and intentions for your relationship on the piece of paper.

The Spell:

1. **Activating the Vanilla Bean:** Start by holding the vanilla bean in your hands. Warm it with your energy, focusing on your intentions for love and romance.
2. **Preparing the Jar:** Place the activated vanilla bean into your jar. If using, add a few drops of vanilla essential oil for an intensified effect.
3. **Adding Sweetness with Honey:** Pour honey into the jar, covering the vanilla bean. As you do this, visualize your relationship being filled with sweetness and joy.
4. **Incorporating Rose Petals:** Sprinkle rose petals into the jar, symbolizing the deepening of romance and affection in your relationship.
5. **Sealing Your Intentions:** Roll up the paper with your written intentions and place it in the jar. Close the jar tightly.
6. **Candle Ritual:** Light the red or pink candles around the jar. Focus on the flame, seeing it as a symbol of the passion and warmth in your relationship.
7. **Affirmation and Visualization:** Recite an affirmation or chant that resonates with your intention for love. Visualize your relationship growing stronger, more passionate, and deeply connected.

After the Spell:

- **Placing the Love Enhancer:** Keep the jar in a special place, such as your bedroom or a shared space, to continuously radiate loving energy.
- **Regular Activation:** Occasionally, shake the jar gently to reactivate its energies and reaffirm your commitment to nurturing love and romance in your relationship.

The Vanilla Bean Love Enhancer is a delightful way to consciously invite more affection, understanding, and sweetness into your love life. Its enchanting scent and symbolic significance make it a potent tool for those wishing to enhance the romantic and emotional aspects of their relationship. Remember, the true magic of this spell lies in the intention and love you infuse into every step of the ritual.

20. Starlit Affection Visualization

The Starlit Affection Visualization is a calming and romantic spell that taps into the tranquil energy of a starlit night sky to foster affection and a deeper emotional connection. This visualization is ideal for individuals seeking to manifest love or couples who wish to strengthen their bond under the romantic and infinite backdrop of the stars.

Purpose: To manifest affection and deepen emotional bonds, using the serene and endless energy of the starlit sky.

Timing: Best performed on a clear night where stars are visible, symbolizing endless possibilities and the vastness of affection.

Materials:

1. A comfortable place to lie down and gaze at the stars (either outdoors or near a window)
2. A blanket or mat
3. Optional: Soft music or nature sounds to enhance the atmosphere
4. Optional: A notebook or journal to record insights or feelings post-visualization

Preparation:

1. Find a quiet and comfortable spot where you can clearly see the night sky, free from artificial lights and distractions.
2. Lie down and make yourself comfortable, allowing the calm of the night to envelop you.

The Visualization:

1. **Connecting with the Stars**: Begin by taking deep, slow breaths, gazing at the stars. Let their twinkling light and vastness fill your vision.
2. **Envisioning Affection**: Close your eyes and start to visualize the qualities of affection and love you desire. Picture these qualities as gentle starlight, softly descending from the sky and enveloping you in a warm, luminous glow.
3. **Manifesting Your Desires**: Imagine this starlight transforming into the affection you seek. If you're in a relationship, envision this light strengthening the bond between you and your partner. If you're single, imagine attracting a partner who resonates with the qualities of the starlight.
4. **Deepening the Connection**: As you bask in this visualization, feel the emotions associated with deep, affectionate love. Allow these feelings to grow stronger, more tangible, and real with each breath.
5. **Affirming the Visualization**: Whisper or think of affirmations that align with your visualization, such as "I am surrounded by love as endless as the stars" or "Our love grows stronger under the starlit sky."

After the Visualization:

- **Reflecting on the Experience**: Take a few moments to come back to the present. If you have a journal, write down any insights, feelings, or realizations that came to you during the visualization.

- **Regular Practice**: Revisit this visualization regularly, especially on clear starry nights, to reinforce your intentions and continue nurturing the affection in your life.

The Starlit Affection Visualization is a peaceful and powerful way to connect with the universal energy of love and affection. It serves as a reminder of the vast and infinite possibilities for love in our lives, mirroring the endless expanse of the night sky. This spell is a beautiful blend of tranquility, hope, and romantic longing, perfect for those who find inspiration and peace in the celestial dimension.

21. Empathic Connection Spell

The Empathic Connection Spell is a deeply intuitive and sensitive ritual designed to enhance understanding and emotional connection between two people. This spell is particularly effective for couples seeking to deepen their empathy towards each other or for individuals wishing to establish a strong emotional connection in a new relationship.

Purpose: To foster deeper empathy and understanding in a relationship, creating a stronger emotional bond.

Timing: Ideal to perform during a waxing moon to grow emotional connections, or when the moon is in Cancer or Pisces for heightened emotional sensitivity.

Materials:

1. Two blue candles (symbolizing communication and emotional depth)
2. A photograph of each person involved in the relationship or a personal item from each
3. A piece of amethyst or moonstone (stones of intuition and empathy)
4. Lavender or chamomile (herbs for calmness and understanding)
5. A small bowl of water (representing emotional fluidity)
6. A piece of paper and a pen

Preparation:

1. Set up a calm and comfortable space for the ritual, ensuring privacy and a peaceful atmosphere.
2. Write a heartfelt intention or prayer for empathy and understanding on the piece of paper.

The Spell:

1. **Candle Arrangement**: Begin by placing the two blue candles on your altar or designated space, symbolizing you and your partner or the person you wish to connect with.
2. **Placing the Photographs/Items**: Between the candles, place the photographs or personal items, creating a physical representation of your connection.
3. **Adding Stones and Herbs**: Place the amethyst or moonstone near the photographs or items, and sprinkle lavender or chamomile around them, enhancing the empathic energy.
4. **Water as a Symbol**: Position the bowl of water in front of the items, signifying the flow and fluidity of emotions between you.
5. **Lighting the Candles**: Light the candles, focusing on opening your heart and mind to deeper understanding and empathy.
6. **Reciting Your Intention**: Read aloud or silently reflect on your written intention or prayer, asking for an open and empathic connection.
7. **Meditation and Visualization**: Spend a few minutes in meditation, visualizing a gentle flow of light and energy between you and the other person, symbolizing the growing empathy and understanding.

8. **Concluding the Spell**: After the meditation, leave the candles to burn down safely. Keep the photographs or items on your altar, along with the stone, as a reminder of your intention.

After the Spell:

- **Ongoing Empathy Practice**: In the days following the spell, make a conscious effort to practice empathy and understanding in your interactions with your partner or the person you are connected with.
- **Reflecting on Changes**: Regularly take time to reflect on any changes or shifts in your emotional connection, acknowledging the growth and depth that has developed.

The Empathic Connection Spell is a beautiful and meaningful way to consciously enhance the emotional depth and understanding in your relationship. It serves as a powerful reminder of the importance of empathy in creating strong, lasting bonds and the transformative effect it can have on our connections with others.

22. Twin Flame Recognition Ritual

The Twin Flame Recognition Ritual is a spiritual and mystical practice designed to aid in recognizing and connecting with your twin flame – a soul believed to be the other half of your spiritual energy. This ritual is ideal for those on a path of profound spiritual partnership and seeking a connection that transcends the ordinary planes of romantic relationships.

Purpose: To facilitate the recognition and connection with your twin flame, enhancing spiritual awareness and harmony.

Timing: Best performed during a new moon to symbolize new beginnings or during a significant astrological event like a solar or lunar eclipse, which symbolizes transformation and deeper understanding.

Materials:

1. Two white candles (representing purity and spiritual connection)
2. A mirror (to reflect and recognize your own soul)
3. Rose quartz and clear quartz crystals (for love and clarity)
4. Lavender or sage (for spiritual cleansing and opening)
5. A piece of paper and a pen
6. A quiet and sacred space where you won't be disturbed

Preparation:

1. Create a tranquil environment conducive to introspection and spiritual connection.
2. Cleanse your space with lavender or sage to purify the energy.

The Ritual:

1. **Setting the Space**: Arrange the two candles in front of the mirror, and place the rose quartz and clear quartz crystals nearby.
2. **Lighting the Candles**: Light the candles, focusing on the flame as a gateway to higher spiritual awareness.
3. **Self-Reflection**: Look into the mirror, taking deep, slow breaths. Reflect on your own soul and the journey that has led you to this point.
4. **Writing Your Intentions**: On the paper, write your intentions and what you seek in your twin flame connection. Be honest and open-hearted about your desires for this spiritual partnership.
5. **Connecting with the Universe**: Hold the paper and read your intentions aloud. Then, fold the paper and place it between the candles.
6. **Meditation and Visualization**: Close your eyes and meditate, visualizing a light connecting you to the universe. Imagine this light reaching out and connecting with the soul that resonates as your twin flame.
7. **Affirmation of Connection**: Affirm your readiness and openness to meet and recognize your twin flame. Trust the universe to guide this soul connection.

After the Ritual:

- **Storing the Intentions**: Keep the written intentions in a safe place, perhaps under your pillow or in a special box.
- **Ongoing Reflection**: Regularly reflect on your journey and stay open to the signs and guidance from the universe regarding your twin flame.

- **Mindfulness and Patience**: Stay mindful and patient, as the connection with a twin flame often unfolds in divine timing and may require spiritual growth and readiness.

The Twin Flame Recognition Ritual is a powerful way to open your heart and soul to the profound connection of a twin flame. It's an acknowledgment of your readiness to explore the deepest spiritual partnership and an invitation to the universe to bring this soul into your life. This ritual is for those who seek a connection that is not just about romance, but about the evolution and growth of the soul.

23. Binding Heartstrings Spell

The Binding Heartstrings Spell is a potent ritual that symbolically binds the heartstrings of two people, fostering a deep and enduring emotional connection. It is particularly effective for couples seeking a stronger bond or for those who wish to secure the affections of a loved one.

Purpose: To strengthen the emotional and spiritual bond between two individuals, creating a lasting and deeply connected relationship.

Timing: Best performed during a full moon for maximum emotional depth and intensity, or on a Friday to align with Venus's energy of love.

Materials:

1. Two strands of ribbon or cord, preferably in red or pink (symbolizing the heartstrings of each individual)
2. A personal item from each person (such as a small photograph, a lock of hair, or a piece of jewelry)
3. A rose quartz crystal (for love and heart connection)
4. A lavender or jasmine incense (for love and harmony)
5. A small container or box
6. A white or red candle (for unity and passion)

Preparation:

1. Create a loving and harmonious atmosphere in your space, perhaps with gentle music or soft lighting.
2. Cleanse the area and your materials with the incense.

The Ritual:

1. **Candle Lighting**: Begin by lighting the candle, setting the intention for a united and passionate bond.
2. **Binding the Ribbons**: Lay out the two strands of ribbon or cord. Place the personal items from each person at opposite ends. Slowly and intentionally, start to braid or twist the ribbons together, symbolizing the intertwining of your heartstrings.
3. **Placing the Rose Quartz**: Once the ribbons are fully intertwined, tie a knot around the rose quartz crystal. This act seals the emotional connection with the energy of love.
4. **Chanting for Connection**: As you tie the knot, chant or say a heartfelt prayer or affirmation, such as "With these heartstrings bound, let our hearts beat as one, in love and harmony."
5. **Securing the Bond**: Place the bound ribbons and rose quartz, along with the personal items, inside the small container or box. This physical act represents the protection and nurturing of your bond.
6. **Concluding the Ritual**: Allow the candle to burn down safely while you meditate on the bond you have created or strengthened. Visualize your relationship being filled with love, understanding, and deep connection.

After the Ritual:

- **Keeping the Bound Heartstrings**: Store the container with the bound heartstrings in a special place, such as your bedroom or a shared space, as a constant reminder of the bond you share.

- **Regular Reinforcement**: Occasionally revisit the container, perhaps on anniversaries or special days, to reinforce your commitment and the strength of your bond.

The Binding Heartstrings Spell is a powerful way to celebrate and solidify the emotional and spiritual connection between two people. It serves as a beautiful and symbolic gesture of commitment and unity, reinforcing the idea that your hearts are inextricably linked in love and harmony.

24. Love's Journey Tarot Spell

The Love's Journey Tarot Spell is a reflective and insightful ritual that uses the symbolic power of Tarot cards to guide and influence your romantic journey. This spell is ideal for gaining clarity on your path to love, whether you're seeking a new relationship or hoping to strengthen an existing one.

Purpose: To gain insight and guidance on your romantic journey, using the wisdom of the Tarot to illuminate the path to love.

Timing: Perform this spell during a waxing moon to draw in new love or during a full moon for clarity in existing relationships.

Materials:

1. A Tarot deck, or specifically selected Tarot cards representing love (such as The Lovers, Two of Cups, Ten of Cups)
2. A pink or red candle (for love and passion)
3. Rose petals or rose quartz crystals (for emotional connection and harmony)
4. A quiet space where you can focus on the ritual
5. A piece of paper and a pen

Preparation:

1. Set up a peaceful area for the ritual, ensuring you won't be disturbed.
2. Lightly cleanse your Tarot deck and space with incense or sage.

The Ritual:

1. **Candle Lighting**: Begin by lighting the pink or red candle, setting an intention for love and emotional clarity.
2. **Selecting Tarot Cards**: If you haven't pre-selected cards, shuffle your Tarot deck with the intention of understanding your love journey. Draw three cards that represent past, present, and future aspects of your love life.
3. **Analyzing the Cards**: Lay the cards in front of you. Reflect on their meanings and how they relate to your experiences and desires in love.
4. **Writing Insights**: On your paper, jot down the insights and feelings each card evokes, focusing on how these can guide you in love. Write down affirmations or actions inspired by the cards.
5. **Surrounding with Rose Elements**: Place the rose petals or rose quartz around the cards, asking for emotional harmony and clarity in your love journey.
6. **Meditation and Visualization**: Spend a few minutes meditating on the cards and your written insights. Visualize your path to love unfolding as guided by the wisdom of the Tarot.

After the Ritual:

- **Contemplation**: Keep the Tarot cards out for a while to remind you of the insights gained. Revisit your notes and reflect on how you can apply the Tarot's guidance to your love life.
- **Regular Tarot Readings**: Consider doing regular Tarot readings focusing on love to continually seek guidance and clarity on your romantic journey.

The Love's Journey Tarot Spell is a thought-provoking and enlightening way to use the ancient wisdom of Tarot as a tool in your romantic life. It offers a unique opportunity to reflect on your past, present, and future in love, providing valuable insights that can help shape your journey toward a fulfilling and harmonious romantic relationship.

25. Harmonic Convergence Amulet

The Harmonic Convergence Amulet is a magical creation designed to harmonize personal energies with those of a desired or existing partner, fostering a deeper and more synchronized connection. This spell is excellent for those seeking alignment in their romantic relationships or looking to attract a partner whose energy resonates harmoniously with their own.

Purpose: To create an amulet that aligns and synchronizes personal energies with a romantic partner, enhancing harmony and understanding in the relationship.

Timing: Ideal to perform when the moon is in Libra for balance in relationships, or during a waxing moon to grow harmonious energies.

Materials:

1. A small locket or amulet container
2. Two small pieces of rose quartz (for love and emotional attunement)
3. Lavender or chamomile (herbs for peace and harmony)
4. A personal item or symbol from each partner (such as a photo, hair strand, or written note)
5. A blue or pink candle (blue for communication, pink for affection)
6. A piece of paper and a pen

Preparation:

1. Find a quiet space where you can perform the ritual without interruption.
2. Cleanse the space and your materials with the scent of lavender or chamomile.

The Spell:

1. **Candle Lighting**: Start by lighting the blue or pink candle, focusing on the intention of creating harmony and understanding in your relationship.
2. **Preparing the Amulet**: Open your locket or amulet container. Place one piece of rose quartz inside, along with the personal item or symbol from one partner.
3. **Adding Herbs for Harmony**: Sprinkle a pinch of lavender or chamomile into the amulet, infusing it with energies of peace and understanding.
4. **Completing the Amulet**: Add the second piece of rose quartz and the other partner's item or symbol. As you do this, visualize the amulet absorbing the essence of each partner, creating a harmonious blend.
5. **Sealing the Amulet**: Close the amulet and hold it in your hands. Recite a prayer or affirmation for harmony and understanding, such as, "In this amulet, our energies converge, bringing harmony, love, and understanding to our union."
6. **Meditation and Visualization**: Spend a few minutes meditating with the amulet, envisioning its energy radiating out and creating a harmonious field around you and your partner.

After the Spell:

- **Wearing the Amulet**: Wear the amulet or keep it in a special place where both partners spend time, like a bedroom or shared living space.
- **Reinforcing the Amulet's Power**: Regularly hold the amulet, reaffirming your intentions for a harmonious and balanced relationship.

The Harmonic Convergence Amulet is a powerful symbol of unity and synchronicity in a relationship. It acts as a constant reminder of the harmonious energies you share with your partner and the balanced connection you aim to maintain. This spell is a beautiful way to celebrate and strengthen the spiritual and emotional bond you share with your significant other.

26. Soulmate Summoning Circle

The Soulmate Summoning Circle is a mystical and profound ritual designed to call forth your soulmate—someone who aligns perfectly with your spirit and essence. This spell is especially suited for those who are ready to welcome their soulmate into their lives, providing a beacon for this profound connection.

Purpose: To draw in your soulmate, creating a spiritual pathway for your paths to meet.

Timing: Best performed during a new moon, symbolizing new beginnings, or on a night of Venus to harness the energy of love and partnership.

Materials:

1. Six pink or red candles (symbolizing love and attraction)
2. Rose petals (for romantic love)
3. A piece of paper and a pen (to write down qualities you seek in a soulmate)
4. Lavender or jasmine incense (for relaxation and spiritual openness)
5. A personal item that holds emotional significance to you
6. A circle of salt (for protection and to create a sacred space)

Preparation:

1. Find a quiet and comfortable space where you won't be disturbed.
2. Cleanse the area with the incense, setting a peaceful and inviting tone.

The Ritual:

1. **Casting the Circle**: Begin by creating a circle with the salt, large enough for you to sit inside comfortably.
2. **Candle Placement**: Arrange the candles around the perimeter of the salt circle, evenly spaced.
3. **Lighting the Candles**: Light each candle, focusing on the flame as a beacon to attract your soulmate.
4. **Writing Down Qualities**: On the paper, write down the qualities you desire in your soulmate—be specific about what you seek in this spiritual partner.
5. **Placing the Personal Item**: Put the personal item in the center of the circle as a representation of yourself and your readiness to connect with your soulmate.
6. **Scattering Rose Petals**: Gently scatter the rose petals within the circle, symbolizing the blossoming of love.
7. **Meditation and Visualization**: Sit in the center of the circle with the paper. Meditate on your qualities list, visualizing the kind of relationship you wish to have. Picture your soulmate coming into your life, ready to share a profound connection.
8. **Closing the Ritual**: Once you feel your intentions have been fully projected, carefully extinguish the candles. Fold the piece of paper and keep it in a safe place, such as under your pillow or in a special box.

After the Ritual:

- **Regular Reflection**: Regularly reflect on the qualities you wrote down, affirming your readiness and openness to meet your soulmate.

- **Patience and Trust**: Be patient and trust in the universe's timing. Stay open to the possibilities and signs that may lead you to your soulmate.

The Soulmate Summoning Circle is a powerful way to actively engage with the universe in your quest for a soulmate. It combines intention-setting with symbolic actions to create a potent magnet for love, drawing your soulmate closer to your sphere. This ritual is a beautiful and hopeful step towards finding a connection that resonates deeply with your spirit.

27. Passionate Ember Incantation

The Passionate Ember Incantation is a spell that kindles and intensifies the flames of passion and desire in a relationship. This spell is perfect for those wishing to revive the spark in their romantic life or to ensure that the fire of passion continues to burn brightly in a new relationship.

Purpose: To ignite or rekindle passion and desire in a romantic relationship.

Timing: Best performed on a Tuesday, associated with Mars, the planet of passion and desire, or during a waxing to full moon to increase the intensity of feelings.

Materials:

1. A red candle (representing passion and desire)
2. Cinnamon sticks or chili pepper (for heat and intensity in love)
3. A piece of paper and a red pen
4. An image or symbol of the relationship (such as a photo of you and your partner)
5. Optional: A few drops of essential oil like ylang-ylang or ginger (to enhance sensuality)

Preparation:

1. Create a space that feels warm and inviting, conducive to the energies of passion.
2. If using, add a few drops of the essential oil to the candle.

The Incantation:

1. **Setting the Atmosphere**: Light the red candle, allowing its warmth to fill your space.
2. **Preparing the Ingredients**: Place the cinnamon sticks or chili pepper near the candle, symbolizing the addition of heat to your relationship.
3. **Writing Your Desires**: On the piece of paper, using the red pen, write down your desires for passion and intimacy. Be specific and open about what you wish to manifest.
4. **Invoking the Incantation**: Hold the paper and read your desires aloud as the candle burns. As you speak, visualize your relationship being infused with renewed passion and intensity.
5. **Focusing on the Image/Symbol**: Place the image or symbol of your relationship in front of the candle. Meditate on it, picturing the relationship filled with vibrant and passionate energy.
6. **Chanting for Passion**: Chant the following or similar words: "With this flame, passion grows, in our hearts, it brightly glows. Heat and desire, come to us, in our love, forever thus."
7. **Concluding the Ritual**: Allow the candle to burn down safely while your desires are set into motion. Keep the written desires in a place where you can see them as a reminder of your intentions.

After the Spell:

- **Revisiting the Incantation**: Regularly revisit the incantation, especially when you wish to reignite the flames of passion in your relationship.

- **Reflecting on the Relationship**: Take time to engage in activities that naturally stimulate passion and connection with your partner, fostering the energy invoked in the spell.

The Passionate Ember Incantation is a potent way to infuse your romantic life with the energy of desire and passion. It serves as a reminder of the vibrancy and intensity that love can bring, keeping the embers of passion alive and glowing.

28. Rosewater Rekindling Potion

The Rosewater Rekindling Potion is a gentle yet powerful spell, using the classic symbol of romance - the rose - to reignite the spark of love and affection in a relationship. This potion is ideal for those who wish to renew the feelings of romance and intimacy in their partnership.

Purpose: To refresh and rekindle the feelings of love and romance in a relationship.

Timing: Best prepared during a waxing moon to grow feelings of love, or on a Friday to align with the energies of Venus, the planet of love.

Materials:

1. Fresh rose petals (preferably from red or pink roses for love and passion)
2. Distilled or spring water
3. A small pot and stove for boiling
4. A strainer or cheesecloth
5. A clean glass bottle or jar for storage
6. Honey or sugar (to sweeten the potion and relationship)
7. A small pink or white candle (for pure affection and love)
8. Optional: A few drops of vanilla extract or essential oil for added sweetness and warmth

Preparation:

1. Select a time and place where you can create your potion undisturbed, infusing it with your focused intent and energy.
2. Gently cleanse your materials and space before beginning.

The Spell:

1. **Boiling the Rose Petals**: Place the rose petals in the pot and cover them with distilled or spring water. Bring the water to a gentle boil, allowing the essence of the roses to infuse into the water.
2. **Adding Sweetness**: Once the water is infused and colored by the petals, add honey or sugar to sweeten the potion, symbolizing the sweetness you wish to bring back into your relationship.
3. **Candle Lighting**: Light the pink or white candle beside your brewing potion to infuse it with energies of love and affection.
4. **Infusing with Intent**: As the potion simmers, focus on your intentions for your relationship. Visualize the love and romance rekindling and blossoming anew.
5. **Straining the Potion**: After the potion has simmered and is infused with the rose essence, strain it using a strainer or cheesecloth into the glass bottle or jar.
6. **Concluding the Ritual**: Allow the potion to cool, and if you choose, add a few drops of vanilla extract or essential oil for an added layer of warmth and affection.

After the Spell:

- **Using the Potion**: Use the rosewater potion as a personal fragrance, add it to a bath, or lightly anoint items around your home, like bedsheets or curtains.
- **Reflecting and Sharing**: Share the potion with your partner, if appropriate, using it in a way that invites romance, such as in a shared bath or as a gentle perfume.

The Rosewater Rekindling Potion is a beautiful, symbolic way to bring back the essence of romance into your relationship. Its gentle energy and the enchanting scent of roses make it a delightful and effective tool for those looking to revive the sweet and tender aspects of their love.

29. Love's Labyrinth Visualization

The Love's Labyrinth Visualization is a meditative and introspective spell that guides you through a symbolic labyrinth to discover the deeper truths and paths in your love life. This visualization is perfect for those seeking clarity and guidance in their romantic journey, whether to find a new love or to navigate the complexities of an existing relationship.

Purpose: To gain insight and direction in your love life through a guided, meditative journey within a symbolic labyrinth.

Timing: Best performed during a waning moon to release confusion and uncertainty, or when Venus is prominent in the night sky, symbolizing love and relationships.

Materials:

1. A quiet and comfortable space for meditation
2. Soft, calming music or sounds of nature (optional)
3. A notebook and pen for recording insights post-visualization

Preparation:

1. Choose a time and place where you will not be disturbed, allowing for full concentration and introspection.
2. If desired, play soft music or nature sounds to aid in relaxation.

The Visualization:

1. **Entering the Labyrinth**: Begin by sitting or lying down in your chosen space. Close your eyes and take deep, steady

breaths. Visualize yourself standing at the entrance of a vast labyrinth. This labyrinth represents your journey in love.

2. **Walking the Path**: In your mind, start walking the path of the labyrinth. With each turn and twist, reflect on your past experiences in love, the lessons learned, and the growth you've achieved.
3. **Center of the Labyrinth**: As you reach the center of the labyrinth, pause. Here, in the heart of the labyrinth, allow yourself to feel the presence of love in its purest form. Ask yourself what you truly seek in love and relationships.
4. **Receiving Insight**: In the center, open yourself to insights or messages. These may come as feelings, words, images, or simply a sense of knowing.
5. **Returning Path**: Begin your journey back through the labyrinth, carrying with you the insights and clarity you've gained. As you walk back, visualize how you will apply these insights to your love life.
6. **Exiting the Labyrinth**: Once you exit the labyrinth in your visualization, gently bring your awareness back to your physical surroundings. Take a few deep breaths and open your eyes.

After the Visualization:

- **Reflecting on the Experience**: Take some time to jot down any insights, feelings, or revelations you experienced during the visualization. Reflect on how these can be applied to your romantic journey.

- **Regular Practice**: Consider revisiting this visualization regularly, especially when faced with decisions or uncertainties in your love life, to gain clarity and guidance.

Love's Labyrinth Visualization is a profound tool for introspection and guidance in matters of the heart. It provides a symbolic journey through the complexities of love, offering a unique and insightful way to understand your path and desires in relationships.

30. Aphrodite's Attraction Elixir

Aphrodite's Attraction Elixir is a bewitching potion inspired by the goddess of love and beauty herself. It's crafted to enhance allure, charm, and the magnetic qualities of the one who consumes it, making it perfect for those seeking to amplify their attractiveness and draw romantic attention.

Purpose: To enhance personal allure and attract romantic interest, embodying the captivating essence of Aphrodite.

Timing: Ideal to concoct during a waxing moon for attraction or on a Friday, the day dedicated to Venus, the Roman equivalent of Aphrodite.

Materials:

1. Rose petals (symbol of love and beauty)
2. A small vial of spring water
3. Honey (for sweetness and allure)
4. A pinch of cinnamon (for warmth and attraction)
5. A few drops of vanilla essence (for sensuality)
6. A small pink or red candle (for passion and desire)
7. A piece of rose quartz (for love energy)
8. A glass jar or bottle for the elixir

Preparation:

1. Set a space that feels luxurious and comfortable, enhancing your connection to beauty and love.
2. Cleanse your space and materials to purify the energy.

The Spell:

1. **Candle Lighting**: Begin by lighting the pink or red candle, invoking the spirit of Aphrodite and her powers of attraction and beauty.
2. **Rose Petal Infusion**: In the glass jar, place the rose petals and pour the spring water over them. Let the petals infuse the water with their essence, symbolizing love and beauty.
3. **Adding Sweetness and Warmth**: Stir in the honey and cinnamon, infusing the elixir with sweetness and a warm allure.
4. **Vanilla for Sensuality**: Add a few drops of vanilla essence to the mixture, enhancing the elixir's sensual energy.
5. **Charging with Rose Quartz**: Place the rose quartz near or in the jar (ensure it's clean and safe to immerse), allowing its energy to charge the elixir with vibrations of love.
6. **Sealing the Intentions**: As the candle burns, focus on your intention to become irresistibly attractive and charming. Visualize yourself radiating a magnetic energy that draws others to you.
7. **Concluding the Ritual**: Once the elixir is charged, extinguish the candle safely. Store the elixir in a cool, dry place.

After the Spell:

- **Using the Elixir**: Before social interactions or dates, dab a little of the elixir on your pulse points, like your wrists or neck. As you apply it, reaffirm your intention to exude allure and attractiveness.

- **Recharging the Elixir**: Occasionally, place the jar in the moonlight, especially during a full or waxing moon, to recharge its powers.

Aphrodite's Attraction Elixir combines the mystique of ancient love potions with modern-day magical practices. It's a delightful way to connect with the timeless energy of attraction and beauty, empowering you to step into your most enchanting and alluring self.

31. Magnetic Desire Mirror Spell

The Magnetic Desire Mirror Spell is a captivating ritual that utilizes the reflective power of a mirror to attract and manifest your deepest romantic desires. This spell is ideal for those who wish to draw in a specific kind of romantic experience or a particular quality in a partner.

Purpose: To use the mirror as a magical tool to reflect and attract your romantic desires into reality.

Timing: Best performed on a Friday, the day associated with Venus, or during a waxing moon to draw in desires.

Materials:

1. A small mirror (representing reflection, clarity, and manifestation)
2. A red or pink candle (symbolizing love and desire)
3. Rose petals (for romance and attraction)
4. A piece of paper and a pen (to write down your desires)
5. A personal item or symbol that represents love to you
6. Optional: A few drops of attraction oil or perfume

Preparation:

1. Create a serene space where you can focus on your intentions without interruption.
2. Cleanse your mirror, candle, and other materials, preparing them energetically for the ritual.

The Spell:

1. **Candle Lighting**: Begin by lighting the red or pink candle, setting the atmosphere for love and desire.
2. **Writing Down Desires**: On the piece of paper, write down the specific romantic desires or qualities you wish to attract. Be as clear and detailed as possible.
3. **Mirror Activation**: Place the mirror in front of the candle, ensuring the flame is reflected in the glass. This act symbolizes your desires being reflected back into the universe.
4. **Rose Petal Circle**: Surround the base of the candle and mirror with rose petals, creating a circle of romantic energy.
5. **Personal Symbol Placement**: Place your personal item or symbol of love in front of the mirror, imbuing the spell with your personal energy and intention.
6. **Visualization and Incantation**: Focus on the mirror and see your written desires being reflected and amplified. Recite an incantation or affirmation that resonates with your intentions, such as "Mirror of love, reflect my heart's desire, bring to me the love that I admire."
7. **Concluding the Spell**: Allow the candle to burn down safely while the mirror continues to reflect the energy of your desires. Keep the paper with your desires in a safe place, such as tucked behind the mirror or in a special box.

After the Spell:

- **Regular Reflection**: Spend a few moments each day in front of the mirror, reaffirming your desires and visualizing them manifesting in your life.

- **Openness to Love**: Stay open and receptive to the opportunities and people that come into your life, trusting that the universe is reflecting your desires back to you.

The Magnetic Desire Mirror Spell is a powerful way to employ the symbolic energy of the mirror in magical practice, focusing and amplifying your intentions to attract love. It's a beautiful blend of reflection, intention, and magical manifestation, making it a potent ritual for those looking to enhance their romantic life.

32. Entwined Destiny Knot Ritual

The Entwined Destiny Knot Ritual is a powerful and symbolic spell designed to intertwine the destinies of two individuals, strengthening the bond and synchronizing their paths. This ritual is particularly meaningful for couples looking to solidify their commitment or for those seeking a deep, fated connection with a future partner.

Purpose: To symbolically bind your destiny with that of your partner or future lover, creating a profound connection and shared path.

Timing: Ideal to perform on a full moon for completion and fulfillment in relationships, or during a significant astrological event like a lunar eclipse, signifying transformation and deep connections.

Materials:

1. Two lengths of red ribbon or cord (symbolizing the individual destinies)
2. A white candle (for purity and new beginnings)
3. Rose oil (for love and emotional connection)
4. A rose quartz crystal (to symbolize love and harmony)
5. A small piece of paper and a pen
6. A bowl of water (representing emotional depth and intuition)

Preparation:

1. Create a peaceful and sacred space where you can perform the ritual without interruption.
2. Cleanse your materials and space, setting a clear and focused intention.

The Ritual:

1. **Candle Lighting**: Begin by lighting the white candle, invoking clarity, purity, and intention.
2. **Anointing the Ribbons**: Anoint each ribbon with a few drops of rose oil while focusing on your intentions to intertwine your destinies.
3. **Writing Intentions**: On the piece of paper, write down your desires for the relationship or qualities you seek in a future partner.
4. **Knot Tying**: Tie the two ribbons together in a knot while visualizing your destinies becoming entwined. As you tie the knot, recite an affirmation or chant that resonates with your intention.
5. **Charging with Rose Quartz**: Place the rose quartz on top of the knot and paper, infusing the ritual with energies of love and harmony.
6. **Water Blessing**: Pass the entwined ribbons over the bowl of water, symbolizing the depth of your emotional connection and intuitive understanding of each other.
7. **Final Affirmation**: Hold the entwined ribbons and affirm your readiness to walk your paths together, united in purpose and love.

After the Ritual:

- **Storing the Knot**: Keep the entwined ribbons and rose quartz in a special place, such as your bedroom or another meaningful area, as a reminder of your connected destinies.

- **Reflect on the Bond**: Regularly revisit your intentions and the symbolic knot, especially during significant moments in your relationship or when seeking to attract a deep connection.

The Entwined Destiny Knot Ritual is a beautiful and meaningful way to celebrate the intertwining of two souls, setting intentions for a shared journey filled with love, harmony, and mutual understanding. It's a powerful symbolic act for those who believe in the magic of connected destinies and the profound bonds that can be forged through ritual and intention.

33. Eternal Flame Candle Enchantment

The Eternal Flame Candle Enchantment is a spell that symbolizes the burning passion and enduring love in a relationship. This enchanting ritual uses the steady flame of a candle to represent the unbreakable bond and eternal affection between partners. It is ideal for couples wishing to affirm their lasting commitment to each other or for individuals seeking a love that endures through time.

Purpose: To strengthen the bonds of love and commitment, symbolizing the eternal nature of your relationship or future love.

Timing: Best performed on a significant anniversary or during a full moon to signify the completion and enduring nature of your love.

Materials:

1. A long-burning candle, preferably in red or pink (symbols of passion and love)
2. A piece of paper and a pen (to write affirmations or intentions)
3. Rose petals (for romantic love)
4. Lavender oil (for harmony and tranquility in the relationship)
5. Two small pieces of rose quartz (to amplify love and emotional connection)
6. A safe candle holder

Preparation:

1. Choose a quiet and comfortable space where you can focus on your intentions without interruption.
2. Set the mood of the space to reflect love and commitment – perhaps with soft music or dim lighting.

The Spell:

1. **Candle Preparation**: Begin by anointing the candle with lavender oil, symbolizing the peaceful and harmonious nature of your love.
2. **Writing Intentions or Affirmations**: On the piece of paper, write down your intentions for the relationship or affirmations of your commitment and love.
3. **Lighting the Candle**: Place the candle in its holder and light it, visualizing the flame as the burning passion and eternal nature of your love.
4. **Surrounding with Rose Petals and Quartz**: Scatter rose petals around the base of the candle holder and place the rose quartz pieces on either side, enhancing the romantic and loving energy.
5. **Affirming Eternal Love**: As the candle burns, read your intentions or affirmations aloud. Visualize the words being absorbed by the flame, radiating out into the universe.
6. **Meditation and Visualization**: Spend some time meditating on the flame. Imagine its light encompassing you and your partner, or surrounding you as you await your future love, reinforcing the bonds of eternal affection.

After the Spell:

- **Let the Candle Burn**: Allow the candle to burn for as long as you safely can, ideally until it extinguishes itself, to signify the endurance of your love.
- **Keep the Intentions**: Store the written intentions or affirmations in a special place, such as a love altar or tucked within a journal.

- **Regular Reaffirmation**: Revisit your intentions and affirmations regularly, and consider repeating the ritual annually or during significant milestones in your relationship.

The Eternal Flame Candle Enchantment is a profound way to honor the everlasting nature of love. It serves as a beautiful reminder of the steady, enduring flame of affection and commitment that exists within a loving relationship.

34. Bewitching Siren's Perfume

The Bewitching Siren's Perfume is a spell that creates a captivating and enchanting fragrance, designed to allure and beguile. Drawing inspiration from the mythical sirens, this potion is for anyone who wishes to enhance their magnetic charm and irresistible allure in romantic pursuits.

Purpose: To craft a bewitching perfume that enhances personal allure, charisma, and seductive qualities.

Timing: Ideal to create during a waxing moon to draw in attraction, or on a Friday, Venus's day, for enhancing love and allure.

Materials:

1. A small glass bottle or perfume vial
2. Essential oils: Jasmine (for sensuality), Rose (for love and passion), and Vanilla (for sweet attraction)
3. Carrier oil like jojoba or almond oil
4. Spring water or alcohol (as a base for the perfume)
5. A small piece of rose quartz (to charge the perfume with loving energy)
6. A pinch of sea salt (for purity and protection)
7. Optional: A few strands of your hair (to personalize the perfume)

Preparation:

1. Create a calming and enchanting atmosphere in your space, perhaps with soft lighting or music.
2. Cleanse your materials and space to prepare them energetically.

The Spell:

1. **Creating the Base**: In your glass bottle, mix the spring water or alcohol with the carrier oil. This mixture forms the base of your perfume.
2. **Adding Essential Oils**: Add a few drops of each essential oil—jasmine, rose, and vanilla—into the bottle. As you do this, focus on imbuing the perfume with qualities of allure and attraction.
3. **Charging with Rose Quartz**: Place the rose quartz near or briefly inside the bottle (ensure it's clean and safe for immersion) to charge the perfume with loving energy.
4. **Personalizing the Perfume**: If using, add the strands of your hair to the mixture, intertwining your essence with the potion.
5. **Sealing with Salt**: Sprinkle a pinch of sea salt into the mixture, setting intentions for purity and protection in your romantic endeavors.
6. **Finalizing the Potion**: Seal the bottle and gently shake it to blend all ingredients. As you shake the bottle, visualize the perfume radiating a bewitching and irresistible aura.
7. **Infusion and Activation**: Allow the perfume to sit in a place where it can be infused with your intentions for a day and night. You might place it on a windowsill to absorb the energies of the moon or sun.

After the Spell:

- **Wearing the Perfume**: Dab the perfume on your pulse points whenever you wish to enhance your allure and charm. Each time you wear it, reaffirm your intention to be irresistibly enchanting.

- **Regular Recharging**: Occasionally, place the bottle near a piece of rose quartz or in the moonlight to recharge its magical properties.

Bewitching Siren's Perfume is a sensual and enchanting tool for those who wish to captivate and charm in their romantic ventures. It's a spell that combines the art of perfumery with the ancient allure of magic, creating a fragrance that is as enchanting as it is irresistible.

35. Lover's Return Lunar Spell

The Lover's Return Lunar Spell is a powerful ritual that calls upon the energy of the moon to help reunite with a lost love or rekindle a past relationship. This spell is particularly resonant for those who feel a deep, lunar connection with a former partner and seek to revive their romance under the moon's guiding light.

Purpose: To facilitate the return of a past love or to rekindle a relationship that has lost its spark, aligning with the moon's powerful energy of emotional renewal and reconciliation.

Timing: Best performed during a full moon, which symbolizes completion and powerful emotional energy, or during the waxing moon phase to draw someone back into your life.

Materials:

1. A photograph of the former lover or a significant item that belonged to them
2. A white candle (symbolizing purity and new beginnings)
3. Moonstone or pearl (stones associated with lunar energy and emotional connection)
4. A piece of paper and a pen
5. A small bowl of water (to represent the moon's influence and emotional clarity)
6. Lavender or chamomile (for calming and healing energies)

Preparation:

1. Find a quiet and comfortable space where you can see the moon or feel its presence.

2. Cleanse your space and materials, preparing them energetically for the ritual.

The Spell:

1. **Candle Lighting**: Begin by lighting the white candle, focusing on the intention of renewal and reunion.
2. **Setting the Photograph/Item**: Place the photograph or item next to the candle as a physical representation of your former lover.
3. **Moonstone or Pearl Activation**: Place the moonstone or pearl near the photograph or item, asking the moon to bless your intentions with its energy.
4. **Writing Intentions**: On the paper, write a heartfelt message to your former lover, expressing your desires for reconciliation and renewed connection.
5. **Water Blessing**: Place the bowl of water in front of the items, symbolizing emotional clarity and the moon's influence in your endeavor.
6. **Herb Offering**: Sprinkle lavender or chamomile around the candle and photograph/item, creating a peaceful and healing atmosphere.
7. **Moon Invocation and Visualization**: Turn your face to the moon (or imagine its presence) and invite its energy into your ritual. Visualize the moon's light enveloping you and your former lover, illuminating the path back to each other.
8. **Concluding the Spell**: Leave the candle burning safely as long as you can, letting the water, stone, and photograph/item absorb the moon's energy. Keep the written message in a safe place.

After the Spell:

- **Regular Reflection**: Spend time under the moonlight, reinforcing your intentions and staying open to the possibilities of reconciliation.
- **Patience and Trust**: Have patience and trust in the power of the moon and the spell. Remember that reconciliation, if it's meant to be, will occur in divine timing.

The Lover's Return Lunar Spell is a beautiful blend of lunar magic and romantic intention. It serves as a potent reminder of the moon's power in guiding hearts and healing past wounds, offering a chance for lovers to reunite and rekindle their once-strong bond.

36. Harmony Binding Sand Ritual

The Harmony Binding Sand Ritual is a serene and grounding spell that utilizes the natural elements of sand to symbolize and strengthen the harmony in a relationship. This ritual is particularly effective for couples seeking to solidify their unity and ensure a balanced, peaceful partnership.

Purpose: To create a tangible symbol of unity and harmony in a relationship, using sand as a representation of blending individual energies into a harmonious whole.

Timing: Best performed during a waxing moon to encourage growth and harmony, or on a day that holds special significance to the relationship.

Materials:

1. Two different colors of sand (representing the individual energies of each partner)
2. A clear glass vessel or jar (to hold the sand and symbolize the relationship)
3. A white or blue candle (white for peace, blue for communication)
4. Lavender or rosemary (herbs for tranquility and loyalty)
5. A piece of paper and a pen (to write down intentions or affirmations)
6. A small piece of amethyst (for spiritual harmony) or agate (for emotional balance)

Preparation:

1. Select a peaceful setting where you can perform the ritual together undisturbed.
2. Cleanse the space, sand, glass vessel, and other materials, setting a tone of harmony and intention.

The Ritual:

1. **Candle Lighting**: Start by lighting the candle, setting the intention for peace and clear communication in the relationship.
2. **Writing Intentions**: On the paper, both partners should write their intentions or affirmations for the relationship, focusing on harmony, understanding, and unity.
3. **Pouring the Sand**: Take turns pouring the sand into the glass vessel, layering the different colors. As you pour, reflect on how your individual qualities contribute to a balanced and harmonious relationship.
4. **Adding Herbs and Crystal**: Sprinkle lavender or rosemary over the sand for tranquility and loyalty. Place the amethyst or agate in the vessel to symbolize the spiritual and emotional harmony of your union.
5. **Sealing the Vessel**: Seal the vessel, symbolizing the secure and protected nature of your relationship.
6. **Affirming Unity**: Together, hold the vessel and recite your written intentions or affirmations, acknowledging your commitment to maintaining harmony and balance.

After the Ritual:

- **Displaying the Vessel**: Place the sand vessel in a prominent place in your home, such as the bedroom or living area, as a constant reminder of your united intentions and harmonious relationship.

- **Regular Reflection**: Regularly revisit the intentions you set during the ritual, using them as guiding principles in your relationship.

The Harmony Binding Sand Ritual is a beautiful and symbolic way to celebrate and strengthen the unity and balance within a relationship. It serves as a visual and physical representation of two individual lives coming together to form a harmonious and cohesive bond, rooted in mutual respect, understanding, and love.

37. Veil of Venus Aura Spell

The Veil of Venus Aura Spell is a mystical enchantment designed to wrap your aura with the captivating and loving energy of Venus, the goddess of love and beauty. This spell is perfect for those who wish to enhance their personal charm, attractiveness, and the energy of love that surrounds them.

Purpose: To envelop your aura with the magnetic and enchanting energy of Venus, enhancing your allure and attractiveness in romantic pursuits.

Timing: Ideal to perform on a Friday, the day associated with Venus, or during a waxing moon to draw in love and positive attention.

Materials:

1. Pink or green candle (colors associated with Venus and the heart chakra)
2. Rose quartz (to amplify love energy)
3. Jasmine or rose incense (for love and attraction)
4. A small mirror (to reflect and enhance your aura)
5. A piece of paper and a pen (to write down your intentions)
6. Rose or ylang-ylang oil (for anointing and enhancing allure)

Preparation:

1. Create a serene and loving atmosphere in your space, conducive to Venusian energy.
2. Cleanse your space and materials to purify the energy.

The Spell:

1. **Candle Lighting**: Begin by lighting the pink or green candle, invoking the loving and beautiful energy of Venus.
2. **Anointing with Oil**: Anoint yourself with a few drops of rose or ylang-ylang oil, focusing on areas like your wrists, neck, and heart chakra.
3. **Writing Intentions**: On the paper, write your intentions to be surrounded by the aura of Venus, focusing on love, beauty, and attraction.
4. **Incense for Attraction**: Light the jasmine or rose incense, letting its fragrance fill the space and enhance the spell's intent.
5. **Mirror Activation**: Hold the mirror in front of you, gazing into it. Visualize a soft, pink or green light (Venusian colors) emanating from the candle and reflecting off the mirror onto you, enveloping your aura.
6. **Affirming Venusian Energy**: Recite an affirmation such as "I am wrapped in the veil of Venus, my aura radiates love and beauty" while continuing to visualize the light surrounding you.
7. **Concluding the Spell**: Place the mirror beside the candle, allowing it to reflect the light as the candle burns. Keep your written intentions near the candle.

After the Spell:

- **Carrying the Energy**: Carry the rose quartz with you to continue harnessing the energy of Venus.
- **Regular Visualization**: Regularly visualize yourself surrounded by the Venusian light, especially before social interactions or romantic encounters.

- **Reflect on the Changes**: Pay attention to how people respond to your enhanced aura and the positive effects it brings to your romantic life.

The Veil of Venus Aura Spell is a magical way to attract the qualities of love and beauty into your life. It serves as a reminder of the enchanting power of Venus and the effect it can have on your personal aura, making you irresistibly alluring and magnetic in your romantic endeavors.

38. Lunar Love Empowerment Ritual

The Lunar Love Empowerment Ritual is a powerful spell that harnesses the energy of the moon to empower your love life. This ritual is ideal for those seeking to strengthen their emotional resilience, enhance their romantic aura, or attract a soulful connection under the moon's mystical influence.

Purpose: To draw upon the moon's energy to empower your romantic endeavors, whether it's strengthening an existing relationship or attracting a new, profound love.

Timing: Best performed during a full moon for its potent emotional energy, or during a waxing moon to grow love and connection.

Materials:

1. A clear space outside under the moonlight, or near a window where the moon is visible
2. A white or silver candle (representing lunar energy)
3. Moonstone or pearl (stones associated with the moon and emotional balance)
4. A bowl of water (to symbolize the moon's influence on emotions)
5. Lavender or jasmine (herbs for love and lunar connections)
6. A piece of paper and a pen (to write down your romantic intentions or desires)

Preparation:

1. Find a quiet space where you can connect with the moon, either outdoors or near a window.

2. Cleanse your space, materials, and yourself to prepare for the ritual.

The Ritual:

1. **Candle Lighting**: Light the white or silver candle, focusing on the lunar qualities of intuition, emotion, and nurturing.
2. **Placing the Stones and Herbs**: Surround the candle with moonstone or pearl and sprinkle lavender or jasmine around it, enhancing the lunar connection.
3. **Water as a Lunar Element**: Place the bowl of water where it can reflect the moonlight, symbolizing the moon's influence on your emotions and love life.
4. **Writing Lunar Intentions**: On the paper, write your desires for your love life, infusing each word with the intention of lunar empowerment.
5. **Moonlight Meditation**: Sit comfortably and meditate under the moonlight. Visualize the moon's rays enveloping you, enhancing your emotional strength and romantic allure.
6. **Affirming Your Desires**: Hold the written intentions in your hands and softly speak them into the night, asking the moon to empower your love life.
7. **Concluding the Ritual**: Leave the candle to burn safely for as long as possible. Keep the paper with your intentions in a place where you can see it, reminding you of the moon's empowerment.

After the Ritual:

- **Regular Reflection**: Revisit your intentions each night when the moon is visible, reaffirming your connection to the lunar energy.

- **Lunar Phases Awareness**: Pay attention to the phases of the moon and how they correlate with your emotional and romantic life, using this awareness to guide your actions in love.

The Lunar Love Empowerment Ritual is a deeply spiritual way to align your romantic intentions with the ebb and flow of the moon's energy. It encourages a harmonious balance between your emotions and your desires, empowering you to navigate your love life with intuition and grace under the moon's guiding light.

39. Sensual Spirit Dance Spell

The Sensual Spirit Dance Spell is a ritual that combines movement, rhythm, and intention to awaken the sensual energies within. This spell is perfect for those looking to enhance their sexual allure, deepen their connection to their body, and embrace their sensuality in a liberating and empowering way.

Purpose: To awaken and amplify sensual energy, connecting deeply with your body and spirit through dance.

Timing: Best performed on a Friday, the day of Venus, the goddess of love and sensuality, or during a waxing moon to increase personal attraction and confidence.

Materials:

1. A private space where you can move freely and dance without inhibition
2. Sensual, rhythmic music that resonates with you
3. Red or pink candles (for passion and love)
4. Fragrant flowers or scented oils like jasmine or ylang-ylang (for sensuality)
5. A mirror (to witness and appreciate your own sensual expression)

Preparation:

1. Create a comfortable, inviting atmosphere in your space, with dim lighting and a sense of privacy.
2. Arrange the candles and flowers or scented oils around the room.

The Spell:

1. **Candle Lighting**: Light the candles to set the intention for love and sensuality.
2. **Starting the Music**: Play the sensual music, allowing its rhythm to guide your movements.
3. **Entering the Dance**: Begin to move your body to the music, letting go of any inhibitions or self-conscious thoughts. Allow the rhythm to flow through you, awakening your sensual energy.
4. **Mirror Gazing**: As you dance, occasionally look into the mirror, observing and appreciating the beauty and sensuality of your movements.
5. **Sensual Affirmations**: While dancing, you can whisper or think of affirmations that reinforce your sensuality, such as "I am a being of passion and desire" or "My sensuality is powerful and liberating."
6. **Embracing the Spirit of Dance**: Let the dance become a ritual in itself, celebrating your body, your spirit, and your sensual energy. Feel how each movement enhances your connection to your sensuality.
7. **Concluding the Dance**: As the music winds down, slowly bring your dance to a close. Stand or sit in front of the mirror, taking a moment to thank yourself for this expression of sensuality.

After the Spell:

- **Reflection and Appreciation**: Spend a few minutes in front of the mirror, appreciating your body and the sensual energy you have released.

- **Regular Practice**: Consider making the Sensual Spirit Dance a regular practice, using it as a tool to continually embrace and express your sensuality.

The Sensual Spirit Dance Spell is a celebration of sensuality, body positivity, and the joy of movement. It's a powerful way to connect with your innermost desires and to express yourself in a deeply personal and sensual way, enhancing your allure and confidence in all aspects of your life.

40. Enchanted Garden Love Growth Spell

The Enchanted Garden Love Growth Spell is a magical ritual that uses the nurturing energies of nature to foster and grow love. This spell is ideal for those who wish to cultivate a blossoming relationship or for anyone seeking to attract new love, using the metaphor of a garden to represent the growth and nurturing of romantic feelings.

Purpose: To symbolically grow and nurture love, whether in an existing relationship or to attract new love, by tending to a garden as a representation of the relationship.

Timing: Best performed during the spring, when the earth is ripe for planting and growth, or during a waxing moon to encourage the growth of new endeavors.

Materials:

1. A small area in a garden or pots for planting
2. Seeds or plants that symbolize love (such as roses, jasmine, or violets)
3. A watering can or water
4. Natural fertilizer or compost
5. Garden tools (like a trowel or spade)
6. A pink or red ribbon
7. A small piece of rose quartz

Preparation:

1. Choose a day where you can spend uninterrupted time in your garden or with your potted plants.
2. Gather all your materials and prepare your planting area.

The Spell:

1. **Preparing the Soil**: Begin by preparing the soil, removing any weeds or debris. As you do this, think of it as clearing away any obstacles to love in your life.
2. **Planting Seeds or Plants**: Plant your seeds or plants that symbolize love. As you plant each one, set an intention for the kind of love you wish to grow and nurture. These could be qualities like understanding, passion, or commitment.
3. **Watering with Intention**: Water your plants, visualizing each drop as nourishment for your growing love. Imagine your relationship (or future relationship) being nurtured and strengthened with each watering.
4. **Fertilizing for Growth**: Add natural fertilizer or compost to help your plants grow. As you do, reflect on the ways you can enrich and support your relationship or prepare yourself for a new love.
5. **Tying the Ribbon**: Tie the pink or red ribbon around one of the plants or a stake in the pot, symbolizing the binding of your intentions to your love life.
6. **Placing the Rose Quartz**: Set the rose quartz near the plants to infuse them with loving energy.

After the Spell:

- **Regular Tending**: Regularly tend to your garden or plants, as this acts as ongoing nurturing of your love intentions. Each act of care symbolizes the care and attention you give to your relationships.
- **Observing Growth**: As the plants grow, take it as a sign of the growth and development happening in your love life. It's

a physical manifestation of the nurturing and energy you're putting into love.

The Enchanted Garden Love Growth Spell is a beautiful and natural way to connect the growth of plants with the growth of love in your life. It's a reminder of the nurturing and attention required to cultivate a healthy and flourishing relationship, much like a garden requires care to bloom.

41. Heart Chakra Alignment Ritual

The Heart Chakra Alignment Ritual is a focused and soothing practice designed to open and balance the heart chakra, the energy center associated with love, compassion, and emotional wellbeing. This ritual is particularly beneficial for those seeking to heal emotional wounds, enhance their capacity for love, or improve their relationships.

Purpose: To balance and energize the heart chakra, enhancing emotional openness, healing, and the ability to give and receive love.

Timing: Ideal to perform on a Friday, the day of Venus, or during a waxing moon to encourage emotional growth and healing.

Materials:

1. Green candles (representing the heart chakra)
2. Rose quartz or green aventurine (crystals associated with heart chakra healing)
3. Lavender or rose incense (for calming and loving energies)
4. Comfortable seating or a peaceful space for meditation
5. Soft, soothing music (optional)
6. A journal and pen for reflections

Preparation:

1. Choose a quiet, comfortable space where you can meditate undisturbed.
2. Set up your materials in a way that creates a serene and sacred atmosphere.

The Ritual:

1. **Candle Lighting:** Begin by lighting the green candles, setting the intention to open and balance your heart chakra.
2. **Crystal Placement:** Hold the rose quartz or green aventurine, feeling its energy, and then place it in front of you or hold it over your heart.
3. **Incense for Atmosphere:** Light the lavender or rose incense, allowing its soothing scent to fill the space and enhance the energy of love and healing.
4. **Meditation and Visualization:** Sit comfortably and begin to meditate. Focus on the area around your heart. Visualize a soft green light emanating from your heart chakra, expanding with each breath. Imagine this light healing any emotional wounds and opening your heart to love.
5. **Chanting or Affirmations:** Optionally, you can chant the mantra "YAM" (the sound associated with the heart chakra) or recite affirmations of love and healing.
6. **Journaling Reflections:** After your meditation, take some time to journal any thoughts, feelings, or insights that arose. Reflect on your emotional state and how you can continue to nurture your heart chakra.

After the Ritual:

- **Regular Practice:** Consider incorporating this ritual into your regular self-care routine to maintain a balanced heart chakra.
- **Mindfulness in Relationships:** Apply the insights and emotional openness from this ritual in your interactions and relationships, fostering deeper connections and understanding.

The Heart Chakra Alignment Ritual is a gentle yet powerful way to connect with and balance your emotional center. Through this practice, you can enhance your emotional wellbeing, deepen your capacity for love, and foster healthier and more harmonious relationships.

42. Celestial Love Alignment

The Celestial Love Alignment is a mystical spell that aligns your romantic aspirations with the energies of celestial bodies, particularly the stars and planets associated with love. This ritual is perfect for those seeking harmony in their love life, guided by the cosmic forces.

Purpose: To harmonize your love life with celestial energies, drawing in cosmic guidance and support for your romantic endeavors.

Timing: Ideally performed on a clear night where the stars and planets are visible, or during significant celestial events such as planetary alignments or meteor showers.

Materials:

1. A star chart or app to identify celestial bodies related to love (such as Venus)
2. A small telescope or binoculars (optional, for stargazing)
3. Blue or silver candles (symbolizing the night sky and celestial energy)
4. Paper and pen (to write down your love intentions and wishes)
5. Amethyst or clear quartz crystal (for clarity and connection to higher energies)
6. Lavender or jasmine incense (for a calming and spiritual atmosphere)

Preparation:

1. Find a location where you have a clear view of the night sky, ideally away from city lights.

2. Set up a comfortable space with your materials, creating a calm and focused atmosphere.

The Ritual:

1. **Candle Lighting**: Begin by lighting the blue or silver candles, representing the connection to the celestial plane.
2. **Identifying Celestial Bodies**: Use the star chart or app to identify and focus on celestial bodies associated with love, like Venus. If available, use a telescope or binoculars for a closer view.
3. **Writing Love Intentions**: Write down your intentions, wishes, or questions related to your love life on the paper. Be as specific and clear as possible.
4. **Connecting with the Cosmos**: Hold the amethyst or clear quartz crystal, and gaze up at the stars and planets. Feel their ancient, vast energy surrounding you and aligning with your love intentions.
5. **Incense Offering**: Light the incense as an offering to the cosmos, asking for guidance and support in your love life.
6. **Affirming Celestial Support**: Recite an affirmation or chant that resonates with seeking love guidance from the stars, such as "Stars above, guide my love, bring alignment from above."
7. **Meditation and Contemplation**: Spend some time in quiet meditation under the stars, open to any insights or feelings that come to you regarding your love life.

After the Ritual:

- **Celestial Observations**: Regularly spend time under the night sky, maintaining your connection to the celestial energies and your love intentions.
- **Reflecting on Insights**: Keep the written intentions in a special place and reflect on them often, especially during significant celestial events.

The Celestial Love Alignment is a deeply spiritual and reflective practice that connects the mysteries of the cosmos with the journey of the heart. It's a way to gain perspective and guidance from the vastness of the universe, reminding us of the interconnectedness between the celestial dimensions and our personal experiences of love.

43. Eternal Devotion Bonding Ceremony

The Eternal Devotion Bonding Ceremony is a deeply meaningful ritual designed for couples wishing to affirm or renew their commitment to each other in a profound and spiritual way. This ceremony symbolizes an unbreakable bond of love and dedication, ideal for partners seeking a deeper connection or to celebrate a significant milestone in their relationship.

Purpose: To celebrate and affirm a deep and lasting commitment between partners, symbolizing an eternal bond of love and mutual devotion.

Timing: Best performed on an anniversary, during a significant lunar phase like a full or new moon, or on a day that holds special meaning to the relationship.

Materials:

1. Two white candles (symbolizing purity and new beginnings)
2. A red candle (representing passion and enduring love)
3. A length of red ribbon or cord (to symbolize the binding of two hearts)
4. Rose petals (for romance and love)
5. A small bowl of water (representing emotional depth and purity)
6. A small bowl of salt (for protection and grounding)
7. Personal vows or affirmations written by each partner

Preparation:

1. Choose a serene and intimate setting for the ceremony, such as a quiet spot in nature or a meaningful place in your home.
2. Arrange the materials on a small table or altar.

The Ceremony:

1. **Lighting the Candles**: Begin by lighting the two white candles, symbolizing each partner's individual light, and then the red candle, representing the union of both lights into one enduring flame.
2. **Binding with the Ribbon**: Tie the red ribbon or cord loosely around both partners' hands, symbolizing the binding of their lives in devotion and love.
3. **Exchange of Vows**: Take turns reading your personal vows or affirmations to each other, expressing your commitment and love.
4. **Rose Petal Circle**: Scatter rose petals around the couple, creating a circle of love and beauty.
5. **Water and Salt Blessing**: Each partner takes a turn to sprinkle a few drops of water and a pinch of salt on the other's hands, representing the purity of their intentions and the grounding of their relationship in reality.
6. **Unbinding and Unity**: Carefully untie the ribbon, signifying that the bond is not one of constraint but a free choice to stay united.

After the Ceremony:

- **Preserving the Ribbon**: Keep the ribbon in a special place, such as a keepsake box, as a reminder of the ceremony and the vows made.

- **Continued Commitment**: Regularly revisit the vows or affirmations made during the ceremony, using them as guiding principles in your relationship.
- **Celebrating Love**: Annually, or on special occasions, consider repeating the ceremony to reaffirm your bond and celebrate your journey together.

The Eternal Devotion Bonding Ceremony is a powerful way to celebrate love and commitment. It serves as a poignant reminder of the deep bond shared between partners, honoring their journey together and the eternal nature of their devotion.

44. Enthralling Love's Vision Quest

The Enthralling Love's Vision Quest is a profound and introspective spell, designed for individuals seeking a deep and meaningful romantic connection. This vision quest involves a meditative journey to discover or understand the qualities of an ideal partner or to gain clarity about a current relationship.

Purpose: To gain insight into one's romantic desires and needs, and to envision the qualities of an ideal partner or the future path of a current relationship.

Timing: Best performed during a new moon for new beginnings, or a full moon for clarity and realization.

Materials:

1. A quiet, comfortable space for meditation
2. Soft, calming music or nature sounds (optional)
3. A journal and pen for recording insights
4. A blue or white candle (for clarity and truth)
5. A crystal associated with intuition and love, such as amethyst or rose quartz
6. Incense or essential oils like lavender or sage (for relaxation and purification)

Preparation:

1. Choose a time and place where you will not be disturbed, allowing for full concentration and introspection.
2. If desired, play soft music or nature sounds to aid in relaxation.

The Vision Quest:

1. **Creating a Calm Atmosphere:** Light the candle and incense or diffuse the essential oils, setting a tranquil and sacred environment.
2. **Comfortable Position:** Sit or lie in a comfortable position, holding the crystal, and begin to focus on your breath.
3. **Meditative State:** Gradually enter a meditative state, allowing your mind to clear and your body to relax deeply.
4. **Envisioning Love:** In your mind, begin to envision the qualities of your ideal partner or the path you wish your current relationship to follow. Consider traits, feelings, and shared experiences that are important to you.
5. **Deepening the Quest:** As you delve deeper into your meditation, open yourself to any insights, feelings, or visions that may arise. Trust in the journey and the messages you receive.
6. **Journaling Insights:** After your meditation, take some time to journal any thoughts, feelings, or revelations you experienced. Reflect on these insights and how they resonate with your current understanding of love and relationships.

After the Vision Quest:

- **Regular Reflection:** Revisit your journal entries regularly to reflect on your vision quest and the insights gained.
- **Applying Insights:** Use the understanding from your vision quest to guide your decisions and actions in your romantic life, whether it involves seeking a new partner or enhancing your current relationship.

Enthralling Love's Vision Quest is an enlightening journey into the depths of your romantic desires and aspirations. It offers a unique way to connect with your innermost feelings about love and relationships, paving the way for a fulfilling and meaningful romantic journey.

45. Mystic Union Astral Journey

The Mystic Union Astral Journey is a profound and transcendent spell that involves an astral projection experience to deepen the spiritual bond between partners or to explore the astral plane for insights into future romantic connections. This spell is for those who are comfortable with advanced metaphysical practices and seek a deeper, spiritual connection in their romantic life.

Purpose: To explore and strengthen the spiritual connection in a romantic relationship through astral projection, or to seek insights about future love in the astral plane.

Timing: Ideally performed during a full moon for heightened intuition and psychic energies, or during significant astrological alignments for deeper cosmic connections.

Materials:

1. A quiet, darkened space where you won't be disturbed
2. Comfortable clothing and a place to lie down
3. Relaxing, ambient music or complete silence, depending on preference
4. Amethyst or clear quartz crystals (for enhancing psychic abilities and protection)
5. Lavender or mugwort (herbs known for aiding astral travel and psychic work)
6. A journal and pen for recording experiences

Preparation:

1. Create a calm and comfortable environment conducive to deep meditation and relaxation.
2. Place the crystals and herbs nearby to enhance your astral journey.

The Astral Journey:

1. **Relaxation and Focus**: Lie down in your quiet space, close your eyes, and focus on deep, steady breathing. Allow your body to relax completely and your mind to become calm and clear.
2. **Setting Intentions**: Mentally set your intentions for the journey, whether it's to strengthen the bond with your current partner in the astral plane or to seek insights about future romantic connections.
3. **Entering the Astral Plane**: As you relax deeper, visualize yourself gently separating from your physical body and entering the astral plane. You may envision a cord of light connecting your astral self to your physical body for safety.
4. **Exploring with Purpose**: In the astral plane, focus on your intention. If you're seeking to connect with your partner, visualize finding and joining them in this space. If you're seeking insights about future love, ask for guidance or signs.
5. **Returning to the Physical**: When you feel it's time to return, gently bring your awareness back to your physical body. Visualize re-entering it and the cord of light dissolving as you become fully present in the physical world again.
6. **Grounding**: Take a few deep breaths and move your fingers and toes to ground yourself. It's important to fully return to your physical senses before getting up.

After the Astral Journey:

- **Journaling**: Write down your experiences, feelings, and any insights or messages received during the astral journey.
- **Reflection and Integration**: Spend time reflecting on your journey and how it relates to your romantic life. Consider ways to integrate any insights or strengthened connections into your physical world relationship.

The Mystic Union Astral Journey is a deeply spiritual and connecting experience, offering a unique perspective on love and relationships from the astral plane. It's a powerful practice for those who are experienced in metaphysical explorations and seek to deepen their romantic connections beyond the physical world.

46. Phoenix Heart Rebirth Spell

The Phoenix Heart Rebirth Spell is a transformative ritual designed for emotional healing and renewal in love. Drawing inspiration from the myth of the Phoenix, this spell symbolizes rising from the ashes of past heartaches to embrace love anew with a rejuvenated heart.

Purpose: To heal from past emotional wounds, release old heartaches, and open up to new beginnings in love, much like the rebirth of the Phoenix.

Timing: Ideal to perform during a new moon, symbolizing new beginnings, or after a significant personal event that marks a need for emotional renewal.

Materials:

1. A red or orange candle (representing the fiery energy of the Phoenix)
2. A bowl of water (symbolizing emotional cleansing)
3. Paper and a fire-safe container (for writing and safely burning past emotional burdens)
4. Healing crystals such as rose quartz (for love) or malachite (for transformation and healing)
5. Incense like sandalwood or dragon's blood (for purification and strength)
6. A feather (symbolizing the lightness and freedom of rebirth)

Preparation:

1. Create a sacred and safe space where you can reflect and focus on your intentions.

2. Cleanse your space and materials, setting a tone of healing and transformation.

The Spell:

1. **Candle Lighting**: Light the red or orange candle, invoking the transformative energy of the Phoenix.
2. **Writing Emotional Burdens**: On the paper, write down past hurts, regrets, or any emotional baggage you wish to release. Be honest and thorough.
3. **Burning the Past**: Safely burn the paper in the fire-safe container, visualizing the flames consuming and transforming your past pains into ashes.
4. **Water Cleansing**: Gently pour water over the ashes (ensure it's safe to do so), signifying the cleansing and cooling of your emotional wounds.
5. **Crystal Healing**: Hold the rose quartz or malachite, feeling its healing energy. Place it near the candle to charge with the intention of love and renewal.
6. **Incense Purification**: Light the incense, allowing its smoke to envelop you and the space, symbolizing purification and preparation for new beginnings.
7. **Feather Symbolism**: Hold the feather, symbolizing your readiness to rise anew. Gently fan the smoke around you, embracing the lightness and freedom of rebirth.

After the Spell:

- **Reflect on Rebirth**: Spend time meditating on the feelings of renewal and openness to new love. Visualize yourself emerging stronger and more open-hearted.

- **Regular Practice**: Consider repeating aspects of this spell regularly, such as the burning of past emotional burdens, to reinforce the ongoing process of emotional healing and renewal.

The Phoenix Heart Rebirth Spell is a powerful way to symbolize and enact emotional healing, allowing you to rise from the ashes of past heartaches with a rejuvenated heart ready for new love. It embraces the transformative power of the Phoenix, guiding you towards a path of emotional renewal and readiness for the love that awaits.

47. Seventh Heaven Harmony Incantation

The Seventh Heaven Harmony Incantation is a magical chant designed to create harmony and bliss in your love life. Inspired by the concept of 'seventh heaven'—a state of utter happiness and peace—this incantation helps align your relationship or your heart's desires with frequencies of joy and harmony.

Purpose: To infuse your love life with harmony, understanding, and bliss, creating a relationship or attracting a love that resonates with the highest forms of happiness and peace.

Timing: Best performed on a night with clear skies, symbolizing clarity and peace, or during a harmonious astrological transit.

Materials:

1. A comfortable and peaceful setting
2. A white or light blue candle (for peace and harmony)
3. Lavender or rose incense (for love and tranquility)
4. A piece of paper and pen (to write your own personalized incantation)
5. A small bell (to symbolize clarity and the dispelling of negative energies)

Preparation:

1. Find a quiet place where you feel at peace and can focus without distractions.
2. Arrange your materials in a way that feels harmonious and calming.

The Incantation:

1. **Candle Lighting**: Light the candle, setting an intention for harmony and bliss in your love life.
2. **Incense for Atmosphere**: Light the incense, allowing its soothing scent to fill the space, enhancing the energy of love and tranquility.
3. **Writing the Incantation**: Reflect on what harmony means to you in love. Write a personalized incantation that resonates with your desires for a harmonious relationship. It could be something like, "In love's embrace, we find our peace, in harmony's light, all discord cease."
4. **Chanting with Intent**: Sit comfortably and begin to softly chant your incantation. Feel each word vibrating through you, aligning your energy with harmony and happiness.
5. **Bell Ringing**: Gently ring the bell at the beginning and end of your chanting session, symbolizing clarity and the dispelling of any negative energy or misunderstandings in your love life.
6. **Meditation and Visualization**: After chanting, meditate for a few minutes. Visualize your love life or future relationship filled with joy, understanding, and a blissful harmony.

After the Incantation:

- **Regular Practice**: Consider incorporating this incantation into your regular meditation or mindfulness practice, reinforcing the energy of harmony in your love life.
- **Reflecting on Harmony**: Regularly reflect on the qualities of harmony and how you can embody them in your relationships or in your journey toward finding love.

The Seventh Heaven Harmony Incantation is a gentle yet powerful way to align your love life with the highest frequencies of joy and peace. It's a reminder of the power of words and intentions in shaping our experiences, especially in the realm of love and relationships.

48. Eros' Arrow Precision Spell

The Eros' Arrow Precision Spell is a targeted love spell invoking the energy of Eros, the Greek god of love and desire. This spell is designed to pinpoint and enhance the focus on a specific aspect of your love life, whether it's attracting a new partner, deepening an existing relationship, or finding clarity in your romantic pursuits.

Purpose: To sharpen focus and intent in a specific area of your love life, guided by the precise and passionate energy of Eros.

Timing: Ideal to perform during a waxing moon to attract new love or a full moon for clarity and fulfillment in love matters.

Materials:

1. A red candle (symbolizing passion and desire)
2. A picture or symbol representing your specific love intention
3. A quill or pointed object (to symbolize Eros' arrow)
4. Rose petals (for romance and attraction)
5. Paper and pen (to write down your focused intention)
6. A small piece of rose quartz (to enhance loving energy)
7. Incense with a sensual fragrance (like musk or rose)

Preparation:

1. Choose a quiet place where you can focus deeply on your love intention.
2. Set up your materials in a way that feels aligned and focused.

The Spell:

1. **Candle Lighting**: Light the red candle, invoking the passionate energy of Eros.
2. **Intention Writing**: On the paper, write your specific love intention. Be as precise as possible, whether it's about attracting a new love, deepening a relationship, or seeking clarity in your love life.
3. **Arrow Symbolism**: With the quill or pointed object, trace over the words you've written, symbolizing Eros' arrow pinpointing your intention.
4. **Rose Petal Circle**: Scatter rose petals around the candle, creating a circle that encapsulates your love intention.
5. **Crystal Charging**: Place the rose quartz near or on top of the written intention, infusing it with loving energy.
6. **Incense Offering**: Light the incense, letting its fragrance enhance the potency and allure of your spell.
7. **Visualizing Eros' Arrow**: Focus on the flame of the candle and visualize Eros' arrow being shot directly to your love target, guided by your clear intention. See the outcome you desire as already manifesting.
8. **Concluding the Spell**: Allow the candle to burn down safely. Keep the written intention and rose quartz in a special place where you can regularly see them, reminding you of your focused love aim.

After the Spell:

- **Reflect and Act**: Stay open to signs and opportunities related to your love intention. Reflect on your desire and take proactive steps that align with your goal.

- **Regular Reinforcement**: Revisit your written intention and the rose quartz regularly, reinforcing your focused aim and keeping your energy aligned with your love goal.

Eros' Arrow Precision Spell is a powerful way to bring concentrated energy and focus to your romantic aspirations, guided by the sharp and passionate energy of Eros. It serves as a reminder of the power of precision and clarity in manifesting your deepest desires in love.

49. Infinite Love Loop Casting

The Infinite Love Loop Casting is a spell designed to create a continuous flow of love energy in your life, symbolizing an unending cycle of giving and receiving love. This spell is particularly effective for those who wish to establish a perpetual exchange of love, warmth, and affection in their relationships or attract ongoing positive love experiences.

Purpose: To establish a perpetual cycle of love in your life, enhancing the constant flow of love energy in and out of your relationships.

Timing: Best performed during a waxing moon to encourage growth in love, or on a Friday, which is associated with the planet Venus and love.

Materials:

1. Two candles, one pink (for affection) and one green (for heart chakra energy)
2. A piece of paper and a pen (to write an affirmation or mantra about love)
3. A loop of ribbon or string (symbolizing the infinite loop of love)
4. Rose quartz (to enhance loving energy)
5. Lavender or rose incense (for harmony and love)
6. A small mirror (to reflect and multiply the love energy)

Preparation:

1. Find a quiet space where you can concentrate on your love intentions without interruptions.
2. Cleanse the space and your materials to purify the energy.

The Spell:

1. **Candle Placement**: Place the pink and green candles in front of you, representing the flow of love.
2. **Writing Affirmation**: Write an affirmation or mantra on the paper that encapsulates your intention for an infinite flow of love. For example, "Love flows endlessly in and out of my life, a perpetual cycle of joy and connection."
3. **Creating the Loop**: Place the loop of ribbon or string around the candles, creating a physical representation of the infinite love cycle.
4. **Crystals for Amplification**: Position the rose quartz within the loop, to amplify the loving energy.
5. **Incense for Atmosphere**: Light the lavender or rose incense, enhancing the spell's intent with its harmonious fragrance.
6. **Activating the Loop**: Light both candles, then read your affirmation aloud while focusing on the concept of infinite love flowing continuously. Visualize this energy moving in a loop, from you to others and back again.
7. **Mirror Reflection**: Place the mirror behind the candles, so it reflects their light. This symbolizes the multiplying effect of your love intentions, sending them out into the world and back to you.

After the Spell:

- **Regular Reinforcement**: Regularly revisit your affirmation and the loop setup, especially when lighting the candles, to reinforce the continuous flow of love energy.
- **Mindfulness in Love**: Be mindful of the love you give and receive in your daily interactions, acknowledging and appreciating this perpetual cycle in your relationships.

Infinite Love Loop Casting is a unique and powerful way to enhance the flow of love in your life, symbolizing an unending cycle of giving and receiving affection, warmth, and connection. It serves as a beautiful reminder of the infinite nature of love and the joy that comes from being part of this continuous exchange.

50. Timeless Love Preservation Ritual

The Timeless Love Preservation Ritual is a deeply moving spell designed to preserve the essence and memories of a cherished love, keeping the connection strong and enduring through time. It's ideal for couples who want to immortalize their love or for individuals cherishing the memories of a past relationship.

Purpose: To capture and preserve the essence of a love that is timeless and enduring, ensuring that the connection and memories remain vibrant and alive.

Timing: Best performed on an anniversary, a significant date that holds special meaning in your relationship, or during a full moon to harness its energy of completion and permanence.

Materials:

1. A keepsake box or a special container
2. Mementos of the relationship (such as photos, letters, or small tokens)
3. A lock of hair or a small personal item from each partner
4. Dried rose petals or lavender (for love and preservation)
5. A white or gold candle (symbolizing purity and eternity)
6. A small piece of paper and a pen (to write down your vows or intentions)
7. Frankincense or myrrh incense (for their preserving qualities)

Preparation:

1. Choose a quiet, intimate space to perform the ritual.

2. Arrange the materials thoughtfully and lovingly in your chosen space.

The Ritual:

1. **Candle Lighting**: Begin by lighting the candle, setting the intention for eternal preservation and love.
2. **Placing Mementos**: One by one, place the mementos into the keepsake box, reminiscing about the significance of each item and the memories it represents.
3. **Adding Personal Items**: Add a lock of hair or small personal item from each partner into the box, symbolizing the personal essence of each individual in the relationship.
4. **Scattering Rose Petals or Lavender**: Scatter the dried rose petals or lavender over the items, ensuring a gentle preservation of the memories and feelings.
5. **Writing and Placing Vows/Intentions**: Write down your vows or intentions for the preservation of your love on the paper. Fold it and place it in the box, sealing your commitment and wishes.
6. **Incense Blessing**: Light the frankincense or myrrh incense, allowing its fragrance and smoke to waft over the box, further sealing in the love and memories for preservation.
7. **Closing the Keepsake Box**: Gently close the box, visualizing your love and memories being safely encapsulated and preserved.

After the Ritual:

- **Securing the Keepsake Box**: Store the keepsake box in a special place, such as a dedicated love altar or a secure, respectful location.

- **Regular Remembrance**: Open the box periodically on special dates or when you wish to reconnect with the memories and essence of your love, keeping the connection alive and cherished.

The Timeless Love Preservation Ritual is a beautiful and heartfelt way to honor and preserve the essence of a love that transcends time. It serves as a tangible reminder of the enduring nature of love and the cherished memories that shape our relationships and lives.

51. Sacred Heart Seal Spell

The Sacred Heart Seal Spell is a protective and nurturing ritual designed to safeguard the heart's emotional well-being, especially after experiencing deep love or heartbreak. This spell is for those seeking to shield their hearts from pain while maintaining an open and loving disposition.

Purpose: To protect the heart from emotional pain and negativity, sealing it with nurturing and loving energy, while remaining open to future positive love experiences.

Timing: Ideal to perform during a waning moon for releasing pain and during a waxing moon for inviting protective love.

Materials:

1. A pink or green candle (representing the heart chakra and emotional healing)
2. A small heart-shaped token or symbol (as a representation of your heart)
3. Rose quartz (for love and healing)
4. Thyme or rosemary (herbs for emotional protection and healing)
5. A piece of paper and pen (to write an affirmation or protective chant)
6. Lavender or rose incense (for calming and loving energies)

Preparation:

1. Create a peaceful and safe space where you can focus on your emotional well-being.

2. Arrange the materials in a way that feels nurturing and protective.

The Spell:

1. **Candle Lighting**: Light the pink or green candle, setting an intention to protect and nurture your heart.
2. **Heart Token Activation**: Hold the heart-shaped token, infusing it with your intention to protect your heart. Place it in front of the candle.
3. **Rose Quartz Empowerment**: Place the rose quartz next to the heart token, asking it to infuse your heart with loving and healing energy.
4. **Herb Offering**: Scatter thyme or rosemary around the candle and heart token, symbolizing emotional healing and protection.
5. **Writing Affirmation**: Write a protective affirmation or chant on the paper, such as "My heart is shielded with love and care, open to joy, closed to despair."
6. **Incense Purification**: Light the lavender or rose incense, allowing its soothing scent to fill the space, enhancing the protective energy.
7. **Reciting the Affirmation**: Read your affirmation aloud, visualizing a protective shield of light around your heart, nurturing it while keeping negativity at bay.
8. **Concluding the Ritual**: Allow the candle to burn down safely. Keep the heart token and rose quartz in a special place, such as near your bed or on a personal altar.

After the Spell:

- **Regular Reflection**: Regularly hold or look at your heart token and rose quartz, reaffirming your intention to protect your heart with love.
- **Emotional Care**: Practice self-care and mindfulness, ensuring that you maintain a balance of openness to love and protection from emotional harm.

The Sacred Heart Seal Spell is a powerful ritual for those seeking to balance the vulnerability of love with the need for emotional protection. It serves as a reminder of the importance of nurturing our hearts and protecting them from unnecessary pain, while still remaining open to the joys and fulfillment love can bring.

52. Mystical Love Oracle Divination

The Mystical Love Oracle Divination is a spell that incorporates the use of oracle cards, or other divinatory tools, to gain insights and guidance about one's love life. This ritual is ideal for those seeking answers or clarity about their romantic path, relationships, or future love prospects.

Purpose: To use divination as a means to gain deeper understanding and guidance in matters of the heart, whether it's about navigating current relationships or uncovering aspects of future romantic endeavors.

Timing: Best performed on a new moon for insights into new beginnings or a full moon for clarity in ongoing matters.

Materials:

1. A deck of love oracle cards or any preferred divinatory tool (like tarot cards, runes, etc.)
2. A pink or white candle (for love and clarity)
3. Rose petals or lavender (for enhancing romantic intuition)
4. A quiet, comfortable space for contemplation
5. A journal and pen for noting insights
6. A crystal for intuition, such as amethyst or moonstone
7. Incense like jasmine or vanilla (for enhancing psychic abilities and love vibrations)

Preparation:

1. Find a quiet and comfortable space where you can focus without interruptions.

2. Lay out your materials in a way that feels intuitive and harmonious.

The Divination:

1. **Candle Lighting**: Light the candle to set the intention for clarity and guidance in your love life.
2. **Preparing the Deck or Tool**: If using oracle cards, shuffle them while focusing on your love questions or concerns. If using another divinatory tool, prepare it according to your tradition.
3. **Drawing Cards or Casting**: Draw cards from the deck or cast your divinatory tool, focusing on your questions about love. Lay them out in a spread that resonates with you.
4. **Interpreting the Messages**: Spend time interpreting the messages or symbols presented. Trust your intuition and allow insights to flow freely. Don't rush the process; let the meanings reveal themselves to you.
5. **Journaling Insights**: Write down your interpretations and any feelings or thoughts that arise in your journal. Note any particular messages or symbols that stand out.
6. **Reflecting with the Crystal**: Hold the crystal, asking for its aid in deepening your understanding or in guiding you to apply the insights in your love life.
7. **Incense to Enhance Intuition**: Light the incense, allowing its fragrance to enhance your intuitive connection and the loving energy of the ritual.

After the Divination:

- **Regular Reflection**: Revisit the insights gained during this divination regularly. Reflect on how they apply to your current situation or future prospects in love.
- **Mindful Application**: Consider ways to apply the guidance from your divination in your daily life, whether it's making changes in your current relationship or preparing yourself for future love.

Mystical Love Oracle Divination is a valuable practice for those seeking spiritual guidance in their romantic life. It offers a reflective and insightful approach to understanding the complexities of love and relationships, providing clarity and direction on the path of love.

53. Tides of Passion Ocean Ritual

The Tides of Passion Ocean Ritual is a potent spell that harnesses the powerful and ever-changing energies of the ocean to amplify passion and desire in your love life. This ritual is perfect for those who feel a deep connection to the sea and wish to invoke its vast energy to enhance romance and passion.

Purpose: To draw upon the ocean's dynamic and powerful energy to heighten passion and desire in your romantic life.

Timing: Ideal to perform during a high tide for intensifying emotions, or during a full moon when the ocean's power is at its peak.

Materials:

1. A beach or coastline where you can safely perform the ritual (alternatively, a bowl of seawater)
2. Red or deep blue candles (representing passion and the depth of the ocean)
3. Sea shells or sea glass (as symbols of the ocean's beauty and power)
4. Sand (to connect with the earth element)
5. A piece of paper and pen (to write down your desires and intentions)
6. A natural object to represent your love or passion (like a red stone or a heart-shaped rock)
7. Ocean-themed incense (like seaweed or sea salt) or essential oil

Preparation:

1. Choose a time when the beach is quiet, allowing for privacy and focus.
2. Set up a small altar in the sand with your materials.

The Ritual:

1. **Candle Lighting**: Light the candles, feeling the connection between their flame and the vastness of the ocean.
2. **Writing Desires and Intentions**: On the paper, write down your deepest desires and intentions for passion and romance in your life.
3. **Creating a Circle with Sand and Shells**: Use the sand and shells to create a circle around your altar, symbolizing the cyclical and eternal nature of the ocean.
4. **Placing the Natural Object**: Place the object that represents your love or passion within the circle, near the candles.
5. **Ocean Offering**: If you're at the beach, stand at the water's edge and read your desires to the ocean. If using a bowl of seawater, pour the water back and forth between your hands as you speak, symbolizing the flow of emotions.
6. **Incense or Essential Oil**: Light the ocean-themed incense or use the essential oil to enhance the connection with the ocean's energy.
7. **Meditation and Visualization**: Close the ritual with a meditation. Visualize the ocean's waves washing over you, each wave intensifying the passion and love in your life.

After the Ritual:

- **Disposal of Materials**: Respectfully dispose of the paper in the ocean or bury it in the sand, letting the ocean's tides carry away your intentions.
- **Reflecting on the Ocean's Power**: Spend time after the ritual contemplating the vast, powerful, and ever-changing nature of the ocean, and how it mirrors the dynamic nature of passion and romance.

The Tides of Passion Ocean Ritual is a magical way to connect with the elemental power of the ocean and channel its vast energy into your love life. It serves as a reminder of the depth, beauty, and strength of your emotions and the ever-flowing nature of passion and desire.

54. Divine Love Crystal Grid Activation

The Divine Love Crystal Grid Activation is a spell that harnesses the power of crystals arranged in a specific grid pattern to attract and enhance divine love. This ritual is ideal for those who seek a spiritually profound connection in their romantic life, aiming to align their relationship with higher vibrational love energies.

Purpose: To create a crystal grid that activates divine love energy, aiding in attracting a soulful, deep romantic connection or enhancing the spiritual bond in an existing relationship.

Timing: Best performed during a new moon for new beginnings in love, or a full moon for manifesting deep, meaningful connections.

Materials:

1. A selection of crystals associated with love, such as rose quartz (for unconditional love), rhodonite (for emotional healing), amethyst (for spiritual connection), and clear quartz (for amplification)
2. A cloth or surface to set up the grid
3. A diagram or pattern for your crystal grid (can be a flower of life, a heart shape, or any pattern that symbolizes love to you)
4. A central crystal or stone, like a large rose quartz, to anchor the grid's energy
5. Lavender or rose incense (for love and harmony)
6. A small piece of paper and pen (to write down your love intention)

Preparation:

1. Cleanse your space and all the crystals to clear any previous energies.
2. Lay out the cloth or select a surface where your grid will remain undisturbed.

The Activation:

1. **Grid Layout**: Place your central crystal in the middle of the cloth or surface. Arrange the other crystals in your chosen pattern around it, focusing on your intention for divine love.
2. **Writing Intentions**: Write your specific intention for love on the paper. Fold it and place it under the central crystal.
3. **Activating the Grid**: Starting from the outer crystals, use a crystal point or your finger to energetically connect each crystal, envisioning a bright light forming between them, creating a network of energy.
4. **Central Crystal Activation**: Focus on the central crystal, imagining it radiating a powerful, loving energy that activates the entire grid.
5. **Incense Offering**: Light the incense, allowing its scent to envelop the grid, further enhancing the loving energy.
6. **Meditation and Visualization**: Sit in front of your grid, meditate, and visualize the divine love energy growing and encompassing your life. Feel its presence filling your space and heart.

After the Activation:

- **Regular Interaction**: Spend time each day near your crystal grid, meditating or simply sitting with it, to reinforce your connection to the divine love energy.

- **Grid Maintenance**: Periodically cleanse and reactivate your grid, especially during new or full moons, to keep its energy strong and clear.

The Divine Love Crystal Grid Activation is a powerful ritual that combines the energies of crystals and sacred geometry to manifest a higher, spiritually attuned form of love. It's an effective way to focus your intentions and draw in the profound, soulful connection that aligns with your highest good.

55. Fateful Lovers' Star Alignment

The Fateful Lovers' Star Alignment is a spell that taps into the cosmic energies of the stars to align fateful encounters and strengthen the bonds of destined love. This ritual is perfect for those who believe in the power of fate and the stars in guiding their romantic destiny.

Purpose: To align one's romantic path with the celestial forces, attracting or strengthening a fated, destined love connection.

Timing: Ideal to perform on a clear starry night, when the cosmos is visibly aligned, or during significant celestial events like meteor showers or planetary alignments.

Materials:

1. A star map or astronomy app to identify key constellations or stars related to love
2. A telescope or binoculars for stargazing (optional)
3. White and blue candles (symbolizing the night sky and celestial energy)
4. A piece of paper and pen (to write down your love intention or desire)
5. A quartz crystal (for clarity and amplification of energy)
6. Night-blooming flowers or jasmine incense (to represent the beauty and mystery of the night)
7. A small bowl of water (to reflect the starlight and symbolize emotional clarity)

Preparation:

1. Choose a location where you have a clear view of the night sky, away from artificial lights.
2. Set up your materials in a way that feels aligned with the celestial energies.

The Ritual:

1. **Candle Lighting**: Begin by lighting the candles, focusing on the vastness of the night sky and your place within the cosmos.
2. **Star Identification**: Use the star map or app to identify and focus on constellations or stars associated with love, such as those in mythological love stories.
3. **Writing Love Intention**: Write your specific love intention or desire on the paper, focusing on attracting or strengthening a fated love.
4. **Quartz Crystal Activation**: Hold the quartz crystal, asking it to amplify your intention and connect it with the celestial energies.
5. **Incense Offering**: Light the night-blooming flowers or jasmine incense, enhancing the ritual's connection to the mysteries of the night.
6. **Starlight Water Reflection**: Hold the bowl of water up to the night sky, allowing it to catch the reflection of the stars, then place it on your altar or near the candles.
7. **Visualizing the Alignment**: Focus on the night sky, visualizing the stars aligning in a way that guides your fated love towards you, or strengthens the bond with your current partner.

After the Ritual:

- **Starlight Contemplation**: Regularly spend time under the stars, reinforcing your connection to the cosmos and your love intention.
- **Reflecting on the Stars and Love**: Keep the written intention and quartz crystal in a place where you can see them at night, reminding you of your alignment with the celestial forces in your romantic life.

Fateful Lovers' Star Alignment is a magical and cosmic ritual that celebrates the belief in destiny and the stars' role in guiding our romantic paths. It's a way to connect with the universe's vast energies and align your love life with the fated courses written in the stars.

56. Astral Love Bridge Construction

The Astral Love Bridge Construction is a spell that involves creating a metaphysical bridge in the astral plane to connect with a current or future lover on a deep, soulful level. This ritual is ideal for those who are comfortable with astral projection and wish to foster or attract a profound, spiritually-connected love.

Purpose: To build a connection or strengthen an existing bond with a lover in the astral plane, enhancing the spiritual and emotional intimacy in the relationship.

Timing: Best performed during the waxing moon to grow connections or on nights when you feel a strong connection to the astral plane.

Materials:

1. A quiet, comfortable space for meditation and astral projection
2. Two candles, preferably pink (for love) and blue (for astral connection)
3. A personal item or photograph of the person you wish to connect with (if applicable)
4. Amethyst or lapis lazuli (crystals that aid in astral projection and spiritual connection)
5. A journal and pen (for recording experiences and insights)
6. Lavender or chamomile incense (for relaxation and heightened intuition)
7. A small bowl of water (to symbolize emotional fluidity and connection)

Preparation:

1. Find a quiet space where you can relax undisturbed for a significant amount of time.
2. Arrange your materials in a way that feels harmonious and conducive to astral work.

The Ritual:

1. **Candle Lighting**: Begin by lighting the pink and blue candles, setting the intention for a loving and deep astral connection.
2. **Item Placement**: If using a personal item or photo, place it between the candles, creating a physical representation of the astral bridge you're about to construct.
3. **Crystal Meditation**: Hold the amethyst or lapis lazuli, meditating on your intention to construct an astral bridge. Feel its energy aiding your journey.
4. **Incense for Intuition**: Light the incense, allowing its soothing scent to fill the space and enhance your intuitive and astral abilities.
5. **Astral Projection and Bridge Construction**: Enter a meditative state and begin your astral projection. Visualize constructing a bridge in the astral plane that reaches out to your current or future lover. See this bridge as a symbol of connection and understanding.
6. **Emotional Water Symbolism**: Dip your fingers into the bowl of water, symbolizing the fluidity and depth of emotional connection that you're fostering.
7. **Journaling Post-Journey**: After returning from the astral journey, write down your experiences and any insights or messages received in your journal.

After the Ritual:

- **Regular Astral Work**: Regularly revisit this astral bridge in your meditations or astral journeys, strengthening the connection and deepening the bond.
- **Reflect on Insights**: Continuously reflect on any insights gained and apply them to your physical world relationship or in preparing for a future love.

Astral Love Bridge Construction is a powerful and mystical ritual, ideal for those seeking to enhance their romantic connections beyond the physical world. It's an exercise in deepening love and understanding through spiritual and astral means, bridging hearts and souls across metaphysical boundaries.

57. Transcendent Love Vortex Spell

The Transcendent Love Vortex Spell is an advanced ritual designed to create a powerful vortex of energy that elevates and transforms your romantic experiences to a higher, more spiritual level. This spell is suited for those who wish to infuse their love life with profound spiritual growth and transcendent connection.

Purpose: To create a vortex of transcendent energy that deepens and elevates the spiritual aspects of love, fostering a connection that goes beyond the physical world.

Timing: Optimal during a full moon for harnessing peak energy, or when you feel deeply connected to your spiritual path.

Materials:

1. A private, quiet space conducive to deep meditation
2. Four candles (representing the cardinal directions and elements)
3. A representation of a vortex or spiral (such as a drawn symbol or a spiraled object)
4. Crystals associated with higher love energies, like pink tourmaline or selenite
5. Essential oils or incense for spiritual connection (such as frankincense or myrrh)
6. A piece of paper and pen to write your intentions or affirmations of transcendent love
7. Soft, meditative music (optional)

Preparation:

1. Create a sacred space where you can focus and meditate without interruptions.
2. Arrange your candles in the cardinal directions, forming a square around your meditation space.

The Spell:

1. **Candle Lighting**: Light each candle, invoking the energy of the corresponding element and direction, creating a balanced and harmonious foundation for your vortex.
2. **Vortex Representation Activation**: Place your vortex representation in the center of your candle square, symbolizing the swirling, dynamic energy you are about to invoke.
3. **Crystals for Amplification**: Position your crystals around or on the vortex symbol, asking them to amplify and purify the love energy.
4. **Incense or Essential Oil**: Use the incense or essential oils to set a deeply spiritual tone, enhancing your connection to higher planes.
5. **Writing Intentions**: Write down your intentions or affirmations focusing on transcendent, spiritual love. Place this paper near or under the vortex symbol.
6. **Meditation and Visualization**: Sit within the square of candles, enter a meditative state, and visualize a powerful vortex of light and energy forming around you, pulling your intentions up and amplifying them.
7. **Chanting or Silent Affirmation**: Use a chant or silently affirm your intentions, imagining the vortex intensifying with each repetition, sending your desires for transcendent love into the universe.

After the Spell:

- **Regular Engagement**: Regularly meditate within your candle square, reinforcing the vortex energy and your connection to transcendent love.
- **Reflection and Application**: Reflect on the nature of transcendent love in your life, finding ways to integrate this higher connection into your everyday interactions and relationships.

The Transcendent Love Vortex Spell is a deeply spiritual practice, ideal for those looking to elevate their love experiences to a more profound and spiritual plane. It's about transcending the ordinary and embracing a love that is as spiritually enriching as it is emotionally fulfilling.

58. Unbreakable Vow Enchantment

The Unbreakable Vow Enchantment is a powerful spell crafted to strengthen the bonds of commitment and fidelity within a relationship. This enchantment is for couples who wish to solidify their commitment to each other, creating a vow that symbolizes unbreakable trust and enduring love.

Purpose: To forge a strong, unbreakable bond of commitment and fidelity between partners, reinforcing the vows of loyalty and enduring love.

Timing: Ideal to perform on a significant anniversary or during a major astrological event that signifies long-term commitments, such as when Venus is in a favorable position.

Materials:

1. A pair of matching rings or tokens representing the relationship
2. A red candle (for passion and commitment) and a white candle (for purity and truth)
3. A small dish of salt (for protection and preservation)
4. A small dish of water (for emotional clarity and purity)
5. A piece of paper and pen (to write down your vows or commitments)
6. Rose or jasmine incense (for love and harmony)
7. A red ribbon or cord (to symbolize the binding of the vow)

Preparation:

1. Choose a quiet, intimate setting, preferably somewhere that holds special meaning to your relationship.
2. Arrange the materials in a meaningful and symmetrical pattern.

The Enchantment:

1. **Lighting the Candles**: Light the red and white candles, setting an intention of creating an unbreakable bond of love and commitment.
2. **Writing the Vows**: Both partners should write their vows or commitments to each other on the paper, focusing on the aspects of fidelity, loyalty, and enduring love.
3. **Exchange of Tokens or Rings**: Exchange the rings or tokens while reading your vows aloud to each other, symbolizing the physical manifestation of your commitments.
4. **Salt and Water Blessing**: Each partner sprinkles a bit of salt and water on the other's token or ring, symbolizing the purification and protection of their vows.
5. **Binding with Ribbon**: Tie the red ribbon or cord around both tokens or rings, binding them together while affirming your commitment to uphold the vows.
6. **Incense Offering**: Light the incense, allowing its fragrance to fill the space, symbolizing the sweetness and harmony of your union.
7. **Sealing the Vow**: Place the bound tokens or rings between the candles until they burn down, symbolizing the sealing and strengthening of the vow.

After the Enchantment:

- **Wearing the Tokens or Rings**: Wear the rings or carry the tokens as a constant reminder of your unbreakable vows.
- **Regular Reaffirmation**: Regularly reaffirm your vows to each other, keeping the essence of the enchantment alive in your daily life.

The Unbreakable Vow Enchantment is a deeply meaningful spell for couples who are committed to strengthening their bond and ensuring the longevity of their love. It serves as a powerful reminder of the vows of fidelity and commitment that form the foundation of a strong, enduring relationship.

59. Love's Eternal Guardian Summoning

The Love's Eternal Guardian Summoning is a spell designed to call upon a spiritual guardian or entity to watch over and protect a love relationship. This ritual is for those who believe in the power of spiritual guardians and seek their guidance and protection to preserve the sanctity and strength of their romantic bond.

Purpose: To summon a guardian spirit or entity to oversee, guide, and protect a love relationship, ensuring its longevity and spiritual harmony.

Timing: Best performed during a significant lunar phase, such as a full moon for protection and clarity, or during spiritual or religious days of significance.

Materials:

1. A sacred space, such as an altar or a special area in your home
2. Two white candles (symbolizing purity and protection)
3. A symbol or representation of the guardian spirit or entity you wish to summon (this can be a statue, a picture, or an emblem)
4. Rose petals or jasmine flowers (for love and harmony)
5. A bowl of water (symbolizing emotional clarity and intuition)
6. Incense associated with spiritual communication (such as sandalwood or myrrh)

7. A small offering, like honey or wine (as a gesture of goodwill towards the guardian)

Preparation:

1. Create a tranquil and respectful atmosphere in your chosen sacred space.
2. Arrange the candles, flowers, water, and the symbol of the guardian in a harmonious layout.

The Summoning:

1. **Lighting the Candles**: Light the white candles to purify the space and set a protective boundary.
2. **Placing the Guardian Symbol**: Position the symbol of the guardian entity in a prominent place on the altar.
3. **Offering Placement**: Place your offering near the guardian's symbol as a sign of respect and invitation.
4. **Incense Burning**: Light the incense to facilitate spiritual communication and to invite the guardian's presence.
5. **Invocation**: Respectfully call upon the guardian spirit or entity. Speak or chant an invocation that resonates with your belief system, inviting the guardian to watch over and protect your love relationship.
6. **Rose Petals or Jasmine Offering**: Scatter the rose petals or jasmine around the symbol, enhancing the loving energy of the summoning.
7. **Water as a Conduit**: Use the bowl of water as a medium to connect with the guardian, symbolizing clarity in your intentions and purity in your request.

After the Summoning:

- **Acknowledging the Guardian**: Regularly acknowledge the presence of the guardian in your relationship, perhaps through small rituals or by simply thanking them in your daily life.
- **Maintaining the Sacred Space**: Keep the sacred space clean and respectful as a sign of honor to the guardian.
- **Observing Changes**: Be mindful of any guidance, signs, or changes in your relationship that may indicate the guardian's influence or advice.

Love's Eternal Guardian Summoning is a deeply spiritual ritual, grounded in the belief that higher powers can oversee and protect our most cherished relationships. It fosters a sense of spiritual support and guidance, adding an extra layer of sanctity and protection to the bonds of love.

60. Dimensional Love Portal Opening

The Dimensional Love Portal Opening is an advanced magical practice that involves opening a metaphysical portal to attract transcendent love energies. This ritual is ideal for those who are experienced in dimensional work and wish to explore more profound, cosmic aspects of love, transcending the physical world.

Purpose: To open a portal that allows higher-dimensional love energies to flow into your life, enhancing your capacity for deep, spiritual connections.

Timing: Optimal during cosmic events like eclipses, meteor showers, or planetary alignments, which are believed to open gateways to higher dimensions.

Materials:

1. A secluded and quiet space for undisturbed focus
2. A large circle drawn on the ground with natural materials (like stones or flowers)
3. Four candles (representing the cardinal directions and elemental energies)
4. Crystals associated with spiritual awakening, such as labradorite, moldavite, or quartz
5. Incense with a cosmic or ethereal scent (like frankincense or star anise)
6. A small mirror (to represent the portal between dimensions)
7. Chimes or a bell (to signify the opening and closing of the portal)

Preparation:

1. Set up your ritual space in an area where you feel a strong spiritual presence.
2. Arrange the candles at the cardinal points of your circle, with the mirror and crystals in the center.

The Ritual:

1. **Candle Lighting**: Light each candle, invoking the energies of the four directions and the elements, creating a balanced foundation for your portal.
2. **Crystal Placement**: Position the crystals around the mirror, asking them to amplify the portal's energy and facilitate the connection to higher dimensions.
3. **Incense Lighting**: Burn the incense to purify the space and elevate the vibrational frequency, preparing for the opening of the portal.
4. **Portal Visualization**: Stand or sit within the circle, focusing on the mirror. Visualize it as a doorway to higher dimensions of love. See it glowing, becoming more tangible.
5. **Chime or Bell Ringing**: Gently ring the chimes or bell, signifying the opening of the portal. Feel the higher-dimensional energies flowing through the portal and into your space.
6. **Meditation and Reception**: Meditate in the presence of the open portal. Open yourself to receive insights, energies, or messages from higher-dimensional beings of love.
7. **Closing the Portal**: When you feel it's time to close the portal, ring the chimes or bell again. Visualize the mirror's glow fading, sealing off the higher dimensions.

After the Ritual:

- **Reflect on the Experience:** Spend time journaling or contemplating the insights and energies received during the ritual.
- **Regular Portal Work:** If you feel called, regularly engage in this ritual to maintain a connection with higher-dimensional love energies.

Dimensional Love Portal Opening is a profound ritual for those seeking to explore the cosmic dimensions of love. It's a practice that stretches beyond the usual boundaries of love magic, tapping into the vast and mysterious energies of the universe and the myriad forms that love can take in higher realms of existence.

61. Cosmic Love Harmony Transmutation

The Cosmic Love Harmony Transmutation is a potent spell that harnesses cosmic energies to transmute and harmonize various aspects of your love life. This ritual is designed for those who wish to bring a sense of cosmic balance and harmony to their romantic relationships or their approach to finding love.

Purpose: To draw on cosmic forces to transmute any negative energies in your love life into harmonious, positive vibrations, aligning your romantic experiences with the harmony of the universe.

Timing: Ideal to perform under a harmonious celestial alignment, such as during a conjunction of Venus and Jupiter, or when the stars and planets are favorably aligned for love and harmony.

Materials:

1. A space under the night sky, or a quiet place with representations of the cosmos (such as star charts or space-themed decor)
2. Various crystals that resonate with cosmic energy, like moonstone, celestite, or meteorite fragments
3. A blue or silver candle (symbolizing the vastness of the cosmos)
4. Incense with a celestial scent, such as stargazer lily or night-blooming jasmine
5. A small dish of water mixed with a few drops of essential oil (like lavender or ylang-ylang) to represent the cosmic ether

6. A representation of the solar system or a cosmic deity (like a model or image)
7. A piece of paper and pen to write down aspects of your love life you wish to harmonize

Preparation:

1. Set up your space in a way that feels open to the cosmos, either outside under the sky or indoors with cosmic representations.
2. Arrange your materials in a circle around you, creating a sacred cosmic space.

The Ritual:

1. **Candle Lighting**: Light the blue or silver candle, invoking the vast and harmonious energies of the cosmos.
2. **Cosmic Representation Activation**: Place the solar system or cosmic deity representation in a prominent position as a focal point for cosmic energy.
3. **Crystal Arrangement**: Surround your space with the crystals, creating a mini cosmos that resonates with universal harmony.
4. **Incense for Atmosphere**: Light the celestial incense to enhance your connection to cosmic energies.
5. **Writing Down Aspects to Harmonize**: Write on the paper aspects of your love life that you wish to bring into harmony. Be specific about the issues or energies you want to transmute.
6. **Water Mixture Activation**: Dip your fingers into the water mixture, and sprinkle a few drops around your space, symbolizing the scattering of cosmic ether for transmutation.
7. **Meditation and Visualization**: Meditate on the aspects you've written down. Visualize the cosmic energies transforming

these aspects, bringing balance and harmony. Imagine the disharmonies dissolving and being replaced with cosmic harmony.

8. **Sealing the Transmutation**: Hold the paper with your written aspects towards the sky or the cosmic representation, asking for the transmutation to be sealed by the cosmic forces.

After the Ritual:

- **Reflect on Cosmic Harmony**: Spend time regularly contemplating the balance and harmony of the cosmos and how it mirrors in your love life.
- **Maintain a Cosmic Perspective**: Keep the written aspects in a place where you can see them, reminding you to maintain a cosmic perspective in your approach to love.

Cosmic Love Harmony Transmutation is a deeply spiritual and mystical ritual, bringing the vast and harmonious energies of the cosmos into your personal love life. It's about aligning your romantic experiences with the balance and order that pervade the universe, creating a love life that resonates with the cosmic dance of harmony and balance.

62. Twin Soul Fusion Ritual

The Twin Soul Fusion Ritual is a deeply spiritual practice aimed at harmonizing and uniting the energies of twin souls, whether in preparation for meeting them or deepening an existing connection. This ritual is for those who believe in the concept of twin souls – two halves of the same soul destined to reunite – and seek a profound spiritual union with theirs.

Purpose: To energetically align and unite with your twin soul, whether to draw them into your life or to deepen an existing connection, fostering a bond that transcends physical dimensions.

Timing: Ideal to perform on significant dates that hold personal or spiritual meaning, such as solstices, equinoxes, or personal milestones.

Materials:

1. A quiet, sacred space conducive to deep meditation and spiritual work
2. Two candles, ideally one representing you and one your twin soul (colors can be chosen based on personal significance or astrological signs)
3. A mirror to symbolize reflection and the concept of twin souls as mirrors to each other
4. Crystals associated with love and spiritual connection, such as pink quartz and twin crystals
5. Fragrant flowers or incense that evoke a sense of love and harmony

6. A piece of paper and pen to write intentions or messages to your twin soul
7. Soft, meditative music (optional)

Preparation:

1. Set up your space in a way that feels harmonious and spiritually inviting.
2. Arrange the candles to face each other with the mirror between them, and place the crystals and flowers or incense around this setup.

The Ritual:

1. **Lighting the Candles**: Light both candles, focusing on the intention of spiritual fusion with your twin soul.
2. **Mirror Placement**: Position the mirror so that it reflects the flames of both candles, symbolizing the mirroring and connection of twin souls.
3. **Crystal Activation**: Arrange the crystals around the candles, asking them to amplify the spiritual connection and harmonize the energies.
4. **Writing Intentions**: Write your intentions or a message to your twin soul on the paper. If you're already in a relationship with them, focus on deepening the connection. If not, focus on attracting them into your life.
5. **Incense or Flowers**: Use the flowers or light the incense to create an atmosphere of love and harmony.
6. **Meditation and Visualization**: Meditate between the candles, visualizing a strong, unbreakable bond forming between you and your twin soul. Imagine energies intertwining and harmonizing, transcending physical space.

7. **Reading Your Intentions**: Read out loud the intentions or message you wrote, sending it out to the universe or directly to your twin soul's higher self.

After the Ritual:

- **Regular Reflection**: Regularly revisit the intentions or messages you wrote, reinforcing the connection and keeping your energies aligned.
- **Meditative Practice**: Continue a regular meditation practice focusing on your twin soul, nurturing the bond and keeping your energies in harmony.

The Twin Soul Fusion Ritual is a sacred practice that taps into the spiritual depths of love and connection. It's a journey of aligning and uniting with your twin soul, whether they are already in your life or you are still waiting to meet them. This ritual helps to foster a bond that is deeply spiritual and transcendent, rooted in the profound belief of twin souls finding and completing each other.

63. Immutable Affection Seal

The Immutable Affection Seal is a potent ritual designed to create an enduring and unchangeable bond of affection and love. This spell is for those who wish to solidify and protect the love in their relationship, making it resilient to external influences and internal fluctuations.

Purpose: To cast a seal of immutable affection, ensuring that the love shared remains constant, unshakable, and protected from any negative influences.

Timing: Best performed during a stable and harmonious astrological period, such as when Venus is in Taurus, or on a date significant to the relationship, like an anniversary.

Materials:

1. A private, intimate space where the ritual can be conducted undisturbed
2. Two red candles (symbolizing enduring passion and love)
3. A binding element, such as a red ribbon or cord
4. Rose petals or essential oil (for love and harmony)
5. A small piece of rose quartz and amethyst (for emotional balance and spiritual connection)
6. A personal item from each partner (to represent each individual in the relationship)
7. A seal or stamp (to symbolize the act of sealing the affection)
8. A parchment or high-quality paper (to write down the seal of affection)

Preparation:

1. Set the space with a romantic and sacred ambiance.
2. Arrange the candles, stones, and personal items on a table or altar.

The Ritual:

1. **Lighting the Candles**: Begin by lighting the red candles, focusing on the enduring strength and passion of your love.
2. **Binding Element Placement**: Place the binding element (ribbon or cord) between the candles, symbolizing the connection between you and your partner.
3. **Rose Petals or Oil**: Scatter rose petals around the candles or anoint them with rose oil, enhancing the loving energy.
4. **Crystal Activation**: Place the rose quartz and amethyst near the candles, asking them to infuse the relationship with balanced and harmonious love.
5. **Writing the Seal**: On the parchment, write down your mutual promise or affirmation of immutable affection. This could be a simple statement or a more elaborate vow.
6. **Sealing the Affection**: Use the seal or stamp on the written promise, symbolizing the solidification and protection of your affection.
7. **Personal Item Exchange**: Exchange the personal items with your partner, each placing the item near the other's candle, symbolizing mutual respect and unity.
8. **Ribbon or Cord Binding**: Tie the ribbon or cord around the sealed parchment, further symbolizing the unbreakable bond of your affection.

After the Ritual:

- **Place of Honor**: Keep the sealed parchment in a place of honor, such as your bedroom or a shared space, as a constant reminder of the unchangeable affection in your relationship.
- **Regular Acknowledgment**: Regularly acknowledge and celebrate the strength and resilience of your bond, keeping the energy of the seal active and powerful.

The Immutable Affection Seal is a profound commitment to maintaining and protecting the love and affection in your relationship. It's a magical way of declaring that the love you share is constant and unwavering, capable of withstanding the test of time and challenge.

64. Quantum Heart Entanglement

The Quantum Heart Entanglement is an advanced spell that draws on concepts from quantum physics to create a deep and unbreakable bond between lovers. This ritual is for those who are not only romantics at heart but also resonate with the mystique of the quantum world, seeking to intertwine their love in a way that defies conventional understanding.

Purpose: To intertwine the energies of two lovers at a quantum level, ensuring that no matter the physical distance, their hearts remain closely connected and in sync.

Timing: Ideal for performing during significant astronomical events, like planetary alignments or during a quantum moon phase, such as a Supermoon or Blood Moon, to amplify quantum energies.

Materials:

1. A secluded and calm environment, free from interruptions
2. Two intertwined rings or pendants made of conductive metals (like silver or copper), symbolizing the quantum entanglement
3. A pair of small mirrors, to reflect and symbolize the concept of quantum states
4. Two candles, one for each individual, in colors that represent personal significance or astrological signs
5. A quartz crystal for each person (for clarity and energy amplification)

6. Scientific diagrams or symbols that represent quantum mechanics (like the Schrödinger equation or a diagram of entangled particles)
7. Soft, ambient music that resonates with cosmic or quantum themes

Preparation:

1. Prepare your space in a way that feels harmonious and conducive to deep, reflective thought.
2. Place the intertwined rings or pendants at the center, flanked by the pair of mirrors and the candles.

The Ritual:

1. **Candle Lighting**: Light each candle, dedicating each one to the individuals involved in the entanglement.
2. **Quantum Symbolism**: Position the scientific diagrams or symbols in a visible spot, focusing on the concept of entanglement and interconnectedness at a quantum level.
3. **Mirror Placement**: Place the mirrors so they reflect the light of the candles and the rings or pendants, symbolizing the infinite reflections and dimensions of your connection.
4. **Crystal Activation**: Hold your quartz crystal, meditating on the clarity and strength of your bond. Place it near your candle.
5. **Entanglement Visualization**: Focus on the intertwined rings or pendants. Visualize an energy field forming around them, representing the entanglement of your hearts at a quantum level.
6. **Ambient Music**: Play the ambient music to deepen the atmosphere of cosmic interconnectedness.

7. **Quantum Heart Connection**: Meditate on the feeling of being deeply connected beyond physical space. Imagine your energies intertwining at a subatomic level, transcending time and space.

After the Ritual:

- **Wearing the Entangled Items**: Each person should wear one of the entangled rings or pendants as a physical representation of the quantum entanglement.
- **Regular Meditation**: Engage in regular meditation sessions focusing on the quantum connection, reinforcing the bond and keeping the energies in harmony.

Quantum Heart Entanglement is a unique and profound way to symbolize and strengthen the deep connection between lovers. It combines the mysteries of love with the fascinating principles of quantum physics, creating a bond that is as spiritually significant as it is scientifically intriguing.

65. Eternal Love's Time Capsule

The Eternal Love's Time Capsule is a magical ritual that involves creating a physical time capsule filled with tokens of love and affection. This spell is for couples who wish to capture the essence of their love in the present, to be revisited and cherished in the future, symbolizing the endurance and evolution of their relationship over time.

Purpose: To create a physical manifestation of a couple's love and affection, preserved to be revisited in the future, symbolizing the lasting and evolving nature of their bond.

Timing: Best performed on a significant date for the relationship, such as an anniversary, or during a meaningful astrological event that represents longevity and endurance, like Saturn's return.

Materials:

1. A sturdy, sealable box or container to serve as the time capsule
2. Personal and sentimental items that represent your relationship (photos, letters, small gifts)
3. A pair of intertwined objects (like rings or woven bracelets) to symbolize your connected paths
4. A love letter or note to your future selves
5. Durable natural items like stones or crystals to symbolize the strength and permanence of your love (e.g., rose quartz for love, amethyst for spiritual growth)
6. Herbs or flowers associated with love and preservation, such as dried roses or lavender

7. A seal or symbol of commitment (like a wax seal or a special emblem)

Preparation:

1. Choose a special place and time to prepare and fill your time capsule, making it a meaningful and intentional activity.
2. Gather all your materials and lay them out in an organized manner.

The Ritual:

1. **Container Blessing**: Begin by holding the container and blessing it, intending that it safely preserves the contents and the essence of your love over time.
2. **Item Placement**: One by one, place the items in the container. As you do so, share memories or thoughts associated with each item, reinforcing the bond and love each represents.
3. **Love Letter Addition**: Write and add the love letter or note to your future selves, expressing your hopes, dreams, and affirmations for your relationship.
4. **Intertwined Objects**: Place the intertwined objects into the capsule last, symbolizing your united journey and enduring connection.
5. **Herbs or Flowers**: Add the herbs or flowers, asking them to maintain the vitality and essence of the items and your love.
6. **Sealing the Time Capsule**: Seal the time capsule with the chosen symbol of commitment, affirming the enduring nature of your bond.

After the Ritual:

- **Choosing a Location**: Decide on a meaningful place to store or bury the time capsule, whether it's in your home or a special outdoor location.
- **Future Opening Date**: Set a future date to open the time capsule, aligning it with another significant milestone in your relationship.
- **Reflective Practice**: Regularly reflect on your relationship's journey, knowing that the time capsule is a physical testament to your enduring love and evolving story.

Eternal Love's Time Capsule is a heartfelt and tangible way to celebrate and preserve the moments, memories, and emotions that define a relationship. It's a promise to the future, a treasure trove of love, waiting to be rediscovered and celebrated in the years to come.

66. Celestial Love Avowal Ceremony

The Celestial Love Avowal Ceremony is a ritual that combines the mystique of the cosmos with the sanctity of love vows. This ceremony is particularly suited for couples who share a fascination with the celestial and wish to incorporate this into their expression of commitment to each other.

Purpose: To affirm love and commitment in a ceremony that intertwines the couple's bond with the celestial energies, symbolizing a love that is as vast and enduring as the universe itself.

Timing: Optimal during a significant celestial event, such as a meteor shower, a planetary alignment, or a particularly meaningful star configuration.

Materials:

1. A location with a clear view of the night sky, like a hilltop or an open field
2. A telescope or star map for stargazing
3. Two candles, one for each partner, ideally in colors that represent their astrological signs
4. A decorative mat or cloth to sit or stand on, adorned with celestial patterns
5. A journal or beautifully bound book to write your love vows
6. Crystals that connect with celestial energies, like moonstone or lapis lazuli
7. Incense or essential oils with ethereal or cosmic scents, such as frankincense or patchouli

Preparation:

1. Set up the space in an open area with minimal light pollution, allowing for an unobstructed view of the cosmos.
2. Arrange the mat or cloth, candles, telescope or star map, and crystals in a harmonious layout.

The Ceremony:

1. **Candle Lighting**: Begin by lighting the candles as symbols of your individual lights coming together in unity.
2. **Stargazing and Celestial Alignment**: Use the telescope or star map to locate and observe celestial bodies or constellations that hold significance for your relationship.
3. **Writing and Reading Vows**: Take turns to write and then read your vows to each other, under the vast canopy of the stars. Let these vows be inspired by the qualities of the celestial bodies you've observed.
4. **Crystal Exchange**: Exchange crystals with each other, symbolizing the exchange of celestial energies and the depth of your connection.
5. **Incense or Oil**: Use the incense or essential oils to enhance the ethereal quality of the ceremony, symbolizing the ascent of your vows to the celestial planes.
6. **Concluding with Celestial Acknowledgment**: Conclude the ceremony by acknowledging the cosmic forces that have witnessed your vows, asking for their blessing on your union.

After the Ceremony:

- **Journal or Book**: Keep the journal or book with your vows in a special place, perhaps alongside the exchanged crystals, as a sacred reminder of your celestial avowal.

- **Celestial Anniversaries**: Celebrate future anniversaries by stargazing or engaging in activities that connect you with the cosmos, reaffirming your celestial love vows.

The Celestial Love Avowal Ceremony is a profound and romantic way for couples to express their commitment, surrounded by the grandeur of the universe. It's a reminder that their love, like the stars and celestial bodies, is a magnificent and enduring force in the vast tapestry of existence.

67. Ancient Lovers' Soul Exchange

The Ancient Lovers' Soul Exchange is a deeply mystical ritual that traces its origins to ancient traditions of soul bonding. This spell is designed for couples who seek to explore the profound depths of their connection by symbolically exchanging fragments of their souls, signifying an eternal spiritual bond.

Purpose: To engage in a sacred exchange of soul energies with a partner, symbolizing the deepest possible connection and unity between two individuals.

Timing: Best performed on a night of a significant lunar or solar event, such as a solstice, equinox, or eclipse, which are traditionally associated with powerful spiritual transformations.

Materials:

1. A quiet, sacred space where the ritual can be conducted in tranquility and reverence
2. Two white candles, representing the purity and essence of each individual's soul
3. A small, symbolic item from each partner (such as a lock of hair, a piece of jewelry, or a personal memento)
4. A bowl of water with flower petals (preferably roses or lilies) for spiritual cleansing and openness
5. Incense sticks with a soothing, sacred scent (like sandalwood or myrrh)

6. A piece of cloth or ribbon to bind the small items together, symbolizing the soul exchange
7. Soft, ambient music or drumming to set a spiritual tone

Preparation:

1. Set up your sacred space in a way that feels intimate and reverential.
2. Arrange the candles, bowl of water, incense, and the small items in a meaningful way.

The Ritual:

1. **Lighting the Candles**: Begin by lighting the candles, focusing on the intention of pure soul connection and unity.
2. **Cleansing with Water and Petals**: Each partner washes their hands in the bowl of water, symbolizing spiritual cleansing and readiness for the soul exchange.
3. **Incense Lighting**: Light the incense to purify the space and invite a sense of the sacred.
4. **Exchange of Personal Items**: Exchange the small symbolic items, holding them as you express your intentions and desires for the soul bond.
5. **Binding with Cloth or Ribbon**: Wrap the cloth or ribbon around the items, physically symbolizing the intertwining of your souls.
6. **Meditation and Visualization**: Sit facing each other with the bound items between you. Enter into a meditative state, visualizing the merging and exchange of your soul energies.
7. **Chant or Affirmation**: Together, chant or affirm your commitment and unity, acknowledging the depth of your bond and the sacred nature of this soul exchange.

After the Ritual:

- **Keeping the Bound Items**: Place the bound items in a special location where they can be honored and respected, symbolizing the ongoing nature of your soul connection.
- **Reflective Practice**: Regularly reflect on the deep connection you have established, and find ways to honor and nurture this bond in your everyday interactions.

The Ancient Lovers' Soul Exchange is a powerful and deeply spiritual ritual, suitable for couples who are committed to exploring the depths of their connection on a soul level. It is a testament to the belief that love, at its highest and most profound, is a union that transcends the physical, merging souls in eternal unity.

68. Universe's Love Convergence Spell

The Universe's Love Convergence Spell is a powerful ritual that aims to align your romantic path with the universal forces of love. This spell is particularly suited for individuals seeking to harmonize their love life with the broader energies of the cosmos, inviting a convergence of universal love into their personal experience.

Purpose: To align oneself with the universal energies of love, facilitating a convergence of romantic opportunities, deeper connections, and a harmonious love life that resonates with the cosmos.

Timing: Ideal for performing during cosmic alignments, such as planetary conjunctions, or when the universe's energy feels particularly vibrant and conducive to love – for instance, during a meteor shower or a rare astronomical event.

Materials:

1. An open space under the night sky, or a quiet place adorned with cosmic symbols
2. A large, circular mat or cloth depicting a starry sky or cosmic motif
3. Several small candles placed around the perimeter of the mat, symbolizing the stars and planets
4. Crystals that connect with cosmic energy, such as meteorite pieces, tektites, or moldavite
5. A small bowl of water mixed with glitter or shimmering particles, representing the Milky Way

6. Incense with a cosmic or mystical scent (such as star anise or galactic orchid)
7. A written list of your desires and intentions regarding love

Preparation:

1. Set up your ritual space in a way that feels open and connected to the vastness of the cosmos.
2. Lay out the mat or cloth, and arrange the candles and crystals around it.

The Spell:

1. **Candle Lighting**: Light the candles, visualizing them as celestial bodies, each flickering flame a star or planet in your cosmic journey of love.
2. **Crystal Placement**: Arrange the crystals on the mat, asking them to channel cosmic energies and facilitate the convergence of universal love.
3. **Water Bowl Centerpiece**: Place the bowl of shimmering water at the center of the mat, symbolizing the galactic center from which cosmic love emanates.
4. **Incense Burning**: Light the incense to elevate the vibrational frequency of the space, enhancing your connection to the universe.
5. **Reading Your Desires**: Read out loud the list of your love desires and intentions, sending them into the cosmos.
6. **Meditation and Visualization**: Sit in the center of the mat, meditate, and visualize the cosmic energies converging around you, aligning your love life with the universal forces of love and harmony.

7. **Affirmation of Convergence**: Conclude by affirming your openness to the universe's guidance and love, trusting in the cosmic journey that lies ahead.

After the Spell:

- **Regular Cosmic Connection**: Spend time stargazing or meditating on cosmic themes, maintaining your connection to the universal energies of love.
- **Reflect on the Cosmic Journey**: Keep the list of desires in a special place, revisiting it to reflect on your journey and the convergence of love in your life.

The Universe's Love Convergence Spell is a magical way to align your personal love journey with the broader, universal forces of love. It is an affirmation that love, in its most magnificent form, is a cosmic journey, intertwined with the vast and mysterious energies of the universe.

69. Heart of the Multiverse Alignment

The Heart of the Multiverse Alignment is an advanced and esoteric spell intended for those who want to explore and align their romantic energies with the multiple dimensions and realities of the universe. This ritual is ideal for individuals seeking a transcendental approach to love that goes beyond the conventional understanding of romantic connections.

Purpose: To align your heart's energies with the infinite possibilities of love across the multiverse, opening up pathways to profound and varied romantic experiences that transcend traditional boundaries.

Timing: Best performed during rare astronomical events that symbolize the vastness and complexity of the universe, such as a cosmic alignment, a comet's appearance, or during significant celestial phenomena.

Materials:

1. A quiet, reflective space, preferably outdoors under the open sky
2. A large circle drawn on the ground, representing the boundary of the known universe
3. Multiple candles of varying colors and sizes, symbolizing the diverse worlds within the multiverse
4. Crystals that resonate with cosmic energy, like clear quartz, labradorite, or opal
5. A reflective surface, such as a mirror or a small pool of water, to represent the portal to different dimensions

6. Incense or essential oils with otherworldly scents, such as mugwort or starflower
7. A notebook or journal to record insights and reflections

Preparation:

1. Create a calm and meditative atmosphere in your chosen space.
2. Arrange the candles and crystals within and around the circle, creating a pattern that resonates with cosmic energy.

The Alignment:

1. **Candle Lighting**: Begin by lighting the candles, each flame a gateway to a different dimension within the multiverse.
2. **Crystal Activation**: Position the crystals strategically around the circle, asking them to act as conduits for multiversal energies.
3. **Mirror or Water Placement**: Place the reflective surface in the center of the circle, symbolizing your access point to the heart of the multiverse.
4. **Incense or Oil**: Use the incense or essential oils to deepen your connection to the cosmos.
5. **Meditation and Visualization**: Sit within the circle, meditate, and visualize your heart's energy extending into the multiverse, connecting with various forms of love across different dimensions.
6. **Affirmation of Multiversal Love**: Affirm your openness to experiencing love in its myriad forms across the multiverse, embracing the complexity and diversity of these connections.

After the Alignment:

- **Journaling**: Record your experiences, thoughts, and feelings in the notebook or journal, noting any particular insights or connections you felt with different dimensions.
- **Ongoing Reflection**: Regularly revisit your notes and meditate on the concept of the multiverse, exploring how it influences your perception and experience of love.

The Heart of the Multiverse Alignment is a deeply mystical and expansive spell, inviting those who practice it to explore the bounty of love beyond our conventional understanding. It acknowledges that love, like the universe itself, is vast, diverse, and infinitely complex, offering endless possibilities for those willing to explore its depths.

70. Love's Infinite Echo Resonance

The Love's Infinite Echo Resonance is a spell that focuses on amplifying and sending your loving intentions and energies across the cosmos, creating echoes that resonate through time and space. This ritual is designed for individuals seeking to magnify their love energy to attract a soulmate or to deepen an existing relationship by resonating with the infinite nature of love.

Purpose: To amplify your love energy and intentions, sending them across the universe in infinite echoes, thereby attracting resonant love energies back into your life.

Timing: Ideal to perform on nights when the universe feels particularly resonant, such as during a harmonic convergence, planetary opposition, or when the stars appear especially bright and clear.

Materials:

1. A serene and open space, preferably under the night sky
2. A central candle, preferably large and white, to symbolize the purity and infinity of love
3. Surrounding candles in a spiral formation, representing the echoing waves of energy
4. A crystal grid using stones associated with love, like rose quartz, garnet, or rhodonite
5. A bowl of water with floating candles or flower petals
6. Incense or essential oils with a deep, resonant scent, like jasmine or rosewood

7. A musical instrument or recorded sounds that evoke the feeling of cosmic resonance (like a singing bowl, chimes, or ambient cosmic music)

Preparation:

1. Create a calm and harmonious setting in your chosen space.
2. Arrange the central candle, surrounded by the spiral of other candles, and set up the crystal grid.

The Ritual:

1. **Lighting the Central Candle**: Begin by lighting the central candle, focusing on the pure, infinite nature of your love intentions.
2. **Spiral Candle Lighting**: Light the surrounding candles in a spiral, visualizing each flame as an echo of your love energy rippling outwards.
3. **Crystal Grid Activation**: Gently touch each stone in the crystal grid, asking them to amplify and carry your love intentions across the cosmos.
4. **Water and Petals**: Place the bowl of water with candles or petals in the center, symbolizing emotional depth and the fluidity of love's journey.
5. **Incense or Oil**: Burn the incense or use the oils to enhance the vibrational quality of the ritual.
6. **Sound Resonance**: Use the musical instrument or play the recorded sounds, creating a resonant atmosphere that embodies the cosmic nature of love.
7. **Meditation and Visualization**: Meditate on the echoes of your love energy traveling through the universe, touching and resonating with similar energies and souls.

After the Ritual:

- **Regular Meditation**: Continue to meditate on this concept, reinforcing the idea of your love resonating through the cosmos.
- **Observation and Openness**: Be open to and observant of the echoes returning in various forms, such as new connections, deepened relationships, or internal insights about love.

Love's Infinite Echo Resonance is a spell that embraces the cosmic and infinite nature of love. It acknowledges that love is not just an emotion confined to our immediate surroundings, but a powerful force that resonates through the entire universe, capable of echoing back to us in beautiful and unexpected ways.

71. Galactic Love Wave Emission

The Galactic Love Wave Emission is a spell that harnesses the vast energies of the galaxy to emit powerful waves of love and affection. This ritual is intended for those who wish to project their love across cosmic distances, attracting universal love energies or strengthening the bond with a partner who may be physically distant but is deeply connected at a soul level.

Purpose: To send out a powerful galactic wave of love, either to attract a profound cosmic connection or to strengthen an existing relationship that transcends physical barriers.

Timing: Most effective when performed under a significant galactic event, such as during a galaxy visibility night, when the Milky Way is clearly visible, or during a cosmic event that feels especially charged with galactic energy.

Materials:

1. An open space under the night sky, allowing for a clear view of the stars and galaxy
2. A large, circular mat with a galaxy or star pattern
3. Multiple candles placed in a spiral galaxy formation
4. Crystals that resonate with cosmic energies, like meteorite, tektite, or blue goldstone
5. A telescope or star map for galactic contemplation
6. Incense with a deep, space-like scent, such as amber or myrrh
7. A journal or piece of paper to write down your galactic love intentions

Preparation:

1. Set up in an area with minimal light pollution to maximize visibility of the night sky.
2. Lay out the mat and arrange the candles and crystals in a formation that mimics a spiral galaxy.

The Ritual:

1. **Lighting the Candles**: Light the candles, envisioning each flame as a star emitting love energy throughout the galaxy.
2. **Crystal Configuration**: Position the crystals in alignment with the candles, enhancing the connection to galactic energies.
3. **Galactic Contemplation**: Use the telescope or star map to observe the galaxy, contemplating the vastness of space and the love it holds.
4. **Incense for Cosmic Connection**: Burn the incense to deepen your connection to the cosmos and set a mystical atmosphere.
5. **Writing Galactic Intentions**: Write your intentions for love on the paper, focusing on the desire to connect with cosmic love energies or to strengthen a distant love bond.
6. **Galactic Wave Visualization**: Meditate in the center of your spiral galaxy formation, visualizing waves of love energy emanating from you and flowing out into the galaxy, reaching far and wide.
7. **Affirmation of Galactic Love**: Conclude by affirming your connection to the cosmos and your openness to receiving or strengthening love on a galactic scale.

After the Ritual:

- **Reflect on the Cosmos**: Spend time stargazing regularly, reinforcing your connection to the cosmic energies of love.

- **Journaling and Contemplation**: Keep the written intentions in your journal and revisit them, meditating on your place in the cosmos and the love that pervades it.

Galactic Love Wave Emission is a spell that transcends the usual boundaries of love magic, tapping into the vast and mystical energies of the galaxy. It acknowledges that love, like the universe itself, is vast and boundless, capable of traversing immense distances and connecting souls across the cosmic expanse.

72. Supernatural Lovers' Pact

The Supernatural Lovers' Pact is a powerful and mystical spell designed for couples who wish to bind their love with the forces of the supernatural, creating a pact that transcends ordinary romance. This ritual is suitable for partners deeply committed to each other and willing to explore the more mystical and arcane aspects of their connection.

Purpose: To forge a supernatural pact between lovers, strengthening their bond with the energies of the mystical and creating a partnership that is protected and empowered by supernatural forces.

Timing: Ideal to perform during nights of metaphysical significance, such as on All Hallows' Eve, during a rare celestial event, or on a date that holds particular spiritual significance for the couple.

Materials:

1. A secluded, intimate space conducive to mystical energies
2. Two black candles, symbolizing the depth and mystery of the supernatural
3. A binding cord or ribbon, preferably in a deep, rich color like purple or red
4. A mix of protective and binding herbs, such as mugwort and vervain
5. Small talismans or amulets that hold personal significance to each partner
6. A chalice of wine or a potion crafted from herbs, symbolizing the blending of lives
7. A parchment or special paper to inscribe the pact

Preparation:

1. Create a mystical and intimate atmosphere in your chosen space.
2. Arrange the candles, herbs, talismans, and chalice in a way that feels sacred and powerful.

The Pact:

1. **Candle Lighting**: Begin by lighting the black candles, invoking the energies of the supernatural.
2. **Herb Circle**: Scatter the protective and binding herbs in a circle around you, creating a protected space for your ritual.
3. **Talisman Exchange**: Exchange the talismans or amulets with each other, symbolizing the exchange of energy and trust.
4. **Binding Cord Ritual**: Use the cord or ribbon to gently bind your hands together, symbolizing your commitment and connection.
5. **Chalice Sharing**: Share the wine or potion from the chalice, representing the union of your spirits and lives.
6. **Pact Inscription**: Write your pact on the parchment, detailing your promises and commitments to each other under the watch of supernatural forces.
7. **Affirmation of the Pact**: Read the pact aloud together, affirming your commitment to uphold it and honor the supernatural bond you have created.

After the Ritual:

- **Pact Preservation**: Keep the inscribed pact in a safe and sacred place, such as a shared altar or a special box.

- **Regular Reaffirmation**: Regularly reaffirm your commitment to each other and the pact, keeping the supernatural energies of your bond alive and strong.
- **Talisman Care**: Cherish and care for the exchanged talismans or amulets, as they are now physical representations of your supernatural lovers' pact.

The Supernatural Lovers' Pact is a spell of deep commitment and mystical bonding, suitable for couples who share a belief in the power of the supernatural and wish to intertwine their love story with the energies of the mystical realms. It's a testament to a love that is not only deep and enduring but also enchanted and protected by forces beyond the ordinary.

73. Ethereal Love Bond Solidification

The Ethereal Love Bond Solidification is a spell focused on strengthening and securing the ethereal, spiritual bonds of love. This ritual is especially meaningful for couples who have experienced a deep spiritual connection and wish to reinforce and solidify this bond at an ethereal level.

Purpose: To solidify and reinforce the spiritual and ethereal bonds of love, making them resilient and enduring beyond the physical plane.

Timing: Most effective when performed during spiritually significant times, such as during a lunar eclipse, on a spiritually significant date, or when both partners feel a heightened sense of spiritual connection.

Materials:

1. A peaceful and private setting conducive to spiritual work
2. Two intertwined quartz crystals, representing the interconnectedness of your spirits
3. A lavender or light blue candle to represent the ethereal nature of your bond
4. Incense with a light, airy fragrance, such as sage or lemongrass
5. A small bowl of purified water infused with petals of a white or pink flower, symbolizing purity and love
6. A soft piece of cloth or a ribbon in a light color, to symbolize the gentle nature of the ethereal bond
7. A piece of paper or parchment to write down your joint spiritual intentions or vows

Preparation:

1. Create a calm and serene atmosphere in your chosen space.
2. Arrange the materials on a table or altar in a way that feels harmonious and connected.

The Ritual:

1. **Candle Lighting**: Begin by lighting the candle, focusing on the lightness and purity of your spiritual bond.
2. **Crystal Intertwining**: Hold the intertwined crystals together, feeling the connection between your spirits.
3. **Incense Burning**: Light the incense, letting its fragrance fill the air and elevate the spiritual energy of the space.
4. **Flower-Infused Water**: Place the bowl of flower-infused water on the altar, symbolizing the nourishment and purity of your love.
5. **Writing Your Intentions**: Together, write your spiritual intentions or vows on the paper or parchment, expressing the depth and sincerity of your ethereal bond.
6. **Ribbon Binding**: Gently wrap the ribbon or cloth around the written intentions and the intertwined crystals, symbolizing the solidification of your spiritual connection.
7. **Meditation and Affirmation**: Meditate together, focusing on the strength and resilience of your spiritual bond. Affirm your commitment to nurturing and honoring this connection.

After the Ritual:

- **Place of Honor**: Keep the intertwined crystals and your written intentions in a place of honor, such as your bedroom or a shared sacred space.

- **Regular Spiritual Practice**: Engage in regular spiritual practices together, such as meditation or shared rituals, to continually nurture and solidify your ethereal bond.

The Ethereal Love Bond Solidification is a deeply meaningful ritual for couples who share a profound spiritual connection. It's a way of acknowledging and honoring the ethereal aspects of love, ensuring that the spiritual bonds you share are as strong and resilient as the emotional and physical aspects of your relationship.

74. Timeless Hearts Union Ritual

The Timeless Hearts Union Ritual is a deeply symbolic spell designed to transcend the constraints of time, celebrating a love that is eternal and unbounded. This ritual is ideal for couples who feel their connection is not just of this lifetime but extends across various dimensions and eras.

Purpose: To honor and solidify a love that transcends time, acknowledging and celebrating a bond that persists beyond the conventional understanding of temporal relationships.

Timing: Most effective when performed during significant temporal events, such as the transition of the New Year, solstices, equinoxes, or during a total solar or lunar eclipse, symbolizing the cyclical and eternal nature of time.

Materials:

1. A quiet, intimate space, preferably outdoors under the open sky
2. Two candles, ideally made of beeswax, to symbolize the natural and enduring light of your love
3. A pair of vintage or ancestral objects (such as jewelry, photographs, or heirlooms) representing the timelessness of your bond
4. A circle of stones or crystals, such as quartz or amethyst, to create a sacred and timeless space
5. A blend of timeless herbs such as rosemary (for remembrance) and thyme (symbolizing the passage of time)

6. A parchment or special paper and quill/pen to write vows or affirmations of your timeless love
7. A small hourglass or a clock as a symbolic representation of time

Preparation:

1. Set up your space in a quiet, secluded area, preferably where you can see the stars or the moon.
2. Arrange the candles, vintage objects, and circle of stones or crystals in a meaningful pattern.

The Ritual:

1. **Lighting the Candles**: Begin by lighting the candles, focusing on the eternal flame of your love that burns across all time.
2. **Arranging Timeless Objects**: Place the vintage or ancestral objects within the circle, symbolizing the connection of your love through different times and generations.
3. **Herb Sprinkling**: Gently sprinkle the timeless herbs around the circle, invoking the essence of eternity and the enduring nature of your bond.
4. **Writing Timeless Vows**: Together, write vows or affirmations on the parchment that reflect the timeless nature of your love and commitment.
5. **Hourglass/Clock Ceremony**: Turn the hourglass or set the clock at a significant time, symbolizing the moment you commit to your timeless union.
6. **Circle Meditation**: Sit within the stone or crystal circle, meditate on the enduring nature of your love, transcending past, present, and future.

7. **Vow Exchange**: Read your vows or affirmations to each other, affirming the timeless and unending nature of your love.

After the Ritual:

- **Keep the Vows Safe**: Store the written vows in a special place, such as a love box or a keepsake container.
- **Regular Remembrance**: Regularly revisit the place where you performed the ritual or engage in activities that remind you of the timeless nature of your love.
- **Celebrate Timeless Moments**: Mark significant dates or anniversaries that reinforce the eternal aspect of your relationship, celebrating your love as a constant through the passage of time.

The Timeless Hearts Union Ritual is a celebration of love that defies the limits of time, a testament to a bond that is as eternal as the universe itself. It's a profound acknowledgment that true love knows no bounds, not even those imposed by the linear progression of time.

75. Endless Love Thread Weaving

The Endless Love Thread Weaving is a ritualistic spell that symbolizes the intricate and continuous weaving of two lives into a harmonious and endless pattern of love. This spell is particularly poignant for couples seeking to reinforce the interconnectivity and enduring nature of their relationship through a symbolic act of unity.

Purpose: To symbolically weave the lives and destinies of two partners together, creating a tapestry of love that is strong, intricate, and unending.

Timing: Optimal when performed on a date that holds special meaning to the relationship, such as an anniversary, or during a significant lunar phase that represents cycles, continuity, and interconnectedness, like the waxing or full moon.

Materials:

1. A quiet, comfortable space for the ritual
2. Two different colored threads or yarns, each color representing one partner
3. A loom or a symbolic framework for weaving, such as a small hand-held loom or even a simple cardboard frame
4. Scissors for cutting and shaping the threads
5. A blend of herbs associated with love and unity, like lavender and rose petals
6. Two candles in colors representing each partner
7. Soft, harmonious music to set a peaceful and collaborative tone

Preparation:

1. Set up the space in a way that feels harmonious and balanced.
2. Arrange the loom, threads, herbs, and candles in an accessible and meaningful pattern.

The Ritual:

1. **Candle Lighting**: Light the candles, each flame representing the individual spirit and energy of each partner.
2. **Herb Blessing**: Sprinkle the herbs around the space, invoking their energies of unity and love.
3. **Thread Selection**: Each partner selects their thread, holding it for a moment to infuse it with their intentions and love.
4. **Weaving Beginnings**: Start the weaving process on the loom or framework, with each partner intertwining their thread with the other's, symbolizing the merging of their lives.
5. **Collaborative Weaving**: Continue weaving together, allowing the pattern to form naturally, representing the unique and beautiful tapestry of your relationship.
6. **Affirmations of Love and Unity**: As you weave, share affirmations or declarations of love and commitment, reinforcing the bond being symbolically created.
7. **Concluding the Weave**: Once the weaving feels complete, cut and tie off the threads, securing the woven piece as a symbol of your intertwined lives.

After the Ritual:

- **Tapestry Placement**: Place the woven tapestry in a significant spot in your home, such as above your bed or in your shared living space, as a daily reminder of your interconnected love.

- **Regular Reflection**: Revisit the tapestry regularly to reflect on your relationship, acknowledging how it has grown and strengthened, just like the woven threads.
- **Anniversary Ritual**: Consider making this a yearly ritual, adding to your tapestry each year to represent the continuous growth and evolution of your love.

The Endless Love Thread Weaving is a deeply meaningful ritual for couples, symbolizing the intricate and beautiful ways in which their lives and destinies are woven together. It's a celebration of unity, harmony, and the ongoing creation of a shared love story that is as unique and enduring as the tapestry they create together.

76. Divine Love Manifestation

The Divine Love Manifestation is a spiritual spell that focuses on invoking and manifesting a love that is aligned with divine guidance and universal harmony. This ritual is ideal for individuals seeking a relationship that not only fulfills earthly desires but also resonates with their higher spiritual purpose.

Purpose: To attract or enhance a love that is in harmony with one's higher self and spiritual path, fostering a relationship that is guided by divine love and wisdom.

Timing: Best performed during spiritually significant times such as during a new moon (for new beginnings) or a full moon (for fruition), or on dates that hold personal spiritual significance.

Materials:

1. A quiet, sacred space conducive to meditation and spiritual work
2. A white or gold candle, symbolizing divine energy and purity of intention
3. Incense or essential oils with uplifting and spiritual scents, like frankincense, myrrh, or rose
4. Crystals associated with love and spiritual connection, such as rose quartz, selenite, or amethyst
5. A journal or piece of paper for writing down intentions and prayers
6. Angelic or spiritual symbols, such as angel figurines, feathers, or mandalas

7. Soft, ambient music that creates a serene and sacred atmosphere

Preparation:

1. Create a peaceful and sacred environment in your chosen space.
2. Arrange the candle, incense/oils, crystals, and spiritual symbols in a way that feels aligned and harmonious.

The Ritual:

1. **Lighting the Candle**: Begin by lighting the candle, focusing on the divine energy and purity of your intentions for love.
2. **Incense or Oil**: Burn the incense or diffuse the oil to create a spiritually uplifting atmosphere.
3. **Setting Intentions**: Write down your intentions for love in the journal or on the paper. Be clear about wanting a relationship that aligns with your higher self and spiritual path.
4. **Crystal Activation**: Hold the crystals, meditating on their properties and asking them to assist in attracting or enhancing divine love.
5. **Invocation of Divine Love**: Use the angelic or spiritual symbols as a focus to invoke divine love. Ask for guidance and clarity in your love life, and for a relationship that enhances your spiritual growth.
6. **Meditation and Visualization**: Meditate on your intentions, visualizing yourself in a loving relationship that is guided and blessed by divine forces. Imagine the feeling of harmony, understanding, and spiritual connection.

7. **Affirmation of Divine Love**: Conclude the ritual with affirmations that reinforce your readiness and openness to receive divine love in your life.

After the Ritual:

- **Regular Reflection**: Revisit your written intentions regularly, meditating on them and remaining open to the guidance and opportunities that come your way.
- **Spiritual Practice**: Incorporate this intention into your daily spiritual practice, allowing your desire for divine love to be a constant in your spiritual journey.

Divine Love Manifestation is a spell for those who understand that love can be a profound spiritual journey, not just an earthly experience. It's about inviting a love that not only fulfills earthly desires but also supports and enhances spiritual growth and alignment with one's higher self.

77. Transdimensional Love Continuum

The Transdimensional Love Continuum is an advanced and mystical spell crafted for those who believe in the existence and power of love across different dimensions. This ritual is particularly resonant for individuals who feel a deep, transcendent connection with a partner, possibly one they perceive as a soulmate or twin flame, transcending the physical plane.

Purpose: To strengthen and affirm a love that extends beyond the physical dimension, embracing the concept of a love that exists across multiple planes of existence.

Timing: Ideally performed during cosmic events that symbolize transcendence and multi-dimensional realities, such as during a planetary alignment, a significant astrological transit, or when the veil between worlds is considered thin.

Materials:

1. A secluded, quiet place, preferably with a view of the night sky
2. A circular arrangement of candles to represent the continuum of dimensions
3. Crystals known for their dimensional properties, like labradorite, celestite, or moldavite
4. Symbols or items that represent the multi-dimensional nature of your relationship (such as intertwined rings or an infinity symbol)

5. A blend of herbs like sage, mugwort, or wormwood to facilitate transcendental awareness
6. A piece of paper or parchment to write down your transcendent love intentions
7. Meditative, ambient music that evokes a sense of cosmic or otherworldly presence

Preparation:

1. Prepare your space in a way that feels open and connected to the cosmos.
2. Arrange the candles in a circle, with the crystals and symbols/items placed thoughtfully within.

The Ritual:

1. **Lighting the Candles**: Light each candle while contemplating the vastness of the universe and the multi-dimensional nature of love.
2. **Crystal Activation**: Hold each crystal, charging it with your intentions of transcendent love and connection.
3. **Herbal Preparation**: Burn the herbs as an incense, allowing their scent to create a transcendent atmosphere.
4. **Writing Intentions**: On the parchment, write down your intentions and desires for a love that transcends dimensions.
5. **Dimensional Meditation**: Sit within the circle, meditate on the concept of a love that exists across different planes of existence. Visualize this love as a powerful force that connects you and your partner beyond the physical plane.
6. **Affirmation and Visualization**: Affirm your connection and visualize a bridge of light that connects you and your partner across dimensions, reaffirming your bond.

After the Ritual:

- **Intention Safekeeping**: Place the written intentions in a special box or area where they will be undisturbed, symbolizing the sacred nature of your transdimensional love.
- **Regular Cosmic Connection**: Engage in regular meditation or practices that reinforce your belief and connection to multi-dimensional love.
- **Celestial Observance**: Take time to observe the night sky or participate in activities that remind you of the vastness of the universe and the transcendent nature of your connection.

Transdimensional Love Continuum is a deeply spiritual and mystical spell that resonates with the belief in a love that is not confined to the physical dimension. It is for those who sense a profound connection with a partner that defies explanation within the physical world alone, embracing the idea that true love knows no bounds, not even those of time and space.

78. Universal Love Frequency Tuning

The Universal Love Frequency Tuning is a spell crafted to harmonize an individual's energy with the universal frequency of love. This ritual is ideal for those seeking to align their personal vibrations with the energies of cosmic love, thereby attracting relationships and connections that resonate with this higher frequency.

Purpose: To tune one's personal energy field to the universal frequency of love, facilitating attraction of relationships and experiences that resonate with this higher vibration of love and harmony.

Timing: Best performed during a cosmic event that signifies universal alignment, such as a planetary conjunction, a significant celestial event, or during a period of personal spiritual significance.

Materials:

1. A quiet, meditative space, ideally under the night sky
2. A tuning fork, singing bowl, or any musical instrument that emits clear, resonant tones
3. Several crystals known for their frequency-tuning properties, such as clear quartz, selenite, or tourmaline
4. Incense or essential oils with a high vibrational scent, like lavender or rose
5. A blue or violet candle, representing the higher spiritual frequencies
6. A comfortable mat or cushion for meditation
7. A journal or notepad for recording insights and affirmations

Preparation:

1. Set up your space in an area where you can be undisturbed and feel connected to the universe.
2. Arrange the candle, crystals, and incense in a way that feels conducive to meditation and spiritual work.

The Ritual:

1. **Lighting the Candle**: Light the candle, focusing on the intention of aligning with the higher frequencies of universal love.
2. **Sound Resonance**: Use the tuning fork, singing bowl, or instrument to create a resonant sound that fills the space, aiding in tuning your energy.
3. **Crystal Activation**: Hold or place the crystals around you, asking them to help harmonize your energy with the frequency of universal love.
4. **Incense or Oil**: Burn the incense or diffuse the oil to enhance the vibrational quality of the ritual.
5. **Meditation and Visualization**: Sit comfortably on the mat or cushion, meditate, and visualize your energy field aligning and resonating with the universal love frequency. Imagine your aura glowing with a harmonious, radiant light.
6. **Affirmation of Alignment**: Repeat affirmations that reinforce your alignment with universal love, such as "I am in harmony with the frequency of universal love" or "My heart resonates with the purest form of cosmic love."

After the Ritual:

- **Journaling**: Write down any insights, feelings, or affirmations in your journal, documenting your journey towards aligning with the universal love frequency.
- **Regular Practice**: Incorporate this frequency tuning into your regular meditation or spiritual practice to maintain alignment.
- **Observation and Openness**: Stay open to the signs and experiences that come your way as a result of this alignment, welcoming relationships and connections that match this higher vibration.

Universal Love Frequency Tuning is a spiritual practice for those who understand that love is not just an emotion but a universal energy. It's about attuning yourself to this energy, embracing the belief that by resonating with the frequency of cosmic love, one can attract relationships and experiences that are in harmony with this profound and universal force.

79. Cosmic Heartbeat Synchronization

The Cosmic Heartbeat Synchronization is a deeply spiritual spell that aims to synchronize an individual's heart rhythm with the metaphorical heartbeat of the cosmos. This ritual is for those who seek a profound connection with the universe, aligning their personal love energy with the vast, rhythmic pulsations of cosmic energy.

Purpose: To harmonize one's personal love energy with the universal energies, symbolically syncing with the cosmic heartbeat for a profound spiritual and emotional alignment.

Timing: Ideally performed during a clear night when the stars and cosmos feel particularly vibrant, or during a significant cosmic event such as a meteor shower or a planetary alignment.

Materials:

1. A serene outdoor location with a clear view of the night sky
2. A large, comfortable mat or blanket to lie on
3. A set of chimes, a drum, or any instrument that can mimic a rhythmic heartbeat
4. Crystals that align with cosmic energies, like lapis lazuli, moonstone, or labradorite
5. Soft, ambient music that emulates the sounds of the cosmos or natural celestial rhythms
6. Incense with a mystical or space-inspired scent, such as star anise or night-blooming jasmine
7. A journal or notepad for reflections and insights

Preparation:

1. Choose a night with minimal light pollution and a clear view of the stars.
2. Set up the mat or blanket in a comfortable spot under the night sky.
3. Arrange the crystals and incense nearby, creating a sacred space.

The Ritual:

1. **Star Gazing**: Begin by lying on the mat and gazing up at the stars, allowing yourself to feel the vastness of the cosmos.
2. **Rhythmic Heartbeat**: Use the chimes or drum to create a steady, rhythmic heartbeat sound, symbolizing the heartbeat of the universe.
3. **Crystal Alignment**: Hold or place the crystals around you, focusing on their connection to the cosmic energies.
4. **Ambient Music**: Play the ambient music softly in the background to enhance the sensation of being in sync with the cosmos.
5. **Meditation and Visualization**: Close your eyes and meditate, visualizing your heart's rhythm aligning with the cosmic heartbeat. Imagine a pulsating energy that connects your heart with the heart of the universe.
6. **Deep Breathing**: Practice deep, rhythmic breathing, further syncing your heartbeat with the cosmic rhythm.

After the Ritual:

- **Journaling**: Reflect on the experience in your journal, writing down any emotions, thoughts, or spiritual insights that arose.

- **Regular Practice**: Incorporate elements of this ritual into your regular meditation or spiritual practice, maintaining the connection with the cosmic heartbeat.
- **Mindful Observation**: Be mindful of the synchronicities and alignments that occur in your life and relationships, as they may be influenced by this cosmic synchronization.

Cosmic Heartbeat Synchronization is more than a spell; it's a profound spiritual practice for those who view love as an integral part of the universe's fabric. This ritual is about attuning yourself not just to another person, but to the universe itself, embracing a love that is as vast and deep as the cosmos.

80. Mystical Love Realm Bridging

The Mystical Love Realm Bridging is a complex spell designed for those who wish to connect and bridge different realms of existence with the power of love. This spell is particularly suited for individuals who believe in the existence of multiple realms or dimensions and seek to establish a profound connection of love that transcends physical boundaries.

Purpose: To establish a mystical bridge between realms, facilitating a connection of love that transcends the physical world and taps into deeper, more esoteric dimensions of affection and understanding.

Timing: Ideal to perform during a significant spiritual alignment or event, such as a solstice, equinox, or during a period of heightened spiritual energy, like a potent astrological transit.

Materials:

1. A tranquil and sacred space, preferably outdoors under the stars
2. Two mirrors placed facing each other, symbolizing the gateway between realms
3. Candles arranged in a circle around the mirrors to create a sacred boundary
4. Crystals that aid in dimensional travel, such as clear quartz, obsidian, or selenite
5. Incense or essential oils that encourage spiritual openness, like sandalwood or copal

6. A piece of ribbon or string to symbolize the connection between realms
7. A written intention or prayer focusing on the desire to bridge realms with love

Preparation:

1. Choose a quiet location where you can connect with the energy of the natural world.
2. Set up the mirrors and arrange the candles and crystals in a way that feels aligned with your intentions.

The Ritual:

1. **Lighting the Candles**: Begin by lighting the candles, envisioning them as beacons guiding the way between realms.
2. **Mirror Alignment**: Adjust the mirrors so they reflect each other, creating an infinite corridor symbolizing endless possibilities.
3. **Crystal Activation**: Place the crystals near the mirrors, charging them with the intention of bridging realms.
4. **Incense or Oil**: Use the incense or oil to enhance your spiritual receptiveness.
5. **Ribbon or String**: Connect the mirrors with the ribbon or string, physically representing the bridge you are creating.
6. **Intention Setting**: Hold your written intention or prayer, focusing deeply on your desire to connect realms through the power of love.
7. **Meditation and Visualization**: Meditate between the mirrors, visualizing a bridge of light forming between realms, guided and supported by your love and intention.

After the Ritual:

- **Maintain the Connection**: Regularly meditate near the mirrors, nurturing the bridge you have created.
- **Reflective Journaling**: Write about your experiences and any signs or messages you receive in your journal, keeping track of your journey in bridging realms.
- **Mindfulness in Love**: Be mindful of how this bridging impacts your relationships and feelings of love, observing changes or deepening connections.

Mystical Love Realm Bridging is a deeply esoteric and profound spell, ideal for those who see love as a force that transcends the physical world. It's about creating a connection that goes beyond the seen, tapping into the unseen realms where love can be just as powerful and transformative.

81. Love's Omnipotent Resonance Ritual

The Love's Omnipotent Resonance Ritual is a profound spell intended to resonate with the omnipotent power of love, magnifying and broadcasting this energy across all planes of existence. This ritual is ideal for practitioners who believe in the boundless and omnipresent nature of love and wish to align themselves with this universal force.

Purpose: To amplify and resonate with the omnipotent power of love, enhancing personal vibrations to attract and emit love in its most potent and universal form.

Timing: Best performed during cosmic events that symbolize universality and boundless energy, such as during a planetary alignment, a significant celestial convergence, or at a moment of personal spiritual epiphany.

Materials:

1. A serene and sacred location conducive to deep meditation
2. A central large candle, preferably white or gold, to represent the pure and omnipotent nature of love
3. Surrounding candles in a circular arrangement, symbolizing the universe
4. Crystals that resonate with universal love energy, such as rose quartz, rhodonite, or kunzite
5. Incense with a rich, all-encompassing scent, like frankincense or ylang-ylang
6. A sound instrument that produces a deep, resonating tone, like a gong or a large singing bowl

7. A piece of paper or parchment to write down your intentions and affirmations of love

Preparation:

1. Settle into your chosen space, ensuring it feels peaceful and sacred.
2. Arrange the central candle, surrounded by the other candles, and place the crystals around them in a pattern that feels harmonious.

The Ritual:

1. **Lighting the Central Candle**: Light the central candle while focusing on the omnipresence of love in the universe.
2. **Candle Circle Lighting**: Light the surrounding candles, visualizing them as points of love energy radiating across the cosmos.
3. **Crystal Charging**: Position the crystals around the candles, asking them to amplify and resonate with the energy of universal love.
4. **Incense Burning**: Light the incense to create an atmosphere of richness and depth, symbolizing the vastness of love.
5. **Writing Intentions**: Write your intentions and affirmations on the paper, focusing on the desire to resonate with and emit universal love.
6. **Sound Resonance**: Use the sound instrument to create deep, resonating tones, symbolizing the vibration of love echoing through the universe.
7. **Meditation and Visualization**: Meditate on the sounds and the candlelight, visualizing your own energy field vibrating in harmony with the omnipotent force of love, sending and receiving love in its most powerful form.

After the Ritual:

- **Intention Keeping**: Place your written intentions in a special place, such as an altar or a sacred box.
- **Regular Resonance Practice**: Incorporate resonant sounds or meditations into your daily practice to maintain your connection with the omnipotent force of love.
- **Observation and Attunement**: Stay attuned to how this ritual influences your interactions and feelings about love, noticing changes or intensifications in your relationships and connections.

Love's Omnipotent Resonance Ritual is a spell that celebrates love as the most powerful and universal force in existence. It's a practice for aligning oneself with this energy, recognizing that to resonate with love is to connect with a power that transcends all boundaries and limitations.

82. Transcendental Love Ascension

The Transcendental Love Ascension is a spiritual ritual designed for those seeking to elevate their experience and understanding of love to a transcendental level. This spell is aimed at individuals who wish to ascend beyond the conventional perceptions of love, tapping into a higher, more spiritually profound aspect of affection and connection.

Purpose: To ascend one's perception and experience of love to a transcendental plane, experiencing and understanding love as a profound spiritual force that goes beyond physical and emotional dimensions.

Timing: Most effective when performed during spiritually significant periods, such as during a lunar eclipse, the zenith of a planetary transit, or on days of personal spiritual enlightenment.

Materials:

1. A peaceful and elevated location, preferably at a higher altitude or a place with a panoramic view
2. A white or silver candle to symbolize spiritual purity and transcendence
3. Incense with ethereal and uplifting scents, such as myrrh, frankincense, or lotus
4. Crystals associated with spiritual ascension, like selenite, celestite, or clear quartz
5. A piece of cloth or scarf to symbolize the lifting of veils to higher understanding

6. A bowl of water mixed with flower petals, representing the fluidity and beauty of spiritual love
7. A journal or parchment for recording insights and revelations about love

Preparation:

1. Choose a location that feels spiritually significant and offers a sense of elevation or expansiveness.
2. Arrange the candle, incense, and crystals in a harmonious pattern conducive to spiritual work.

The Ritual:

1. **Candle Lighting**: Begin by lighting the candle, focusing on your intention to transcend to a higher understanding of love.
2. **Incense Burning**: Light the incense to enhance the spiritual ambiance and elevate your senses.
3. **Crystal Placement**: Arrange the crystals in a way that feels aligned with spiritual ascension and clarity.
4. **Veil Lifting**: Gently drape and then lift the cloth or scarf, symbolizing the unveiling of higher love wisdom.
5. **Water and Petals**: Use the bowl of water and petals as a focus for meditation, contemplating the spiritual essence of love.
6. **Meditation and Contemplation**: Meditate on the concept of love as a spiritual force, opening yourself to insights and understandings that transcend the ordinary.
7. **Recording Revelations**: Write any insights, feelings, or revelations about love in your journal or on the parchment.

After the Ritual:

- **Reflective Practice**: Regularly revisit your written insights, using them as a basis for further meditation and contemplation.
- **Continued Spiritual Work**: Integrate the insights gained from this ritual into your daily spiritual practice, allowing them to guide and deepen your understanding of love.
- **Mindful Application**: Apply the transcendent aspects of love in your relationships and interactions, embodying the spiritual essence of love in your daily life.

Transcendental Love Ascension is a profound ritual that invites practitioners to experience love as a deeply spiritual force. It's about elevating love from the realm of the physical and emotional into the spiritual, recognizing its power to transcend, transform, and enlighten.

83. Eternal Love Essence Infusion

The Eternal Love Essence Infusion is a ritual designed to infuse one's being with the essence of eternal love, transcending time and physical boundaries. This spell is particularly suited for individuals seeking to embody love in its most enduring and timeless form, enhancing their capacity to give and receive love unconditionally.

Purpose: To infuse oneself with the essence of eternal love, fostering an enduring, timeless capacity for deep, unconditional love in all relationships and interactions.

Timing: Ideal to perform on a date of personal significance that symbolizes enduring love, such as an anniversary, or during a cosmic event that reflects eternity, like a meteor shower or a significant planetary alignment.

Materials:

1. A serene, comfortable space for deep meditation
2. A large heart-shaped candle, symbolizing the eternal essence of love
3. Incense with a deep, enduring scent, like rose or patchouli
4. Crystals that embody timeless love, such as rose quartz, emerald, or diamond
5. A bowl of water with floating rose petals, symbolizing the purity and beauty of love
6. A small vial or container for collecting a portion of the infused water post-ritual

7. A piece of comfortable, heart-emblazoned clothing or accessory to wear during the ritual

Preparation:

1. Create a peaceful and loving atmosphere in your chosen space.
2. Arrange the heart-shaped candle, incense, and crystals in a way that feels harmonious and conducive to love.

The Ritual:

1. **Candle Lighting**: Light the heart-shaped candle, focusing on the concept of eternal and enduring love.
2. **Incense Burning**: Burn the incense to enhance the ambiance with the essence of deep, lasting love.
3. **Crystal Charging**: Place the crystals around the candle, asking them to absorb and amplify the energy of eternal love.
4. **Water and Rose Petals**: Set the bowl of water with rose petals nearby, symbolizing the purity and beauty of love.
5. **Meditation and Infusion**: Sit comfortably and meditate on the candle flame, visualizing the essence of eternal love flowing from the flame into your heart and being. Feel yourself becoming a vessel of timeless love.
6. **Vial Filling**: Towards the end of the ritual, collect some of the rose petal-infused water in your vial or container, symbolizing the physical embodiment of the love essence.

After the Ritual:

- **Wear the Infused Item**: Regularly wear the heart-emblazoned clothing or accessory as a reminder of your connection to eternal love.

- **Use the Infused Water**: Use the rose petal-infused water in future rituals, baths, or as a personal essence to reconnect with the energy of the ritual.
- **Reflective Practice**: Incorporate reflections on eternal love into your daily meditations and mindfulness practices, reinforcing the essence of timeless love in your life.

Eternal Love Essence Infusion is a powerful ritual for those who seek to embody love in its most profound and enduring form. It's about internalizing the concept of love as a timeless, universal force, enhancing one's capacity to engage in deep, unconditional love that transcends the limitations of time and space.

84. Celestial Soulmates Reunion

The Celestial Soulmates Reunion is a potent ritual aimed at reuniting or strengthening the bond between soulmates, whether they are currently together, separated, or yet to meet. This spell is designed for those who believe in the concept of soulmates and wish to enhance their connection on a celestial level.

Purpose: To facilitate the reunion or fortification of the bond between soulmates, drawing upon celestial energies to guide and strengthen their connection.

Timing: Best performed under a significant celestial event such as a full moon, a comet sighting, or during a rare astronomical alignment, symbolizing the rare and profound nature of a soulmate connection.

Materials:

1. A quiet and intimate outdoor setting under the night sky
2. Two candles, ideally silver or white, representing the celestial light guiding soulmates together
3. A pair of crystals known for enhancing spiritual connections, like twin quartz points or two pieces of amethyst
4. Incense or essential oils that resonate with high spiritual frequencies, such as frankincense or neroli
5. A small telescope or stargazing app to observe celestial bodies as symbolic guides
6. A locket or small box to symbolize the safekeeping of the soulmate bond
7. A written letter or poem expressing your intentions and feelings towards your soulmate

Preparation:

1. Select a peaceful location where the night sky is visible and inviting.
2. Arrange the candles, crystals, and incense in a way that feels aligned with the purpose of uniting soulmates.

The Ritual:

1. **Candle Lighting**: Begin by lighting the candles, focusing on the celestial light as a beacon for soulmates.
2. **Crystal Connection**: Place the crystals near the candles, charging them with the intention of enhancing your spiritual connection with your soulmate.
3. **Incense or Oil Burning**: Light the incense or diffuse the oil to create an atmosphere conducive to spiritual and emotional openness.
4. **Celestial Observation**: Use the telescope or app to gaze at the stars or celestial bodies, contemplating their guidance in your soulmate journey.
5. **Locket or Box**: Place the letter or poem inside the locket or box, symbolizing the safeguarding of your love and intention.
6. **Meditation and Visualization**: Meditate on the connection with your soulmate, visualizing a celestial light surrounding both of you, strengthening your bond across any distance.

After the Ritual:

- **Keep the Locket or Box Safe**: Store the locket or box in a place where it will be undisturbed, keeping your intentions secure.

- **Regular Celestial Connection**: Regularly spend time under the night sky, reinforcing your connection with the celestial energies and your soulmate.
- **Reflective Writing**: Continue to write letters or poems, even if only for yourself, as a way to express and reinforce your feelings and intentions towards your soulmate.

Celestial Soulmates Reunion is a spell that transcends the ordinary, tapping into the cosmic forces to reunite or strengthen the bonds between soulmates. It's a practice for those who believe in the destined and celestial nature of profound connections, and who seek to foster these connections under the guidance of the stars and the universe.

85. Love's Divine Essence Embodiment

The Love's Divine Essence Embodiment is a deeply spiritual ritual that focuses on embodying the essence of divine love within oneself. This spell is particularly suitable for individuals seeking to deepen their capacity for unconditional love and to radiate this love to others, thereby enhancing their relationships and personal spiritual growth.

Purpose: To internalize and embody the essence of divine love, enriching one's ability to love unconditionally and to extend this love to others in their life.

Timing: Optimal to perform during spiritual peaks such as during a significant religious or spiritual holiday, a lunar eclipse, or at a time of personal spiritual awakening.

Materials:

1. A calm, sacred space, ideally adorned with symbols of divine love
2. A heart-shaped candle or a candle in a soft, loving color such as pink or green
3. Incense or essential oils that evoke a sense of divinity and unconditional love, like rose or jasmine
4. Crystals that embody love, such as rose quartz, rhodonite, or green aventurine
5. A small bowl of water with rose petals, symbolizing purity and the flow of divine love
6. A comfortable seating arrangement for meditation
7. A journal or piece of paper to write down affirmations or intentions of love

Preparation:

1. Create a peaceful and loving atmosphere in your chosen space.
2. Arrange the candle, incense/oils, and crystals in a way that feels sacred and conducive to the embodiment of love.

The Ritual:

1. **Candle Lighting**: Light the heart-shaped or colored candle, focusing on the pure, divine essence of love.
2. **Incense or Oil**: Burn the incense or diffuse the oil to fill the space with a fragrance that uplifts and opens the heart.
3. **Crystal Activation**: Place the crystals around you, asking them to aid in channeling and embodying divine love.
4. **Rose Petal Water**: Gently touch the water with rose petals, contemplating the fluid and pure nature of divine love.
5. **Meditation and Visualization**: Sit comfortably and meditate, focusing on your heart center. Visualize it filling with a radiant, divine light, representing the essence of pure love.
6. **Affirmations of Divine Love**: Recite affirmations or intentions that reinforce your desire and commitment to embody divine love, such as "I am an embodiment of divine love" or "My heart radiates with the light of unconditional love."

After the Ritual:

- **Reflective Writing**: Write down your experiences and affirmations in your journal, solidifying your intentions and insights.
- **Regular Practice**: Incorporate practices that reinforce divine love into your daily routine, such as loving-kindness meditation or heart-centered prayers.

- **Conscious Application**: Strive to apply the essence of divine love in your interactions and relationships, being a beacon of love, compassion, and understanding.

Love's Divine Essence Embodiment is not just a ritual but a transformative practice, ideal for those who aspire to live with a heart full of divine, unconditional love. It's about more than just feeling love; it's about becoming an embodiment of it, and in doing so, enriching not only one's own life but also the lives of those around them.

86. Infinite Love Vibration Amplification

The Infinite Love Vibration Amplification is a ritual designed to amplify the vibrational frequency of love within oneself and to radiate this amplified love to the world. This spell is ideal for individuals seeking to enhance their capacity to love unconditionally and to positively impact their surroundings through the power of love.

Purpose: To magnify the vibration of love within oneself, thereby enhancing one's ability to love unconditionally and to spread this elevated love to others.

Timing: Optimal when performed during phases of high cosmic energy, such as during a full moon, a significant planetary alignment, or during a personal moment of high spiritual energy and clarity.

Materials:

1. A peaceful, harmonious space, ideally in a natural setting
2. A large, radiant candle, preferably in a hue representing love, such as pink or red
3. Incense or essential oils with uplifting and love-enhancing properties, like rose, ylang-ylang, or vanilla
4. An array of love-affirming crystals, such as rose quartz, kunzite, or pink tourmaline
5. A tuning fork, singing bowl, or any musical instrument that emits a clear, resonant sound
6. Comfortable seating for meditation and contemplation

7. A journal or piece of paper for writing down intentions and reflections on love

Preparation:

1. Choose a location that feels energetically positive and nurturing.
2. Set up your space with the candle, incense/oils, and crystals, arranging them in a manner that creates a harmonious and inviting energy.

The Ritual:

1. **Candle Lighting**: Light the candle while focusing on your intention to amplify the vibration of love within you.
2. **Incense or Oil**: Burn the incense or diffuse the oil to create an atmosphere that supports a heightened state of love and positivity.
3. **Crystal Arrangement**: Place the crystals around your meditation space, asking them to assist in amplifying your love vibration.
4. **Sound Vibration**: Use the tuning fork, singing bowl, or instrument to create a resonant sound that symbolizes the vibration of love. Allow this sound to permeate your space.
5. **Meditation and Visualization**: Sit comfortably and meditate, visualizing your heart center expanding and glowing with a brilliant light. Imagine this light representing an amplified vibration of love, extending outwards from you.
6. **Intention Setting**: Write down your intentions or reflections on how you wish to amplify love in your life and the lives of others.

After the Ritual:

- **Journaling**: Keep a record of your experiences and intentions in your journal, using it as a guide and reminder of your commitment to living a life amplified by love.
- **Regular Vibrational Practices**: Incorporate practices that enhance your vibrational frequency into your daily routine, such as positive affirmations, heart-centered meditations, or acts of kindness and love.
- **Mindful Living**: Be mindful of your interactions, aiming to infuse them with the amplified love energy cultivated through this ritual.

Infinite Love Vibration Amplification is a powerful practice for those who believe in the transformative and healing power of love. It's about elevating one's own vibration to resonate with the highest frequencies of love and using this energy to bring about positive change and harmony in one's environment.

87. Galactic Heart Chakra Activation

The Galactic Heart Chakra Activation is a profound spiritual ritual designed to align and activate the heart chakra at a galactic level, tapping into cosmic energies of love and compassion. This spell is especially suitable for those seeking to expand their heart's energies beyond earthly bounds, embracing and emitting the universal love that connects all beings across the cosmos.

Purpose: To activate and align the heart chakra with the galactic frequency, expanding one's capacity for universal love and deepening the connection with all forms of life throughout the cosmos.

Timing: Ideal to perform under a starlit sky, particularly during astronomical events that evoke a sense of cosmic interconnectedness, such as meteor showers, planetary alignments, or when the Milky Way is visible.

Materials:

1. A tranquil outdoor space where the night sky can be observed
2. A green or pink candle, representing the heart chakra
3. Incense or essential oils that resonate with heart energy, like rose or green tea
4. Crystals that facilitate cosmic connections, such as moldavite, lapis lazuli, or malachite
5. Comfortable seating for meditation, preferably facing the night sky
6. Soothing, ambient music that evokes a sense of the universe or cosmic journey
7. A journal or notepad for recording experiences and insights

Preparation:

1. Select a peaceful location with minimal light pollution and a clear view of the stars.
2. Set up your space with the candle, incense/oils, and crystals, creating a sacred and inviting environment.

The Ritual:

1. **Candle Lighting**: Begin by lighting the candle, setting your intention to open and align your heart chakra with galactic energies.
2. **Incense or Oil**: Use the incense or oil to enhance the atmosphere, inviting a sense of universal love and compassion.
3. **Crystal Arrangement**: Place the crystals around you, focusing on their ability to connect your heart energy with the cosmos.
4. **Stargazing Meditation**: Sit comfortably and gaze up at the stars, allowing the vastness of the cosmos to fill your heart with awe and interconnectedness.
5. **Heart Chakra Visualization**: Visualize your heart chakra expanding, its energy extending out into the galaxy, connecting with the cosmic energy of love.
6. **Ambient Music**: Play the music softly in the background, letting it guide your meditation and enhance your cosmic journey.

After the Ritual:

- **Journaling**: Document your experience and any insights or feelings that emerged during the ritual.

- **Regular Cosmic Connection**: Regularly spend time under the night sky, continuing to meditate and align with the cosmic heart energy.
- **Heart-Centered Practices**: Incorporate heart-centered practices into your daily life, such as compassion meditation or acts of kindness, reinforcing your connection to universal love.

Galactic Heart Chakra Activation is a powerful practice for those who are drawn to the idea of universal love and interstellar connectedness. It's about transcending personal and earthly limitations of love, opening the heart to the boundless compassion and unity that exists within the vast expanse of the cosmos.

88. Ultimate Love Force Field Creation

The Ultimate Love Force Field Creation is a potent and protective ritual designed to create a powerful force field of love energy around oneself or a loved one. This spell is ideal for those seeking to establish a protective barrier fueled by the strength and purity of love, safeguarding against negative energies and influences.

Purpose: To generate a protective force field powered by love, which acts as a shield against negativity and harm, while also nurturing and strengthening the bonds of love.

Timing: Best performed during a time of personal significance when protection is most needed, such as during a challenging phase in life, or during a full moon to harness its energy of culmination and protection.

Materials:

1. A quiet, safe space where you can focus and meditate
2. A pink or white candle to symbolize love and purity
3. Protective incense or essential oils, such as rosemary or cedar
4. Crystals known for their protective and loving properties, like rose quartz, amethyst, or black tourmaline
5. A small bowl of salt water for purification
6. A photograph or personal item belonging to the person (yourself or a loved one) you wish to protect
7. Calming, protective music or sounds to enhance the ritual

Preparation:

1. Create a peaceful environment conducive to concentration and spiritual work.
2. Arrange the candle, incense/oils, crystals, and salt water in a way that feels protective and nurturing.

The Ritual:

1. **Candle Lighting**: Begin by lighting the candle, setting an intention for creating a loving and protective energy field.
2. **Incense or Oil Burning**: Use the incense or oil to cleanse the space and to set a protective atmosphere.
3. **Crystal Activation**: Place the crystals around the candle, asking them to aid in forming a strong love-based protective field.
4. **Salt Water Purification**: Sprinkle a bit of salt water around the area and over the photograph or item, purifying the space and the focus of your protection.
5. **Visualization and Energy Work**: Focus on the candle flame and visualize a radiant, protective force field of love energy emanating from the flame, surrounding and permeating the space or person you wish to protect.
6. **Protective Music or Sounds**: Play the music or sounds to deepen the sense of safety and protection.

After the Ritual:

- **Maintain the Protective Energy**: Regularly visualize and reaffirm the love force field whenever you feel the need for protection.

- **Carry a Crystal**: Keep a piece of rose quartz, amethyst, or black tourmaline with you as a physical reminder and extension of the protective love energy.
- **Reflective Practice**: Note any changes or feelings of increased safety and love in your journal, acknowledging the power of your protective ritual.

Ultimate Love Force Field Creation is a deeply nurturing and protective spell, ideal for those who believe in the strength and purity of love as a shield against negativity. It's about harnessing the power of love to create a sanctuary of safety, peace, and positive energy, both for oneself and for loved ones.

89. Time-Transcending Love Anchor

The Time-Transcending Love Anchor is a mystical spell designed to establish a powerful, enduring connection of love that transcends the boundaries of time and physical separation. This ritual is especially meaningful for those who feel a deep, timeless bond with someone, whether they are currently apart, have yet to meet, or wish to strengthen an existing connection.

Purpose: To create an anchor of love that remains steadfast and strong, unaffected by the constraints of time and physical distance, ensuring a deep and enduring emotional and spiritual connection.

Timing: Most powerful when performed during significant temporal transitions, such as New Year's Eve, solstices, equinoxes, or during personal moments of significant life change or reflection.

Materials:

1. A peaceful and reflective setting
2. A durable, timeless token, such as a locket, a stone, or a piece of jewelry, to serve as the physical representation of the love anchor
3. Two candles, ideally one black and one white, symbolizing the continuum of time
4. Incense or essential oils with deep, enduring scents, like patchouli or myrrh
5. Crystals associated with enduring strength and love, such as garnet, onyx, or diamond

6. A piece of paper or parchment for writing a love intention or vow
7. A container or box to safely store the token and intention

Preparation:

1. Choose a setting that feels calm and undisturbed, suitable for deep contemplation.
2. Set up the candles, incense/oils, crystals, and the token in a meaningful arrangement.

The Ritual:

1. **Candle Lighting**: Begin by lighting the candles, acknowledging the passage of time and the enduring nature of love.
2. **Incense or Oil**: Burn the incense or diffuse the oil to create a deeply reflective and grounding atmosphere.
3. **Token Empowerment**: Hold the token in your hands, infusing it with your intentions for a love that transcends time.
4. **Writing Intention or Vow**: Write your intention, vow, or message of timeless love on the paper or parchment.
5. **Crystal Charging**: Surround the token and written intention with the crystals, asking them to imbue both with lasting strength and connection.
6. **Meditation and Visualization**: Meditate on the token, visualizing it as a powerful anchor grounding your love across all times and spaces.

After the Ritual:

- **Token Safekeeping**: Place the token and written intention in the container or box, and store it in a place of significance.

- **Regular Connection**: Regularly hold the token and revisit your written intention, reaffirming your connection and commitment to transcendent love.
- **Reflective Journaling**: Write about your experiences and feelings in your journal, documenting your journey in creating and maintaining this timeless love anchor.

The Time-Transcending Love Anchor is a deeply moving and powerful ritual, suitable for anyone who believes in the enduring power of love beyond the physical world. It's about establishing a connection that is not hindered by time or distance, creating a bond that is as enduring as it is profound.

90. Cosmic Love Elixir Synthesis

The Cosmic Love Elixir Synthesis is a mystical ritual that involves creating an elixir imbued with the energies of cosmic love. This spell is tailored for individuals who wish to tap into the vast, universal energies of love, creating a potion that encapsulates these powerful, celestial vibrations.

Purpose: To synthesize an elixir that captures the essence of cosmic love, enhancing one's ability to connect with and radiate this profound, universal energy.

Timing: Optimal when performed under a clear night sky, especially during significant cosmic events such as meteor showers, planetary alignments, or during a new or full moon.

Materials:

1. A clear, starry night for preparing the elixir outdoors
2. A small cauldron or heat-resistant bowl for mixing the elixir
3. Moon water (water left out under the full moon) as the elixir's base
4. Crystals like moonstone, rose quartz, or amethyst, known for their connection to cosmic love
5. Herbs associated with love and the cosmos, such as damiana, rose petals, or lavender
6. A small bottle or vial to store the elixir
7. A silver spoon or stirrer, symbolizing the connection to lunar and cosmic energies

Preparation:

1. Choose a location where you can clearly see the night sky and feel connected to the cosmos.
2. Arrange your materials in a sacred space where you can work undisturbed.

The Ritual:

1. **Cauldron Preparation**: Place the moon water in the cauldron or bowl, ready to be transformed into your elixir.
2. **Crystal Charging**: Surround the cauldron with your chosen crystals, charging the water with cosmic love energies.
3. **Herb Infusion**: Add the herbs to the moon water while focusing on your intention to capture the essence of cosmic love.
4. **Stirring the Elixir**: Use the silver spoon or stirrer to mix the elixir, doing so under the night sky, allowing the cosmic energies to infuse the mixture.
5. **Elixir Blessing**: Hold your hands over the cauldron and recite a blessing or chant, asking the universe to imbue the elixir with the purest form of cosmic love.
6. **Bottling**: Carefully pour the elixir into your bottle or vial, sealing the cosmic energies within.

After the Ritual:

- **Storage**: Store the elixir in a place where it can continue to absorb cosmic energies, like a windowsill under the night sky.
- **Usage**: Use the elixir in future rituals, baths, or as a personal essence to connect with cosmic love energies.

- **Journaling**: Document the process and your feelings in your journal, noting any changes or insights you experience when using the elixir.

Cosmic Love Elixir Synthesis is a magical practice for those who are drawn to the concept of universal love and seek to embody and radiate this profound energy. It's about creating a physical manifestation of the vast, celestial love that binds the universe, bringing its powerful essence into one's personal spiritual practice.

91. Dimensional Love Cascade

The Dimensional Love Cascade is a spell intended to unleash a cascade of love energy across multiple dimensions. It's designed for practitioners who believe in the multidimensional nature of the universe and wish to send and receive love through various planes of existence.

Purpose: To create a multi-dimensional cascade of love, enhancing one's ability to send and receive love across different planes of existence and to experience love in its many forms.

Timing: Ideal to perform during significant cosmic events that symbolize multidimensionality, such as during a planetary retrograde, a solar eclipse, or when the veil between worlds is believed to be thin.

Materials:

1. A quiet, sacred space conducive to deep meditation
2. Candles in various colors to represent different dimensions and aspects of love
3. Incense or essential oils that evoke feelings of expansiveness and interconnectedness, like sandalwood or sage
4. Crystals that facilitate multidimensional travel and connection, such as quartz, labradorite, or shungite
5. A diagram or representation of the different dimensions or planes you wish to connect with
6. A comfortable seating arrangement for meditation
7. A notebook or journal for recording experiences and insights

Preparation:

1. Set up your space in an area that feels energetically aligned and peaceful.
2. Arrange the candles, incense/oils, and crystals around the dimensional diagram in a way that feels harmonious.

The Ritual:

1. **Candle Lighting**: Light each candle while contemplating the multidimensional nature of love and its manifestation in different dimensions.
2. **Incense or Oil**: Burn the incense or diffuse the oil to create an atmosphere that supports spiritual expansion and connectivity.
3. **Crystal Activation**: Position the crystals around the dimensional diagram, charging them with the intention of bridging connections across dimensions.
4. **Dimensional Contemplation**: Sit comfortably and meditate on the diagram, visualizing love energy cascading from you and flowing through various dimensions.
5. **Visualization and Energy Flow**: Visualize a flow of love energy moving through the different planes, touching and connecting with various forms of existence and consciousness.
6. **Journaling**: After the meditation, write down any experiences, feelings, or insights you have in your notebook or journal.

After the Ritual:

- **Regular Meditation**: Incorporate this multidimensional meditation into your regular practice to maintain and strengthen the connections.

- **Reflective Writing**: Continue to document your journey and experiences with this practice, noting any changes or deepened understandings about love.
- **Mindfulness in Daily Life**: Apply this multidimensional perspective of love to your daily interactions, recognizing the interconnectedness of all beings across different planes of existence.

The Dimensional Love Cascade is a deeply spiritual practice, ideal for those who view love as a force that transcends the physical world, reaching into the very fabric of the universe across multiple dimensions. This ritual allows practitioners to explore and experience the vastness and diversity of love beyond the constraints of their immediate reality.

92. Universe's Heart Echo Spell

The Universe's Heart Echo Spell is a powerful ritual aimed at harmonizing one's personal love energy with the heartbeat of the universe. This spell is crafted for individuals seeking to resonate with the universe's profound and all-encompassing love, amplifying their personal love energy to echo across the cosmos.

Purpose: To align and resonate one's love energy with the universe's heartbeat, creating an echo of love that reverberates throughout the cosmos and enhances personal connections with universal love.

Timing: Best performed during cosmic events that represent universality and connectivity, such as during a planetary conjunction, a cosmic alignment, or on a night where the Milky Way is clearly visible.

Materials:

1. A serene location under the night sky
2. A large, heart-shaped crystal or a set of smaller heart crystals
3. Candles in shades of deep blue or purple, symbolizing the vastness of the cosmos
4. Incense with a celestial scent, like star anise or frankincense
5. A drum, a set of chimes, or any musical instrument that can produce a rhythmic, heartbeat-like sound
6. A journal or parchment for writing down cosmic love intentions or affirmations
7. A comfortable place to sit or lie down for meditation

Preparation:

1. Choose a peaceful outdoor setting with a clear view of the sky.
2. Arrange the candles and heart crystals in a circular pattern, creating a sacred space for the ritual.

The Ritual:

1. **Candle Lighting**: Light the candles, setting the intention to connect with the cosmic heartbeat of love.
2. **Incense Burning**: Use the incense to create a celestial atmosphere, inviting the energy of universal love.
3. **Crystal Charging**: Place the heart crystals within the candle circle, asking them to amplify and resonate with the cosmic love energy.
4. **Rhythmic Sound**: Begin a rhythmic beat with the drum or chimes, mimicking the heartbeat of the universe.
5. **Meditation and Visualization**: Sit or lie comfortably, meditate, and visualize your heart's rhythm syncing with the cosmic heartbeat, feeling your love energy expand and echo throughout the universe.
6. **Affirmations and Intentions**: Speak or write your love intentions and affirmations, focusing on the desire to resonate with and contribute to the universe's love.

After the Ritual:

- **Reflective Journaling**: Document your experiences and insights in your journal, noting the feelings and revelations about cosmic love.

- **Regular Practice**: Integrate this cosmic heartbeat meditation into your regular spiritual routine to maintain your connection with universal love.
- **Conscious Awareness**: Carry the awareness of this connection into your daily life, recognizing the reflections of cosmic love in your relationships and experiences.

The Universe's Heart Echo Spell is an expansive and spiritually enriching practice, perfect for those who wish to deeply connect with the universal energy of love and to understand their part in the vast cosmic tapestry of affection and connection. It's a spell that transcends the personal, reaching into the heart of the universe itself.

93. Love's Quantum Entanglement

The Love's Quantum Entanglement ritual is a spell that utilizes the concept of quantum entanglement to create a deep and unbreakable bond of love. This spell is particularly suited for those who believe in the power of deep, soul-level connections that transcend space and time.

Purpose: To entangle the energy of love at a quantum level, ensuring a profound and inseparable bond between two souls, regardless of physical distance or circumstance.

Timing: Best performed during a new moon or solar eclipse, signifying new beginnings and the powerful unseen forces that connect the universe.

Materials:

1. A private, quiet space conducive to focused meditation
2. Two matching crystals, such as twin quartz points, symbolizing the two individuals involved in the entanglement
3. A black and a white candle, representing the duality and balance in the universe
4. Incense or essential oils with grounding and connecting properties, like vetiver or myrrh
5. Two pieces of string or ribbon, to physically represent the entanglement
6. A detailed diagram or representation of quantum entanglement
7. A journal or notepad for recording intentions and insights

Preparation:

1. Set up a peaceful area where you can meditate without interruptions.
2. Arrange the candles, incense/oils, and the quantum entanglement diagram in your space, along with the crystals and strings.

The Ritual:

1. **Candle Lighting**: Light the black and white candles, acknowledging the complex nature of the universe and the interconnectedness of all things.
2. **Incense or Oil**: Burn the incense or diffuse the oil to enhance your focus and deepen your connection to the universal energies.
3. **Crystal Connection**: Hold one crystal in each hand, feeling the energy of each and visualizing them becoming quantumly entangled with each other.
4. **String or Ribbon Entanglement**: Tie the strings or ribbons to each crystal, then intricately entwine them together, symbolizing the quantum entanglement of your souls.
5. **Meditation and Visualization**: Focus on the diagram or representation of quantum entanglement, meditating on the concept of being deeply connected at a quantum level, beyond the physical world.
6. **Setting Intentions**: Write down your intentions for this entanglement in your journal, focusing on the strength, depth, and unbreakable nature of this bond.

After the Ritual:

- **Keep the Entangled Crystals Safe**: Place the entangled crystals in a special location where they won't be disturbed, maintaining the integrity of the entanglement.
- **Regular Meditation**: Frequently meditate with the entangled crystals, reinforcing the quantum connection and deepening your bond.
- **Reflective Journaling**: Regularly write in your journal about your experiences and feelings related to this deep connection, observing how it manifests in your life.

Love's Quantum Entanglement is a spell for those who are ready to experience a love that transcends the usual boundaries of space and time, embodying the concept that two souls can be connected on a level that defies conventional understanding. This ritual is about embracing the mysteries of the universe and the profound connections that exist within it.

94. Eternal Love Nexus Formation

The Eternal Love Nexus Formation is an advanced ritual crafted to establish a nexus, or central point, of eternal love energy. It is designed for those who wish to create a powerful, enduring focal point for love energy that can nourish and sustain their relationships over time, regardless of external circumstances.

Purpose: To form a nexus of eternal love energy, serving as a perpetual source of love, support, and connection for oneself and loved ones.

Timing: Ideally performed during a significant celestial event, such as a rare planetary alignment, which symbolizes rare and extraordinary connections, or during a personal milestone that signifies enduring commitment and love.

Materials:

1. A peaceful, sacred space where you won't be disturbed
2. A central large crystal, such as a quartz cluster or a large rose quartz, to act as the nexus point
3. Multiple smaller crystals to form a grid around the central crystal, such as amethyst, moonstone, or jade
4. Candles in shades of pink and green, symbolizing love and heart energy
5. Incense or essential oils that resonate with lasting love, like rose or lavender
6. A bowl of water with rose petals, symbolizing purity and the flow of love
7. A written declaration of love, commitment, and intention

Preparation:

1. Select a quiet and comfortable location where you feel a strong, positive energy.
2. Set up the central crystal and arrange the smaller crystals around it to form a grid. Place the candles and bowl of water nearby.

The Ritual:

1. **Candle Lighting**: Light the candles, focusing on their light as a symbol of enduring love and warmth.
2. **Incense or Oil**: Burn the incense or diffuse the oil to create an atmosphere of deep, abiding love.
3. **Crystal Grid Activation**: Begin by holding your hands over the central crystal, charging it with your intentions for eternal love. Then, activate the surrounding crystal grid, envisioning each crystal strengthening and supporting the energy of the central nexus.
4. **Declaration Reading**: Read your written declaration aloud, affirming your commitment to fostering and nurturing a nexus of eternal love.
5. **Water and Petals Ritual**: Gently sprinkle rose petals into the bowl of water, visualizing each petal infusing the nexus with pure, loving energy.
6. **Meditation and Visualization**: Sit quietly and meditate, focusing on the crystal nexus. Visualize it glowing with a radiant, warm light that symbolizes the eternal nature of your love.

After the Ritual:

- **Maintain the Nexus**: Regularly cleanse and recharge the crystal nexus and the surrounding grid, ensuring its energy remains strong and clear.
- **Reflective Practice**: Spend time near the nexus for meditation and reflection, drawing upon its energy to nurture your relationships and love intentions.
- **Journaling**: Keep a record of your experiences, feelings, and insights related to the nexus in your journal, observing how it influences your life and relationships.

Eternal Love Nexus Formation is a deeply meaningful practice for those who believe in the power of love as a guiding and sustaining force in their lives. It's about creating a physical and spiritual focal point that constantly radiates love and positive energy, reinforcing the connections and bonds that are most important to you.

95. Supreme Love Energy Conductor

The Supreme Love Energy Conductor is a spell focused on creating a powerful conduit for love energy, channeling this force to magnify and enhance love in all its forms. This ritual is for practitioners who believe in actively directing and amplifying love energy for the highest good of all involved.

Purpose: To construct a powerful conductor for love energy, amplifying and directing this force to enhance personal relationships, self-love, and universal love.

Timing: Best performed during a lunar event that symbolizes growth and expansion, like the waxing moon phase, or during Venus transits that heighten love energy.

Materials:

1. A quiet and comfortable space for the ritual
2. A central focus object, such as a large crystal wand or a beautifully crafted staff, to serve as the conductor
3. Candles in shades of pink and red, representing various aspects of love
4. Incense or essential oils with properties of attraction and amplification, such as jasmine or rose
5. Crystals that resonate with love energy, like rose quartz, ruby, or garnet
6. A piece of paper or parchment to write down your intentions and goals related to love
7. Soft, harmonious music to enhance the ambiance of the ritual

Preparation:

1. Set up your ritual space in an area where you feel a strong connection to love energy.
2. Arrange the candles, incense/oils, and crystals around the central focus object in a pattern that feels harmonious and powerful.

The Ritual:

1. **Candle Lighting**: Light the candles, focusing on the illumination of love in various aspects of your life.
2. **Incense or Oil**: Burn the incense or use the oil to create an atmosphere conducive to love and attraction.
3. **Conductor Charging**: Hold the focus object, channeling your intentions and desires related to love through it, visualizing it as a powerful conductor of love energy.
4. **Intention Setting**: Write your specific goals and intentions on the paper or parchment, focusing on what you wish to attract or amplify in your love life.
5. **Crystal Activation**: Place the crystals around the focus object, asking them to aid in amplifying and directing the love energy.
6. **Visualization and Meditation**: With the focus object in hand, meditate on your intentions, visualizing the love energy flowing through the conductor, magnifying, and reaching your goals.

After the Ritual:

- **Regular Use of the Conductor**: Use the focus object in future love-related rituals or meditations, continuously channeling and directing love energy.

- **Reflective Journaling**: Keep a record of your experiences, feelings, and the changes you observe in your love life in your journal.
- **Mindful Practices**: Incorporate practices into your daily life that align with the intentions set during the ritual, actively working towards attracting and nurturing the love you desire.

The Supreme Love Energy Conductor ritual is a powerful practice for those who wish to play an active role in harnessing and directing love energy. It's about using focused intent and spiritual tools to amplify love in your life, creating positive changes and deeper connections.

96. Celestial Love Symphony Conduction

The Celestial Love Symphony Conduction is an enchanting ritual that intertwines the harmonies of celestial bodies with the essence of love. This spell is ideal for practitioners who seek to align their romantic aspirations with the cosmic orchestra, creating a symphony of love that resonates with celestial frequencies.

Purpose: To harmonize personal love energy with the celestial bodies, creating a symphony of love that resonates with the universe's natural rhythm and harmony.

Timing: Optimal when performed under a starry night sky, particularly during astronomical phenomena like meteor showers or planetary alignments, which symbolize celestial harmony.

Materials:

1. An open space under the night sky
2. A collection of musical instruments or recorded celestial sounds
3. Candles in celestial colors, such as deep blues and purples, to represent the cosmos
4. Incense or essential oils that evoke a sense of the vastness and mystery of space, like myrrh or frankincense
5. Celestially aligned crystals such as meteorite fragments, tektite, or moldavite
6. A telescope or stargazing app to observe and connect with celestial bodies
7. A journal or parchment for writing down celestial insights related to love

Preparation:

1. Choose a location with a clear view of the night sky.
2. Set up your candles, incense/oils, and instruments in a way that feels aligned with the celestial theme.

The Ritual:

1. **Candle Lighting**: Begin by lighting the candles, focusing on the vastness of the cosmos and the celestial bodies.
2. **Incense or Oil**: Burn the incense or diffuse the oil to enhance your connection with the cosmos.
3. **Celestial Observation**: Use the telescope or stargazing app to connect with the stars, planets, and other celestial bodies, contemplating their influence on love.
4. **Musical Harmony**: Play the instruments or celestial sounds, allowing the music to symbolize the harmony you wish to achieve in your love life.
5. **Crystal Charging**: Arrange the celestially aligned crystals around you, asking them to resonate with the celestial love symphony.
6. **Meditation and Contemplation**: Meditate on the music and the celestial bodies, visualizing their harmonies intertwining with your personal love energy.

After the Ritual:

- **Journaling**: Document your experiences and insights in your journal, focusing on how the celestial energies influence your perception and experience of love.
- **Regular Celestial Engagement**: Regularly engage with the night sky, maintaining your connection to the celestial symphony and its influence on your love life.

- **Integration into Daily Life**: Integrate the harmony and insights gained from this ritual into your relationships, striving for balance, understanding, and cosmic alignment in love.

Celestial Love Symphony Conduction is a spell that seeks to blend the mystique of the cosmos with the universal language of love. It's a unique practice for those who find romance in the stars and seek to align their love life with the celestial dance of the universe.

97. Love's Infinite Reservoir Tapping

The Love's Infinite Reservoir Tapping is a powerful ritual designed to connect with and draw upon the limitless reservoir of love that exists in the universe. This spell is ideal for practitioners who wish to tap into this vast source to replenish their own capacity for love, compassion, and connection.

Purpose: To access and draw from the infinite reservoir of universal love, replenishing one's own heart and soul with this boundless energy.

Timing: Best performed when feeling a need for rejuvenation in love—perhaps during a new moon to symbolize new beginnings in love or when Venus is visible in the night sky, representing love and beauty.

Materials:

1. A tranquil setting, ideally in a place that feels spiritually vibrant
2. A large bowl filled with pure water, symbolizing the reservoir of universal love
3. Rose petals to represent love and compassion
4. Candles in shades of pink or green, embodying love and heart energy
5. Incense or essential oils with uplifting properties, such as rose or bergamot
6. Crystals associated with love and emotional healing, like rose quartz or emerald
7. A small cup or chalice to symbolize receiving love

Preparation:

1. Create a serene and inviting atmosphere in your chosen location.
2. Arrange the bowl of water, rose petals, candles, incense/oils, and crystals in a harmonious pattern.

The Ritual:

1. **Candle Lighting**: Begin by lighting the candles, focusing on the intention of filling your heart with love.
2. **Incense or Oil**: Use the incense or oil to create a space filled with the energy of love and healing.
3. **Rose Petal Infusion**: Gently place the rose petals in the bowl of water, visualizing them infusing the water with the essence of love.
4. **Crystal Charging**: Position the crystals around the bowl, asking them to amplify and purify the love energy within the water.
5. **Meditation and Contemplation**: Focus on the bowl of water, meditating on the concept of an infinite reservoir of love. Visualize this love flowing into the water, turning it into a potent source of emotional replenishment.
6. **Receiving Love**: Dip the cup or chalice into the bowl, scooping up some water. Drink the water, imagining it filling you with the boundless love from the universe.

After the Ritual:

- **Regular Connection**: Make it a practice to regularly connect with the concept of the universe's infinite reservoir of love, especially during times of emotional depletion.

- **Journaling**: Record your experiences and feelings in a journal, noting how the ritual impacts your capacity for love and compassion.
- **Incorporate in Daily Life**: Apply this newfound sense of love and fullness in your interactions and relationships, aiming to spread the love you have tapped into with others.

Love's Infinite Reservoir Tapping is a deeply nurturing and replenishing ritual, perfect for anyone seeking to deepen their connection to the universal source of love. It's about recognizing the vastness of love available to us and learning to open ourselves to this endless supply for healing, growth, and connection.

98. Multiverse Love Beam Projection

The Multiverse Love Beam Projection is an advanced metaphysical spell intended to project love energy across multiple dimensions and universes. It is especially suited for practitioners who embrace the concept of a multiverse and seek to send positive, loving vibrations beyond the confines of their own reality.

Purpose: To project a powerful beam of love energy into the multiverse, thereby spreading love, healing, and positivity across different dimensions and planes of existence.

Timing: Ideal for casting during astronomical events that evoke a sense of cosmic expansiveness, such as during a meteor shower, a galactic alignment, or when witnessing a particularly clear and star-filled night sky.

Materials:

1. A secluded and quiet outdoor space with a clear view of the night sky
2. A large crystal or crystal grid set up for amplifying and directing energy
3. Candles in white or silver to symbolize purity and the vastness of the cosmos
4. Incense or essential oils with a celestial or ethereal quality, like myrrh or star anise
5. A powerful laser pointer or a directed light source to symbolize the beam of love
6. A map or representation of the multiverse or cosmic realms
7. A meditation mat or cushion for comfort during the ritual

Preparation:

1. Select an outdoor location that feels connected to the wider universe.
2. Set up your crystal or crystal grid, candles, incense/oils, and the map in your chosen space.

The Ritual:

1. **Candle Lighting**: Light the candles, setting your intention to connect with and project love across the multiverse.
2. **Incense or Oil**: Burn the incense or diffuse the oil to create an atmosphere that resonates with high vibrational cosmic energy.
3. **Crystal or Grid Activation**: Activate the crystal or grid, focusing your intention on using it as a conduit for projecting love energy.
4. **Beam Projection**: Use the laser pointer or directed light source, pointing it towards the sky, visualizing it as a powerful beam of love energy traveling across different dimensions and universes.
5. **Multiverse Meditation**: Sit on the meditation mat or cushion, focusing on the map or representation of the multiverse. Visualize your love energy as a radiant beam, reaching far into the cosmos and touching multiple dimensions and realms.
6. **Affirmation of Love Spread**: Affirm your intention to spread love and healing throughout the multiverse, visualizing the beam impacting and uplifting countless beings and realities.

After the Ritual:

- **Stargazing Reflection**: Spend time after the ritual stargazing, reflecting on the vastness of the universe and your connection to it.
- **Regular Cosmic Engagement**: Incorporate this practice into your regular spiritual routine, continuously sending love into the multiverse.
- **Journaling**: Document your experiences and any insights or feelings in a journal, especially any intuitive responses you receive from the cosmos.

Multiverse Love Beam Projection is a deeply profound and expansive ritual, perfect for practitioners who embrace the idea of interconnectedness across all planes of existence. This ritual symbolizes the practitioner's desire to be a source of love and positivity, not just in their own world, but across the vast and infinite multiverse.

99. Omniversal Love Harmonization

The Omniversal Love Harmonization is a spell that aims to align and harmonize the practitioner's personal love energy with the love energy of the entire omniverse. It's particularly suited for advanced practitioners who recognize the interconnectedness of all things across multiple universes and dimensions and wish to attune their personal vibrations to these vast energies.

Purpose: To harmonize personal love energy with the omniversal energies, creating a balanced and fluid exchange of love that transcends all boundaries and dimensions.

Timing: Most potent when performed during cosmic events that symbolize unity and interconnectedness, such as during a rare planetary conjunction or a significant celestial alignment.

Materials:

1. A peaceful, sacred space, ideally under the night sky
2. A large central crystal or a crystal grid for channeling and balancing energies
3. Multi-colored candles to represent the diversity and unity of the omniverse
4. Incense or essential oils that evoke a sense of universal connection, such as sandalwood or frankincense
5. A representation of the omniverse, like a mandala or a complex geometric pattern
6. Comfortable seating for meditation and contemplation
7. A journal or parchment for recording experiences and insights

Preparation:

1. Find a location that feels connected to the broader universe.
2. Arrange the central crystal or crystal grid, candles, incense/oils, and the omniversal representation in a harmonious setup.

The Ritual:

1. **Candle Lighting**: Light the candles, acknowledging the diversity and unity of the omniverse.
2. **Incense or Oil**: Use the incense or oil to create an atmosphere conducive to universal energy and connection.
3. **Crystal/Grid Activation**: Activate the crystal or grid, setting the intention to use it as a channel for harmonizing your personal love energy with that of the omniverse.
4. **Omniverse Meditation**: Sit comfortably and focus on the representation of the omniverse. Visualize your personal love energy aligning and harmonizing with the energies of all realms and dimensions.
5. **Energetic Flow Visualization**: Imagine a flow of love energy moving through you and the omniverse, creating a balanced and harmonious exchange.
6. **Affirmation of Harmonization**: Affirm your commitment to maintaining this harmonious state, contributing positively to the universal fabric of love.

After the Ritual:

- **Regular Meditation**: Integrate this meditation into your regular practice, continually aligning and harmonizing your love energy with the omniverse.

- **Journaling**: Document your journey and any significant experiences or insights related to this practice.
- **Daily Application**: Apply the concept of harmonization in your daily life, striving to interact with others and the world in a way that reflects universal love and interconnectedness.

Omniversal Love Harmonization is an expansive and unifying practice, ideal for those who view love as a universal force that connects all dimensions and beings. It's a deeply spiritual exercise in aligning personal energy with the vastness of the omniverse, fostering a sense of unity, balance, and cosmic love.

100. Cosmic Love Network Connection

The Cosmic Love Network Connection is a spiritual ritual designed to connect the practitioner with the cosmic network of love energy. This spell is particularly suitable for individuals who believe in the interconnectedness of all beings through a universal network of love and seek to consciously engage with this cosmic web.

Purpose: To connect and engage with the cosmic network of love, enhancing the practitioner's ability to give and receive love on a universal scale.

Timing: Ideal to perform during astral events that signify connectivity, such as during a full moon, when the stars are exceptionally bright, or during planetary alignments.

Materials:

1. A quiet, comfortable space for meditation, preferably outdoors under the night sky
2. A crystal grid arranged with stones known for their connectivity and love properties, like rose quartz, amethyst, and clear quartz
3. Candles in shades of violet or silver, representing the cosmic energy
4. Incense or essential oils that inspire a sense of unity and interconnectedness, such as lavender or lotus
5. A detailed star map or a representation of the cosmic network
6. Comfortable seating or a meditation cushion
7. A journal or parchment for recording insights and experiences

Preparation:

1. Choose a location where you feel a deep connection to the cosmos.
2. Set up your crystal grid, candles, incense/oils, and star map in a way that feels aligned and harmonious.

The Ritual:

1. **Candle Lighting**: Light the candles, focusing on the vastness of the cosmos and your intention to connect with the cosmic network of love.
2. **Incense or Oil**: Burn the incense or diffuse the oil to create an atmosphere conducive to spiritual connectivity.
3. **Crystal Grid Activation**: Activate the crystal grid, envisioning it as a physical representation of the cosmic love network.
4. **Cosmic Network Meditation**: Sit comfortably and meditate, focusing on the star map or cosmic representation. Visualize yourself connecting with a vast network of love energy that spans the cosmos.
5. **Visualization of Love Exchange**: Imagine love energy flowing through this network, reaching out to distant stars, galaxies, and beings, and receiving love in return, creating a dynamic exchange.
6. **Affirmation of Connectivity**: Affirm your connection to this cosmic network and your role in the continuous flow and exchange of universal love.

After the Ritual:

- **Regular Meditation**: Incorporate this cosmic love network meditation into your daily practice, continually nurturing your connection to this universal energy.

- **Journaling**: Write down your experiences, feelings, and any insights gained during the ritual in your journal.
- **Conscious Connectivity**: Apply the concept of cosmic love in your everyday interactions, embodying the idea of being connected to a vast network of love.

Cosmic Love Network Connection is a profound practice for those who view love as a cosmic force that binds all existence. It's about consciously connecting with this universal network, playing an active role in the exchange of love across the cosmos, and reinforcing the notion that we are all connected through the fabric of love.

101. The Ultimate Love Spell: Heart of the Cosmos

The Ultimate Love Spell: Heart of the Cosmos is an immensely powerful ritual designed to connect the practitioner's heart directly with the heart of the cosmos. This advanced spell is for those who wish to experience and embody the most profound and unconditional form of love that the universe has to offer.

Purpose: To align one's heart with the cosmic heart, experiencing a profound connection with the universe and tapping into the deepest wellspring of universal love.

Timing: Most effective when performed under a significant celestial event that symbolizes unity and connection, such as a total solar eclipse, a rare planetary alignment, or during a significant astrological transit.

Materials:

1. A secluded and quiet place where the cosmos can be observed
2. A large and powerful crystal, like a quartz geode, to symbolize the cosmic heart
3. Candles in cosmic colors like deep blue, purple, and silver
4. Incense or essential oils that evoke a sense of cosmic expansiveness, such as frankincense, myrrh, or star anise
5. A large, circular representation of the cosmos, like a mandala or astrological chart
6. Comfortable seating for deep meditation
7. A journal or parchment for recording your experience

Preparation:

1. **Location**: Choose a location where you feel a strong spiritual connection, preferably where you can see the night sky.
2. **Cosmic Representation**: Place a large circular representation of the cosmos, like a mandala or astrological chart, in the center of your space. This serves as a focal point for your meditation and symbolizes the universe.
3. **Materials Setup**: Surround this cosmic representation with your candles, incense or oils, and the large crystal. The arrangement should feel harmonious and conducive to meditation, with the cosmic representation and crystal at the heart of your setup.

The Ritual:

1. **Candle Lighting**:
   - Light the candles around your cosmic representation.
   - As you do this, set your intention to deeply connect with the cosmic heart. This act of lighting candles symbolizes igniting the light within you and preparing to connect with the universal source of love.
2. **Incense or Oil**:
   - Burn incense or use essential oils that help open your mind and spirit.
   - This step is to create an atmosphere that is receptive to cosmic energies, enhancing your sensory experience and helping you to attune to higher frequencies.
3. **Crystal Placement**:
   - Place your large crystal (like a quartz geode) centrally on the cosmic representation.

- This crystal acts as a physical symbol of your direct connection to the cosmic heart, serving as a conduit for cosmic energy during your meditation.

4. **Cosmic Heart Meditation**:
    - Sit comfortably in front of your setup, focusing on the crystal and the representation of the cosmos.
    - Engage in deep meditation, envisioning your heart's energy extending outwards and connecting with the heart of the cosmos. This visualization is key to establishing a profound emotional and spiritual connection with the cosmic heart.
5. **Visualization of Love Exchange**:
    - Imagine a dynamic exchange of love between your heart and the cosmic heart.
    - Feel the unconditional, infinite love of the cosmos flowing into you, filling you with pure love. Then, visualize projecting your own love back into the universe, creating a cycle of giving and receiving love.
6. **Affirmation of Cosmic Love**:
    - Conclude your meditation with an affirmation of your unity with the cosmic heart.
    - Acknowledge that you are an integral part of the boundless universe, filled with and radiating pure love. This affirmation is a powerful statement of your deep connection to universal love.

After the Ritual:

- **Reflective Journaling**: Document your experiences, emotions, and any insights or revelations in your journal.

- **Regular Practice**: Regularly meditate on this connection, maintaining and deepening your bond with the cosmic heart.
- **Daily Application**: Bring this sense of universal love into your daily life, allowing it to guide your actions, thoughts, and interactions with others.

The Ultimate Love Spell: Heart of the Cosmos is a transformative and profound ritual, ideal for those who are ready to experience love in its most expansive and universal form. It is about transcending personal limitations and understanding love as the fundamental, connecting force of the universe, a force that binds and permeates all existence.

CHAPTER 5.

DAILY PRACTICES FOR LOVE ATTRACTION

Following on from the 101 Love Spells, we embark on a journey on the profound power of incorporating daily rituals into our lives to attract and nurture love. Within this chapter we look at the magic hidden in the ordinary moments of our day, revealing how small, consistent practices can create a significant impact of drawing love into our lives.

The art of attracting love is not confined to grand gestures or elaborate spells; it can often be found in the little things we do every day. These practices are like planting seeds in a garden; with regular care and attention, they grow, flourish, and eventually bloom into the love we desire. This chapter is a guide to cultivating such a garden of love through simple, daily rituals.

Why are these small rituals so powerful? Because they work subtly yet consistently, aligning our energies with the frequency of love. Each practice, be it a morning affirmation or a nightly gratitude ritual, acts as a gentle nudge to the universe, signaling our readiness and openness to love. Over time, these rituals build upon each other, creating a cumulative effect that manifests love towards us.

The beauty of these daily practices lies in their simplicity and accessibility. They can be easily integrated into the fabric of our daily lives, regardless of how busy or chaotic our schedules might be. Whether it's sipping a cup of herbal tea infused with intention, carrying a love-attracting crystal, or spending a few quiet moments in meditation, each act is a step towards inviting more love into our existence.

Moreover, these practices aren't just about attracting a partner; they are also about nurturing self-love and strengthening existing relationships. Love, in all its forms, is the cornerstone of a fulfilled life, and by dedicating a few moments each day to its pursuit, we open ourselves to experiencing more profound connections and joy.

In the following sections, we will delve into various practices, each designed to be easily integrated into your daily routine. From morning affirmations that set the tone for your day to journaling exercises that help clarify your desires, each practice is a thread in the tapestry of love you are weaving. We will explore how visualization techniques can shape your reality, how the right crystals can enhance your love energy, and how simple herbal magic can transform your perspective on love.

The goal of this chapter is not to overhaul your life with complex rituals but to introduce small changes that make a significant difference. It's about finding magic in the mundane and recognizing that every day holds the potential for love and wonder.

Remember that the path to love is as unique as you are. Feel free to adapt these practices to suit your personal beliefs, lifestyle, and love aspirations. Embrace them as tools to not only attract love but also to become a beacon of love, radiating warmth and affection in all your interactions.

Let this chapter be your guide to infusing your daily life with the magic of love, one small ritual at a time. As you incorporate these practices into your routine, watch as the seeds of love you plant today blossom into the beautiful, fulfilling relationships of tomorrow.

Morning Affirmations for Love

Morning affirmations are a powerful way to start your day with intention and positivity. They can be especially transformative, setting the tone for attracting and nurturing love in all its forms. Here, we delve into five affirmations that can be recited each morning to open your heart and align your energies with the vibrations of love.

1. **Affirmation of Self-Love**: "I am worthy of love and joy. I embrace myself fully and radiate love from within." This affirmation is a reminder of your intrinsic worthiness of love. Reciting this affirmation encourages self-acceptance and self-love, the bedrock upon which all other forms of love are built. It instills confidence and a deep sense of self-worth that is essential for attracting genuine, nurturing relationships.

2. **Affirmation for Attracting Love**: "The universe is filled with endless love, and I open my heart to receive it in abundance." This affirmation taps into the universal supply of love, inviting it into your life. It helps to dissolve any barriers or walls you might have built around your heart, encouraging a receptive and open stance towards love in all its manifestations.

3. **Affirmation for Nurturing Relationships**: "I nurture my relationships with kindness, understanding, and unconditional love." This affirmation focuses on the active role you play in cultivating and sustaining love in your relationships. It's a promise to approach your interactions with compassion, empathy, and an open heart, fostering deeper connections and understanding with those around you.

4. **Affirmation for Healing and Release**: "I release past hurts and open myself to new and healthy love." It's essential to let go of past wounds to make room for new love to enter. This affirmation supports the healing process, aiding you

in releasing any lingering pain or bitterness from past relationships and preparing you for new, healthy experiences of love.

5. **Affirmation for Joy and Gratitude in Love**: "Every day, I find joy in love and am grateful for the love that surrounds me." This affirmation encourages you to recognize and appreciate the love that already exists in your life. By acknowledging and being grateful for these moments of connection, you attract more such experiences, creating a cycle of love and gratitude.

Integrating these affirmations into your morning routine sets a powerful intention for the day. They act as gentle yet potent reminders of your desires and aspirations in love. Say them out loud, write them in your journal, or meditate on them – find what resonates with you. Over time, these affirmations will not only shift your mindset but also transform the energy you emit, drawing love into your life like a magnet.

Mindful Love Meditation

One of my personal favorite daily meditation practices is the "Mindful Love Meditation," a simple yet profound exercise that focuses on cultivating feelings of love, compassion, and openness both towards oneself and others. This meditation can be practiced in the morning to set a loving tone for the day or at any time when you feel the need to center yourself in the energy of love.

Duration: 10-15 minutes

Setting: Choose a quiet and comfortable space where you won't be disturbed. Sitting on a cushion or chair, ensure your back is straight but not stiff. If you prefer, this meditation can also be done lying down.

Process:

1. **Centering Yourself**: Begin by taking three deep, slow breaths. With each inhalation, feel yourself becoming more present in the moment. With each exhalation, release any tension or stress you may be holding in your body.
2. **Heart-Focused Breathing**: Shift your focus to your heart area. Visualize your breath flowing in and out of your heart center. Imagine each breath as a warm light, filling your heart with peace and warmth. Continue this heart-focused breathing for a few minutes, allowing yourself to feel calm and centered.
3. **Cultivating Self-Love**: Now, gently introduce a loving-kindness phrase directed towards yourself, such as "May I be happy, may I be healthy, may I be filled with love." Silently repeat this phrase to yourself, letting the words resonate within your heart. Feel the sincerity of the wish for your own happiness and well-being.
4. **Expanding Love Outward**: Gradually extend this loving energy outward. First, think of someone close to you, then friends, acquaintances, and eventually even those you may have difficulties with. For each person or group, silently repeat, "May you be happy, may you be healthy, may you be filled with love." Visualize sending a warm light from your heart to theirs, connecting you through these wishes of love and kindness.

5. **Universal Love**: Finally, extend this loving-kindness to all beings in the world. Imagine this warm light expanding further and further, enveloping your community, city, country, and eventually the entire globe. Hold the intention of universal love and compassion, silently repeating, "May all beings be happy, may all beings be healthy, may all beings be filled with love."
6. **Closing the Meditation**: As you conclude your meditation, take a moment to acknowledge the love and peace you've cultivated. Take a few deep breaths and, when you feel ready, gently open your eyes. Carry this feeling of love and openness with you throughout your day.

This meditation practice not only helps in fostering feelings of love and compassion towards others but also significantly enhances your own sense of inner peace and connectedness. It's a reminder that love, in its purest form, starts from within and radiates outward, touching lives and creating a ripple effect of positivity and warmth.

Journaling for Love

Journaling is a potent tool in all magickal practices, serving as a bridge between your innermost desires and the tangible world. Keeping a love-focused journal is more than just a method of record-keeping; it's an intimate process of self-exploration, intention setting, and manifestation. Here, I'll delve into how journaling can be a transformative practice in attracting love, enhancing relationships, and clarifying your romantic aspirations.

Purpose and Power of a Love Journal: A love journal acts as a dedicated space for your thoughts, feelings, and intentions about love and relationships. It's a safe haven where you can express yourself freely, exploring your deepest desires and fears without judgment. This practice of self-expression is not only therapeutic but also clarifying. It helps in identifying what you truly seek in a relationship, be it romantic love, a deeper connection with your partner, or a journey towards self-love.

Manifesting Romantic Desires: Journaling is a manifestation tool. By writing down your desires, you're sending a clear and focused message to the universe. It's like placing an order with the cosmos. Whether you're scripting detailed scenarios of your ideal relationship, listing qualities you seek in a partner, or visualizing romantic encounters, each entry serves as a powerful affirmation of your intentions. The act of writing imbues your desires with energy, transforming them from mere thoughts into potential realities.

Clarity in Relationship Goals: A love journal helps in bringing clarity to your relationship goals. It encourages introspection, prompting you to consider what you truly want and need in a relationship. Are you seeking companionship, emotional support, shared growth, or passion? Writing about these aspects can uncover hidden truths about your relationship needs and desires, guiding you towards more fulfilling connections.

Tracking Emotional Growth and Patterns: Journaling offers insights into your emotional growth and relationship patterns. By regularly documenting your feelings and experiences, you begin to notice patterns - both healthy and unhealthy ones. This awareness is crucial for personal development. It allows you to celebrate progress, recognize areas needing change, and make conscious decisions in your love life.

Techniques for Love Journaling:

1. **Daily Reflections**: Dedicate a few minutes each day to write about your feelings, experiences, and learnings related to love. Reflect on both the joyful and challenging aspects.
2. **Gratitude Entries**: Regularly jot down things you're grateful for in your relationships or your journey towards love. Gratitude shifts your focus to abundance, inviting more of it into your life.
3. **Dream and Desire Scripts**: Write detailed narratives about your ideal love scenario. Describe your dream partner, ideal dates, or the qualities of a strong, healthy relationship.
4. **Affirmations and Intentions**: Use your journal to write powerful love affirmations and intentions. Revisit and rewrite them to reinforce your desires.
5. **Letters to Future or Past Self/Partner**: Write letters to your future partner, expressing your hopes and intentions for your relationship. Alternatively, write to your past self or partner, offering forgiveness, understanding, or gratitude.

Your love journal is a sacred repository of your heart's journey. It's both a mirror reflecting your inner world and a map guiding your path in love. Treat it as a companion on your journey towards love. Let it be a testament to your growth, a blueprint of your desires, and a catalyst for manifesting the love you deserve and desire.

Love Visualization Techniques

Visualizing love is a powerful technique in the world of magic and manifestation. It involves creating a vivid mental image of the love life you desire, thereby aligning your energy with that vision. Here,

I'll guide you through three effective daily visualization exercises designed to attract love and paint a picture of your ideal relationship. These practices not only help in manifesting love but also in nurturing a positive and hopeful mindset towards relationships.

1. The Ideal Partner Visualization:

- **Technique**: Find a quiet, comfortable space where you won't be disturbed. Close your eyes and take a few deep breaths to relax. Now, visualize your ideal partner. Imagine their physical appearance, but more importantly, focus on their qualities and how they make you feel. Do they make you laugh? Are they kind, understanding, supportive?
- **Details to Focus On**: Imagine scenarios where you are both interacting. It could be a simple conversation, a laugh shared during a date, or a supportive embrace. Pay attention to the emotions these interactions evoke. Feel the joy, the love, the connection.
- **Duration and Frequency**: Practice this visualization for about 5-10 minutes daily. The key is consistency, as it reinforces your intention and desire.

2. The Love-Filled Day Visualization:

- **Technique**: In this exercise, imagine a day in your life, but filled with love and affection. Start from the moment you wake up to when you go to bed. Visualize small moments of love throughout your day – a loving text message, a thoughtful gesture from a stranger, or a warm hug from a friend.
- **Details to Focus On**: Include details that feel significant to you. Maybe it's the warmth of the sun on your face, symbolizing

love's warmth, or the sight of couples around you, reflecting the love you wish to attract.

- **Duration and Frequency**: Spend about 10 minutes each morning on this visualization. It sets a positive tone for the day, opening your heart to receive love.

3. The Future Relationship Visualization:

- **Technique**: This visualization takes you into the future. Imagine yourself in a loving, committed relationship. What does it look like? How does it feel to be in a secure, loving partnership?
- **Details to Focus On**: Think about the aspects that matter most to you in a relationship. It might be mutual respect, shared laughter, or deep emotional connection. Visualize scenarios like a holiday together, a quiet evening at home, or supporting each other through challenges.
- **Duration and Frequency**: Practice this visualization for about 5 minutes before you go to sleep. It allows these positive images to seep into your subconscious, reinforcing your belief in the possibility of such love.

Conclusion: Visualization is a tool that harnesses the power of your mind to shape your reality. By consistently practicing these exercises, you not only refine your vision of what you want in love but also attract the energy needed to manifest it. Remember, the clearer and more emotionally charged your visualizations are, the more powerful they become. So, embark on these visual journeys with an open heart and a strong belief in the love that awaits you.

Using Crystals for Love

Crystals have been used for centuries as tools for healing, protection, and manifestation, with each crystal possessing unique energies and properties. Certain crystals, like rose quartz, are revered for their ability to enhance and attract love. Incorporating these love-enhancing crystals into your daily routines can be a beautiful and effective way to focus your intentions on attracting love, healing from past heartaches, and strengthening existing relationships. Here's a detailed guide on how to use crystals, particularly rose quartz, in your daily life to foster love.

Understanding Rose Quartz: Rose quartz, known as the 'stone of love', radiates gentle, nurturing energy that promotes love in all its forms: romantic, platonic, and most importantly, self-love. This pink-hued crystal is associated with the heart chakra and is believed to open the heart to give and receive love.

Incorporating Rose Quartz into Daily Routines:

1. **Morning Affirmation Ritual:**
    - Start your day by holding a piece of rose quartz in your hand.
    - As you hold the crystal, close your eyes and take a few deep breaths to center yourself.
    - Recite a love-focused affirmation, such as "I am open to love," or "I radiate love and love returns to me."
    - Visualize the crystal's energy enveloping you in a warm, pink light, symbolizing love entering your life.
2. **Rose Quartz Meditation:**
    - Find a quiet space where you can sit undisturbed.

- Hold a rose quartz crystal in your hands or place it over your heart.
- Meditate for 10-15 minutes, focusing on the sensation of the crystal and the feeling of love it embodies.
- Envision yourself surrounded by love and imagine the qualities of your ideal relationship.

3. **Carrying Rose Quartz:**
    - Carry a small rose quartz stone in your pocket or wear it as jewelry (like a pendant or bracelet).
    - Throughout the day, whenever you touch or see the crystal, let it remind you of your intention to find love or enhance your current relationship.
4. **Rose Quartz Bath:**
    - Create a love-attracting bath by placing rose quartz crystals around your bathtub.
    - As you soak, visualize the water being infused with the loving energy of the crystals.
    - Focus on letting go of any barriers to love and filling your heart with the crystal's warm energy.
5. **Bedtime Crystal Placement:**
    - Before going to sleep, place rose quartz under your pillow or on your bedside table.
    - This placement helps facilitate loving dreams and promotes a sense of peace and contentment in your heart.
6. **Healing Heartache:**
    - If you're healing from a past relationship, hold a piece of rose quartz over your heart and visualize mending and healing any emotional wounds.

  - Pair this with affirmations of self-love and worthiness.

7. **Crystal Grid for Love:**
   - Create a crystal grid using rose quartz, along with other love-attracting stones like amethyst and moonstone.
   - Arrange the stones in a grid pattern that resonates with you, focusing on your intention of attracting or enhancing love.

Caring for Your Rose Quartz: To maintain the effectiveness of your rose quartz, it's important to cleanse it regularly. This can be done by rinsing it under running water, placing it in moonlight, or smudging it with sage. Cleansing removes any absorbed negative energies and recharges the crystal.

Incorporating rose quartz into your daily routines is a beautiful, tangible way to enhance your focus on love. Its gentle energy supports emotional healing, encourages self-love, and assists in attracting and maintaining loving relationships. By setting intentions and regularly interacting with this crystal, you align yourself more closely with the energies of love and compassion, paving the way for more fulfilling and loving interactions in your life.

Herbal Magic

Herbal magic is a time-honored practice, deeply rooted in the belief that plants hold powerful energies that can aid in various aspects of life, including love and affection. Incorporating herbs into your daily practices can be a simple yet potent way to harness their natural magic to attract love, enhance romance, and foster emotional connections. Here are three accessible and effective ways to use herbs in your daily routines to promote love and affection:

1. **Drinking Herbal Teas for Love:**
    - **Herbal Teas for Love**: Certain herbs are known for their properties in enhancing love, romance, and emotional connections. Some of these include rose petals, jasmine, lavender, and hibiscus. Each of these herbs resonates with the energy of love and can be used to brew teas that invoke feelings of affection and warmth.
    - **Preparation and Ritual**: To prepare a love-enhancing herbal tea, steep your chosen herb (or a blend of herbs) in hot water. As you wait for it to brew, focus on your intention of attracting love or strengthening your current relationship. You can even recite a small affirmation or chant as the tea steeps, such as, "With each sip, love flows within and around me."
    - **Daily Practice**: Incorporate this ritual into your morning routine or enjoy it in the evening as you wind down. Let each sip remind you of your worthiness of love and the love you wish to attract or nurture.
2. **Using Essential Oils for Affection:**
    - **Love Attracting Essential Oils**: Essential oils like rose, ylang-ylang, patchouli, and sandalwood are famed for their love-drawing properties. These oils can be used in various ways to set the tone for romance and affection.
    - **Application Methods**: You can add a few drops of these oils to your bath, use them in a diffuser to fill your space with their loving essence, or dab a little on your pulse points. When using them on your skin, ensure they are properly diluted with a carrier oil to avoid irritation.

- **Intention Setting**: As you use these oils, set a clear intention for love. For instance, while applying rose oil, you might think, "I attract loving, harmonious relationships."

3. **Creating Herbal Sachets for Love:**
   - **Herbal Sachets**: Small pouches or sachets filled with love-promoting herbs are a traditional and discreet way to carry the magic of herbs with you throughout the day.
   - **Making a Love Sachet**: Choose herbs that align with your love intentions, such as rose petals for romance, lavender for calmness in relationships, or cinnamon for passion. Place these herbs in a small cloth pouch, and if you like, add a few drops of a corresponding essential oil.
   - **Utilization and Placement**: Carry the sachet with you in your purse or pocket, or place it under your pillow. You can also place it in areas of your home where you wish to enhance love energies, such as the bedroom.

Integrating herbs into your daily practices is a beautiful and natural way to enhance your connection to the energies of love and affection. Whether it's through a calming cup of herbal tea, the soothing aroma of essential oils, or the discreet magic of a herbal sachet, these practices help to align your energy with the vibration of love. Embrace these simple herbal practices as part of your journey in love magic, and let them serve as daily reminders of your intentions and desires in love.

Creating a Love Altar

Creating a love altar is a deeply personal practice, serving as a focal point for your intentions and desires in the realm of love and relationships. An altar dedicated to love can act as a daily reminder of your quest for love, whether it's about attracting a new relationship, enhancing an existing one, or fostering more self-love. Here's how you can create and utilize a small, personal love altar for focus and inspiration in your daily life.

1. **Choosing a Space for Your Altar:**
    - **Location**: Select a quiet, private space in your home where you can set up your altar. It could be a small table, a shelf, or even a dedicated corner of a room. The key is to choose a spot that feels special and peaceful to you, a place where you can sit or stand comfortably and reflect.
    - **Setting the Mood**: Ensure the area is clean and uncluttered. You might want to drape a cloth in colors associated with love, such as pink or red, over your altar space. This helps create a serene and inviting atmosphere.
2. **Selecting Items for Your Altar:**
    - **Symbols of Love**: Place items that symbolize love and affection on your altar. This could include rose quartz crystals, heart-shaped stones, or figurines representing partnership or affection.
    - **Personal Touches**: Add personal items that hold meaning for your love intentions. These could be photographs of you and your partner, a love letter, or even a list of qualities you desire in a future partner.
    - **Candles and Incense**: Incorporate candles to bring warmth and light to your altar, signifying the illumination and warmth of love. Pink or red candles are particularly suitable. Scented candles or incense with romantic

fragrances like rose, jasmine, or vanilla can also enhance the ambiance.

3. **Activating Your Altar:**
    - **Setting Intentions**: When your altar is set up, spend some time in front of it to set your intentions. Speak or think clearly about what you want to manifest or nurture in your love life.
    - **Regular Rituals**: Use this space for regular rituals like lighting candles, saying affirmations, or meditating. These practices help to reinforce your intentions and keep the energy of your altar vibrant and aligned with your desires.
4. **Maintaining Your Altar:**
    - **Keeping It Fresh**: Regularly change or rearrange items on your altar to keep the energy fresh and relevant to your current intentions in love.
    - **Cleansing**: Cleanse your altar space periodically. This can be done by wiping down the surface, using a sage smudge stick, or placing a bowl of saltwater on it temporarily to absorb any stagnant energies.
5. **Using Your Altar for Focus and Inspiration:**
    - **Daily Visits**: Make it a habit to spend a few moments at your altar each day. This could be for a morning affirmation, a brief meditation, or simply to reflect on your love intentions.
    - **Journaling**: Keep a journal near your altar. Use it to write down your thoughts, experiences, and progress in love. This practice can offer insights and keep you inspired on your journey.

Your love altar is more than just a physical space; it's a sacred place that holds your aspirations and dreams in love. It's a testament to your commitment to finding, nurturing, and celebrating love in its many forms. As you interact with your altar daily, let it be a source of inspiration and a constant reminder of the love that exists within and around you. Embrace this practice as a beautiful part of your magical journey in love.

Crafting a Charm Bag

Creating a love charm bag is a great way to attract love into your life. This small, portable pouch can be filled with various items that resonate with love energies, making it a personal talisman for attracting or enhancing love. Here's how you can create and utilize a love charm bag in your daily routine.

1. **Selecting Your Bag:**
    - Choose a small pouch or bag that resonates with love. This could be in shades of pink, red, or any color you associate with love. The material can be anything from silk to cotton, as long as it feels special to you.
2. **Gathering Love-Attracting Items:**
    - Fill your bag with items that symbolize love and are meaningful to your intention. Here are some suggestions:
    - **Crystals:** Rose quartz is a classic choice for love, promoting romance, self-love, and emotional healing. Other crystals like rhodonite, moonstone, or garnet can also be used.
    - **Herbs:** Consider adding dried herbs like lavender for calm and loving communication, rose petals for romance, or basil for harmony.

- **Personal Tokens:** This could be anything that represents love to you personally. It might be a small heart-shaped object, a piece of jewelry, or a written affirmation of love.
- **Symbols:** Add symbols that represent love, such as a small heart charm or a piece of paper with a love sigil drawn on it.

3. **Assembling Your Charm Bag:**
   - As you place each item in the bag, hold it in your hand and focus on your intention for love. Visualize each item radiating with love energy and contributing to your overall intention.
   - Once all items are placed, close the bag securely. You can do this by tying it with a ribbon or simply pulling the drawstring if it has one.
4. **Activating Your Charm Bag:**
   - To activate your charm bag, hold it in your hands and meditate on your intention. You might visualize yourself surrounded by love or in a happy, loving relationship.
   - You can also recite an affirmation or chant, such as "This charm bag attracts love and joy into my life."
5. **Using Your Love Charm Bag:**
   - Carry your charm bag with you as much as possible. It can be placed in your purse, pocket, or even under your pillow while you sleep.
   - Occasionally, take the bag out and remind yourself of your intention for love. Feel the energy of the bag and let it uplift you.

6. **Maintaining Your Charm Bag:**
   - Over time, you may want to recharge your charm bag. This can be done under a full moon, by passing it through incense smoke, or by re-anointing it with a love-focused essential oil.
   - You can also update or change the contents of your bag as your intentions or desires evolve.

A love charm bag is a powerful, personal tool in your love magic arsenal. It serves as a daily reminder of your intentions and carries the energy of love with you wherever you go. Treat it with care and respect, and it will become a cherished ally in your journey of attracting and nurturing love.

Nighttime Gratitude Practice

Each night, before going to sleep, I take a few moments for a reflective gratitude exercise centered on love. This practice involves journaling, which I find deeply therapeutic and a powerful way to end the day on a positive note. Here's how it works:

1. **Creating the Right Atmosphere:**
   - Before I begin, I make sure my surroundings are calm and peaceful. I might light a candle or dim the lights to create a serene ambiance, conducive to introspection and reflection.
2. **Focusing on Love:**
   - With my journal in hand, I settle into a comfortable position, usually in bed or a cozy chair, and start by taking a few deep breaths to center myself.
   - I then turn my thoughts to the day that has passed, specifically focusing on moments where I experienced

love. This includes love received from others, love I've given, and instances of self-love.

3. **Journaling with Gratitude:**
    - For each instance of love, I jot down a few sentences in my journal. This might include a kind word from a friend, a loving gesture from a family member, or a moment of self-care I gave myself.
    - As I write, I consciously feel grateful for these moments. I acknowledge the love that exists in my life and appreciate its presence in various forms.
4. **Reflecting on Love's Impact:**
    - After writing down these instances, I spend a few minutes reflecting on how they impacted my day and my feelings. I consider how even small acts of love can significantly uplift my mood and outlook.
5. **Closing the Practice:**
    - To conclude, I often read back what I've written and allow myself to absorb the feelings of gratitude and love fully. I might also recite a short affirmation like, "I am grateful for love in my life, and I welcome more each day."
    - I then close my journal, feeling content and filled with positive, loving thoughts as I turn off the light and settle in for the night.
6. **Regular Practice:**
    - Making this a nightly routine helps cultivate a consistent awareness and appreciation for love. Over time, it builds a mindset that naturally looks for and cherishes loving moments.

This practice of reflective gratitude journaling focusing on love is a powerful way to end each day. It fosters a sense of contentment, reinforces the positive role of love in daily life, and prepares the mind and heart for restful sleep filled with positive thoughts.

Reflecting on Love's Journey

It's essential to recognize that the path of love is not static but dynamic, constantly evolving as we grow and change. Reflecting on this journey helps us appreciate our progress and adapt our practices to align with our current needs and desires.

Reflecting on Love's Journey: The journey of love is as much about self-discovery and personal growth as it is about finding and nurturing relationships with others. By engaging in daily love attraction practices, you embark on a path that not only draws love into your life but also deepens your understanding of what love means to you. Regular reflection on this journey is vital. It allows you to recognize the shifts in your perceptions, feelings, and experiences of love. Whether it's through journaling, meditation, or simply taking a few moments each day to contemplate your experiences, reflection helps you acknowledge and celebrate your growth. It also offers insights into how these practices are impacting your love life. Perhaps you've noticed a newfound confidence in your interactions, a deeper sense of self-love, or a more profound connection in your relationships. These changes, whether big or small, are milestones on your journey and deserve recognition.

Adapting Practices Over Time: As you continue on your path, it's important to remember that your needs and circumstances may change, and your practices should evolve accordingly. The rituals and exercises that resonated with you at the beginning of your journey might need adjustments as you grow. Stay attuned to your inner self and be open to modifying your practices. For instance, the affirmations that once empowered you might need rephrasing to reflect the new aspects of love you are exploring. The crystals or herbs you use in your rituals might change as your focus shifts from attracting new love to deepening an existing relationship. This adaptability ensures that your practices remain relevant and effective.

Moreover, as your understanding of love deepens, you might find yourself drawn to more complex rituals or exploring different aspects of love magic. This progression is a natural part of your growth in love magic. It reflects an expanding awareness and a deeper connection to the energies of love. Embrace these changes, and allow your practices to be a true reflection of your journey.

The Importance of Patience and Perseverance: It's also important to approach this journey with patience and perseverance. Changes, especially those influenced by magic, often happen subtly and over time. Trust in the process and know that each step you take is contributing to your growth. The seeds of love you plant and nurture daily will eventually bloom in their own time.

Celebrating Progress and Embracing Challenges: Remember to celebrate your progress, no matter how small it may seem. Acknowledge the efforts you've made and the strides you've taken in understanding and manifesting love. At the same time, be prepared to face challenges. Love's journey is not without its obstacles, but each challenge is an opportunity for growth and learning. Embrace these experiences as part of your evolution, knowing that they contribute to your strength and understanding of love.

Encouragement for Continued Growth and Exploration: As you continue with your daily practices for love attraction, keep an open heart and mind. Be willing to explore new facets of love magic, to deepen your understanding and enhance your experiences. Love is a vast and multifaceted emotion, and its magic is equally diverse and profound. Your journey is unique, and your exploration of love magic is a personal and deeply enriching experience.

In conclusion, the journey of love, aided by daily magical practices, is a continuous path of discovery, growth, and adaptation. Reflect regularly on your journey, celebrate your progress, embrace challenges, and remain open to evolving your practices. This approach will not only enhance your experiences in love but also contribute to a deeper understanding and appreciation of the magic of love in your life. Remember, the journey itself is as important as the destination, and each step you take enriches your experience of love in all its beautiful forms.

CHAPTER 6.

CREATING LOVE POTIONS AND ELIXIRS

Welcome to the fascinating world of love potions and elixirs, a practice where the mystique of ancient recipes blends with the intentions of the heart to create magical brews. Love potions, steeped in history and culture, have been a cornerstone of love magic from time immemorial. Their allure lies not just in their mystical properties but in the way they encapsulate the timeless desire for love, connection, and emotional depth.

The mystique of love potions stretches back to ancient civilizations, where they were often steeped in mythology and surrounded by tales of gods and mortals influenced by these powerful concoctions. From the love-inducing draughts of Greek mythology to the aphrodisiacs of medieval lore, love potions have always captured the human imagination. They symbolize the mysterious and often elusive nature of love itself, offering a tangible means to tap into its profound energies.

But beyond their allure and historical charm, love potions serve varied and significant purposes in the practice of love magic. These magical brews can be crafted to attract love, enhance desirability, or deepen an existing romantic connection. They can also be used for fostering self-love and emotional healing, serving as tools for personal empowerment and inner harmony.

In love potions and elixirs, we find a unique blend of herbal wisdom, magical symbolism, and the power of intention. Each ingredient is carefully chosen not just for its physical properties but for its symbolic resonance with aspects of love and affection. When these elements combine, they create more than just a potion; they weave a spell in liquid form, imbued with the power to touch hearts and open pathways of emotional connection.

As we delve into this chapter, we'll explore how to create your own love potions and elixirs. From selecting the right ingredients to imbuing your concoction with intention, you'll learn the art of crafting these magical liquids. Whether you're a seasoned practitioner or new to the craft, this journey into the world of love potions will enhance your magical practice, offering new ways to explore the depths and delights of love magic.

Magical Properties of Ingredients

In the craft of creating love potions and elixirs, the ingredients you choose are the foundation of your magical work. Each element you add to your potion carries its own unique set of symbolic meanings and energetic properties, contributing to the overall effectiveness and intent of your concoction.

Herbs and Plants

1. **Roses**: Symbolize deep romantic love. Use dried rose petals in potions to invoke passion and a strong emotional connection.
2. **Lavender**: Known for promoting peace, tranquility, and emotional healing. Add lavender to elixirs to create a calming love atmosphere.
3. **Basil**: Attracts love and happiness. Basil leaves can be used in potions to bring joy and harmony into a relationship.
4. **Jasmine**: Encourages prophetic dreams and spiritual love. Jasmine flowers are great in teas or as an infusion in oils for spells focusing on spiritual connections.

Crystals and Gemstones

1. **Rose Quartz**: The quintessential stone of love, healing heartaches, and attracting new love. Place rose quartz crystals in your potion or elixir during brewing for gentle love energy.
2. **Garnet**: Ignites passion and desire. Use garnet in spells when you want to spice up your love life.
3. **Amethyst**: Brings clarity and emotional balance. Ideal for potions that aim to deepen understanding in a relationship.
4. **Moonstone**: Revered for its connection to the moon and feminine energy. Moonstone is ideal for spells focusing on intuition in love, fertility, and balancing emotions.

Essential Oils

1. **Ylang-Ylang**: Enhances sensual and romantic feelings. Add a few drops to potions or baths for an instant love boost.
2. **Vanilla**: Invokes warm, comforting feelings. Vanilla is perfect for spells that aim to nurture and stabilize love.
3. **Patchouli**: Known for its grounding and sensual properties. Patchouli oil can be used in love spells to deepen physical attraction and emotional connection.
4. **Rose**: The quintessential oil for love, representing deep, romantic, and unconditional love. Rose oil is perfect for spells aimed at attracting true love or enhancing romantic feelings.

Colors

1. **Pink**: Symbolizes gentle, nurturing love. Use pink candles or pink-colored ingredients in spells for budding romance or healing emotional wounds.

2. **Red**: Represents passion and deep desire. Red elements in a potion can amplify sexual energy and attraction.
3. **Green**: Represents the heart chakra and emotional healing. Utilize green elements in your potion for healing past wounds and preparing for new love.
4. **Gold**: Symbolizes divine love and spiritual enlightenment. Gold accents in a potion can elevate the spiritual aspect of love and attraction.

Sourcing Ingredients Ethically

The potency and integrity of your love potions are significantly influenced by how you source your ingredients. Ethical sourcing ensures that your magical work is harmonious not just with your intentions, but also with the environment and the energies of the earth.

1. **Respect for Nature**: When gathering herbs, flowers, or other natural ingredients, do so with respect for the earth and its ecosystems. Harvest responsibly and sustainably, taking only what you need and leaving no harm behind.
2. **Fair Trade and Ethical Practices**: If purchasing ingredients, opt for suppliers who follow fair trade and ethical practices. This ensures that the products are obtained in a way that honors the labor and resources involved.
3. **Organic and Pure Sources**: Whenever possible, use organic ingredients to avoid the influence of pesticides and chemicals. Pure, natural ingredients carry clearer and more potent energies, making them more effective in your magical work.
4. **Personal Connection**: Whenever you can, personally connect with the source of your ingredients. Growing your own herbs or personally picking them can enhance their

magical properties, as it imbues the ingredients with your energy and intent.

Understanding and respecting the properties and sources of your ingredients is crucial in the art of potion making. It not only ensures the efficacy of your potions but also aligns your magical practice with ethical and harmonious principles, making your work a true act of love and respect for the forces of nature and magic.

Types of Love Potions

1. **Infusions**: Infusions are among the simplest and most common types of love potions. They involve steeping herbs, flowers, or other ingredients in hot water. For instance, a rose petal infusion can be used to attract romantic love.
2. **Tinctures**: Tinctures are concentrated herbal extracts made by soaking herbs in alcohol or vinegar. A few drops of a tincture can be potent. For example, a vanilla tincture might be used to enhance sensual energy.
3. **Teas**: Teas are a gentle way of drawing out the magical properties of herbs. A blend of jasmine and lavender in a tea can be used for calming emotions and opening the heart.
4. **Scented Oils**: Scented oils involve infusing oil with herbs, flowers, or essential oils. These can be used in anointing or as part of a ritual bath. Ylang-ylang oil, for instance, is excellent for enhancing romantic and sensual feelings.
5. **Magical Syrups**: Syrups, made by simmering ingredients in water with sugar, can be used in love magic for sweetening relationships. A syrup made with cinnamon and honey can be used to attract affection.

6. **Potion Sprays**: Potion sprays, which involve diluting a magical blend with water and alcohol, can be used to spritz around a space to set the mood for love and harmony.

Safety and Allergy Considerations

When crafting love potions and elixirs, safety and awareness of potential allergies are paramount. Whether your potion is for ingestion, like a tea or syrup, or for topical application, like scented oils, ensure all ingredients are safe and non-toxic. Be particularly cautious with any allergies, either known or potential, to avoid adverse reactions. If a potion is to be applied to the skin, it's wise to perform a patch test first. Using high-quality, organic ingredients where possible can also reduce the risk of reactions. Always prioritize safety in your magical practice to ensure that your love spells bring joy and fulfillment, free from harm.

Crafting a Basic Love Potion

Ingredients:

- 2 cups of spring water
- Rose petals (fresh or dried)
- A pinch of cinnamon
- A few drops of vanilla extract
- Honey (optional, for sweetness)

Equipment:

- A small pot or cauldron
- A strainer
- A clean bottle or jar for storage

Steps:

1. **Cleanse Your Space**: Begin by cleansing your workspace and equipment. You can do this by burning some sage or simply visualizing a bright light purifying the area.
2. **Set Your Intentions**: As you prepare to make the potion, focus on your intention. Whether it's to attract love, enhance an existing relationship, or foster self-love, keep this intention clear in your mind.
3. **Heat the Water**: Pour the spring water into your pot and gently heat it over a low flame. Avoid boiling - the aim is to warm the water.
4. **Add Rose Petals**: Once the water is warm, add the rose petals. Roses are a classic symbol of love and are believed to attract affection and enhance romantic feelings.
5. **Include Cinnamon and Vanilla**: Sprinkle in the cinnamon and add a few drops of vanilla extract. Cinnamon is used for its properties of attraction and passion, while vanilla adds an element of comforting sweetness.
6. **Simmer Gently**: Allow the mixture to simmer gently for about 10 minutes. As it simmers, visualize the potion absorbing your intentions, becoming a liquid embodiment of love.
7. **Add Honey**: If desired, add a teaspoon of honey to sweeten the potion and enhance its loving properties.
8. **Strain and Store**: After simmering, take the pot off the heat. Strain the potion to remove the petals and any residue, pouring the liquid into your clean bottle or jar.
9. **Seal with an Affirmation**: As you seal the potion, affirm your intentions once more. You might say something like, "May

this potion bring love and joy into my life, in harmony with my highest good."

10. **Store Safely**: Store your potion in a cool, dark place. It can be used in ritual baths, as an anointment, or simply placed on your altar as a magical tool.

Remember, the effectiveness of your love potion relies not just on the ingredients or the process, but on the energy and intention you put into it. Approach this practice with respect, love, and a positive mindset, and you'll create a potion that truly embodies the magic of love.

For those ready to advance their potion-making skills, here's a step-by-step guide to creating a more complex love potion. This potion incorporates additional elements for a deeper, more nuanced effect.

A Slightly More Complex Love Potion

Ingredients:

- 1 cup of rose water
- A handful of dried hibiscus flowers
- 3 drops of jasmine essential oil
- A small piece of rose quartz crystal
- A teaspoon of honey
- A pinch of ground cardamom

Equipment:

- Heat-resistant glass jar or cauldron
- Wooden spoon
- Strainer or cheesecloth
- A small bottle for storage
- A candle (pink or red for love)

Steps:

1. **Prepare Your Space**: Begin by preparing your workspace. Cleanse the area and all your tools. Light the candle to set the intention for love and passion.
2. **Charge the Rose Quartz**: Before starting, hold the rose quartz crystal in your hand. Visualize it glowing with a soft pink light, charged with your intention for love. Place it beside the candle.
3. **Warm the Rose Water**: In your jar or cauldron, gently warm the rose water. Rose water is used for its strong association with love and emotional healing.
4. **Add Hibiscus Flowers**: Add the dried hibiscus flowers to the warm rose water. Hibiscus is known for attracting love and enhancing sensuality.
5. **Infuse with Jasmine Oil**: Stir in the jasmine essential oil. Jasmine is believed to draw spiritual love and enhance prophetic dreams.
6. **Blend in Honey and Cardamom**: Add the honey for sweetness, symbolizing the sweetening of a relationship or attraction. Sprinkle the ground cardamom for its properties of love and desire.
7. **Simmer and Stir**: Allow the mixture to simmer gently for about 15 minutes, stirring occasionally with the wooden spoon. As you stir, maintain focus on your intention, infusing the potion with your desires.
8. **Strain and Energize**: After simmering, remove the potion from heat. Strain it to remove the hibiscus flowers. While the

potion is still warm, hold the bottle containing the potion near the rose quartz to imbue it with the crystal's energy.

9. **Seal with an Incantation**: As you seal the potion, recite an incantation or affirmation that encapsulates your intention, such as, "May this potion bring deep and lasting love, in perfect harmony with my heart's true desire."
10. **Store and Use Mindfully**: Store the potion in a cool, dark place. Use it in ritual baths, anointing, or as part of a broader love spell, always respecting the free will and well-being of all involved.

This more complex love potion, with its blend of symbolic ingredients and focused intention, offers a deeper exploration into the art of magical potion-making. Its creation is not only an act of love magic but a meditation on the qualities and energies you wish to attract or strengthen in your love life.

Aligning Potions with Astrological Events

In the world of love magic, aligning your potion-making with astrological events and lunar phases can significantly enhance the effectiveness of your concoctions. This practice taps into the ancient wisdom of astrology, allowing you to harness specific cosmic energies to empower your potions.

Lunar Phases

1. **New Moon**: The new moon, symbolizing new beginnings, is an ideal time for crafting potions focused on attracting new love or starting a fresh chapter in your love life.
2. **Waxing Moon**: As the moon grows, it's a powerful time for potions that increase things – such as growing affection,

deepening desire, or strengthening a bond in an existing relationship.

3. **Full Moon**: The full moon is a peak time for magical potency. Potions made during this phase can be charged with powerful energy for significant love manifestations, especially those focused on fulfillment and realization.
4. **Waning Moon**: This phase is suitable for potions intended to diminish or release – such as letting go of past loves, healing from heartbreak, or removing obstacles in your love life.

Astrological Alignments

1. **Venus Transits**: Venus, the planet of love, plays a crucial role in love potion crafting. Creating potions when Venus is strong in the sky (such as when it's in Taurus or Libra) can amplify their romantic and harmonious energies.
2. **Mars Alignments**: For potions aimed at enhancing passion and desire, consider aligning your potion-making with Mars transits, tapping into the planet's fiery, passionate energy.
3. **Jupiter Aspects**: Jupiter, the planet of expansion and blessings, can enhance the abundance and growth aspect of your love potions. Crafting potions during favorable Jupiter aspects can bring generosity and expansiveness to your love life.

Practical Application

1. **Astrological Calendars**: Keep an astrological calendar handy to plan your potion-making according to the lunar phases and significant planetary transits.

2. **Intention Setting**: When crafting your potion, set your intentions in alignment with the specific astrological energy you're harnessing. For instance, during a Venus transit, focus on harmony, beauty, and attraction.
3. **Ritual Timing**: Plan your potion-making ritual to coincide with the exact phase of the moon or the peak of an astrological transit for maximum effect.
4. **Astrological Correspondences**: Incorporate ingredients into your potions that correspond to the astrological event. For example, using rose (associated with Venus) during a Venus transit can add an extra layer of power to your love potion.

By aligning your love potions with the rhythms of the cosmos, you not only infuse them with potent energies but also connect your magical practice with the ancient dance of the celestial bodies. This harmonious alignment brings a deeper sense of purpose and effectiveness to your potion-making, embedding your love spells with the wisdom and power of the universe.

Enhancing Magic with Love Potions

Love potions, while potent on their own, can be integrated into broader magical practices for an enhanced effect. Understanding how to weave these concoctions into rituals and self-care routines can amplify their power and deepen your connection to the magic of love.

Incorporating Potions into Rituals

1. **Ritual Baths**: Infuse your bathwater with a love potion, transforming it into a ritual bath. This is especially effective for self-love spells or preparing yourself energetically before

a romantic encounter. The act of bathing in potion-infused water symbolizes the absorption of the potion's qualities.

2. **Anointing and Dressing Candles**: Use your potion to anoint candles used in love spells. This can be done by lightly rubbing the potion on the candle while focusing on your intention. For instance, a candle dressed with a passion-enhancing potion can intensify the energy of a love spell.
3. **Altar Offerings**: Place a small bowl or vial of your love potion on your altar as an offering to deities or spirits associated with love. This act can be a part of a larger ritual to seek divine assistance in your love endeavors.
4. **Potion as a Consecration Tool**: Use the potion to consecrate tools, talismans, or amulets used in love magic. By doing so, you're charging these items with the specific energies of the potion, aligning them more closely with your magical objectives.

Love Potions for Self-Care

1. **Self-Love Rituals**: Create potions specifically designed for self-love and incorporate them into your self-care rituals. For instance, a potion made with rose petals and lavender can be used in a self-bath ritual to promote self-acceptance and emotional healing.
2. **Meditation and Visualization**: Use love potions as an aid during meditation or visualization exercises. Sipping a small amount of a self-love potion before meditation can set the stage for a powerful self-affirmation practice.
3. **Potion-Infused Tea Time**: Integrate your love potion into a daily tea ritual. This act of self-care not only nurtures your

body but also continually reinforces your intentions for love and personal fulfillment.

4. **Journaling with Potion**: Anoint your journal or writing tools with a love potion while working on entries related to your love life or personal growth. This can help align your thoughts and reflections with your magical goals.

The Art and Heart of Potion Making

Incorporating love potions into rituals and self-care practices is about more than just the physical act; it's about embedding your magical intentions into your daily life. Whether you're using potions in elaborate rituals or simple self-care routines, they serve as powerful tools, weaving the magic of love into your everyday existence and enhancing your overall practice of witchcraft.

Potion making in love magic is far more than a mere craft; it is an art form that beautifully intertwines creativity, intention, and magical practice. It's a deeply personal process that involves not just the mixing of ingredients but the blending of your own energies and desires into a harmonious whole.

Potion making allows for immense creativity. Each brewer brings their unique touch to their concoctions, selecting ingredients not just for their magical properties but also for their personal significance. The choice of herbs, the blend of scents, and even the color of the potion can be a reflection of the potion maker's personality and magical style. This creative freedom turns each potion into a unique work of art, a liquid embodiment of individual expression and intention.

At the heart of every love potion is intention. This focused thought and desire is what charges the potion with magical energy. It's the practitioner's intention that transforms a simple mixture of ingredients into a potent magical tool. The process of stirring a cauldron or brewing a tea becomes a meditative practice, where thoughts and energies are concentrated and infused into the brew.

Potion making is a magical practice that connects the practitioner to the ancient traditions of witchcraft. It's a ritual that honors the natural world and its bounty, celebrating the connection between the earth and the esoteric. Each potion is a testament to this enduring bond, a reminder of the magic that flows through all things.

In love magic, potion making holds a special place. It's an act of love in itself – love for the craft, love for the natural world, and love for the people the potions are intended for. Whether it's a potion to attract love, enhance a relationship, or cultivate self-love, each concoction is a manifestation of the heart's deepest desires.

CHAPTER 7.

CHANTS AND INCANTATIONS FOR LOVE

In the world of love magic, words and sounds are more than mere expressions; they are potent tools imbued with energy. Chants and incantations, when uttered with intention and focus, harness vibrational energies, transforming them into powerful vehicles for manifesting love and desire. The rhythm, tone, and resonance of these spoken elements play a critical role in amplifying the effectiveness of a spell, aligning the practitioner's desires with the universal energies of love.

The use of chants and incantations in love magic spans across various cultures and epochs, each contributing its unique perspective to this mystical art. From the enchanting love songs of ancient Greece to the mystical Vedic hymns of India, chants have always been a cornerstone in love rituals. These practices evolved over time, with each culture adding its nuances. For instance, the ancient Egyptians used elaborate love spells inscribed in scrolls, while during the Renaissance, poets crafted sonnets with magical properties to influence matters of the heart.

In modern times, these traditions have adapted to contemporary witchcraft practices. Today's practitioners draw inspiration from ancient lore, infusing chants and incantations with personal energies and modern understandings. This rich lineage of using words as magical tools in love magic shows a lasting belief in their power to influence the realms of love and affection. As we explore the art of love chants further, we connect with a legacy that transcends time, continuing the narrative of love magic in our own unique ways.

Chanting and incantation form a core part of love magic, with their power often lying in the nuances of rhythm, rhyme, voice modulation, and pronunciation. These elements combine to create a harmonious and potent expression of intent.

Understanding Rhythm and Rhyme

Rhythm and rhyme play a pivotal role in the effectiveness of magical chants. They are not just poetic devices but tools that create energetic patterns and vibrations.

1. **Rhythm**: The rhythm of a chant helps in building energy and focus. A steady, repetitive rhythm can induce a trance-like state, making the practitioner more receptive to the energies being summoned. It helps in syncing the practitioner's energy with that of the universe, creating a powerful conduit for manifesting intentions.
2. **Rhyme**: Rhymes make chants easier to remember and recite, and they add to the aesthetic and energetic appeal. Rhyming words in a chant can act like a spell's heartbeat, giving life and rhythm to the practitioner's desires. The sonic harmony created by rhyme can also enhance the spell's ability to tap into the vibrational energies of love.

Voice and Pronunciation

The way a chant is vocalized is equally important. Voice modulation and proper pronunciation can significantly amplify a spell's potency.

1. **Voice Modulation**: Using different tones and volumes can imbue a chant with emotional depth and energy. A soft, whisper-like tone can be used for gentle, nurturing love spells, while a stronger, more assertive voice might be suited for spells that seek to overcome obstacles in love.

2. **Pronunciation**: Clear and deliberate pronunciation ensures that each word's vibrational energy is fully realized. Mispronouncing words in a spell can lead to unintended results. Taking the time to learn the correct pronunciation, especially in chants derived from ancient or foreign languages, is crucial.

The practice of chanting and incantation in love magic is an art that requires attention to these subtleties. It's about aligning your vocal expressions with your magical intent, creating a symphony of words that resonates with the energies of love and desire you wish to manifest. By mastering rhythm, rhyme, voice, and pronunciation, you can turn your chants and incantations into powerful tools in your love magic repertoire.

Traditional Incantations in Love Magic

By delving into the domain of traditional love incantations, we are able to discover a rich tapestry of magical words passed down through generations. These incantations, originating from diverse cultures, carry deep meanings and have been used for centuries to invoke the powers of love and attraction.

1. Ancient Greek Love Charm

Origin: Dating back to ancient Greece, this incantation was often inscribed on amulets or recited in rituals dedicated to Aphrodite, the goddess of love.

Incantation: "Eros, bright and beautiful, bring to me a love that's dutiful. By Aphrodite's tender hand, let my heart's desire expand."

Usage: This chant was used to attract a devoted and passionate love. The invocation of Eros, the god of love, and Aphrodite symbolizes a plea for divine assistance in matters of the heart.

Meaning: The incantation expresses a desire for love that is not only passionate but also respectful and committed, under the guidance of divine forces.

2. Celtic Binding Spell

Origin: Stemming from ancient Celtic traditions, this spell was used in rituals to symbolize the binding of two hearts in love.

Incantation: "By the knot of one, the spell's begun. By the knot of two, my love is true. By the knot of three, so mote it be."

Usage: This incantation, often accompanied by the physical act of tying knots in a cord, was believed to strengthen the bond between lovers.

Meaning: Each knot and corresponding line in the chant symbolizes a deepening commitment and the weaving together of two lives.

3. Egyptian Love Invocation

Origin: From the sands of ancient Egypt, this incantation was recited to invoke the powers of Isis, the goddess of love and fertility.

Incantation: "Isis, goddess of mystical might, bring to me sweet love's light. Through moon's glow and star's gaze, let love find me in its blaze."

Usage: Used in rituals under the night sky, this spell calls upon Isis to manifest a love that is as enduring as the stars.

Meaning: The invocation is a plea for a love that is not only passionate but also illuminated with wisdom and cosmic power, reflecting the eternal nature of the stars.

4. Japanese Love Enchantment

Origin: Rooted in ancient Japanese folklore, this enchantment was often associated with rituals of love and affection, evoking the delicate balance of nature and emotion.

Incantation: "Kokoro no kizuna, ai no hikari, tsunagu tamae, musubi no chikara."

Translation: "Bond of the heart, light of love, connect us, with the power of binding."

Usage: This incantation, often recited with offerings at shrines, was believed to create a spiritual bond between lovers, drawing upon the natural forces of harmony and connection.

Meaning: The chant speaks of the deep bond of the heart and the light of love as powerful forces that bind and connect individuals, echoing the Shinto belief in the sacredness of natural bonds.

5. West African Love Prayer

Origin: Stemming from West African traditions, this prayer was used to invoke the benevolence of ancestral spirits and deities in matters of the heart.

Incantation: "Ancestors of old, guide my heart to love bold. In your wisdom, I trust, bring to me love that is just."

Usage: Accompanied by rituals involving ancestral altars and natural elements, this prayer was a plea for ancestral guidance and blessing in finding true and just love.

Meaning: The invocation reflects a deep trust in the wisdom of ancestors and the spiritual world to guide one towards a love that is righteous and fair, emphasizing the community's role in supporting and validating love.

Modern Love Incantations

The following are five powerful and popular modern love incantations, each crafted to address different aspects of love in contemporary times. These incantations blend traditional magical concepts with modern expressions of love and relationships.

1. Incantation for Attracting New Love

"By the light of the moon's waxing grace,
Bring to me a loving face.
Across the stars, through time and space,
May love come forth in gentle pace."

This incantation is designed to attract new love into your life, focusing on a gentle and natural progression of a relationship. It is best recited under a waxing moon, signifying growth and new beginnings.

2. Incantation for Deepening an Existing Relationship

"In this bond, we grow and thrive,
With each breath, our love's alive.
Deeper roots, let our hearts dive,
Together strong, our love shall strive."

This chant focuses on deepening the connection and strengthening the bond in an existing relationship. It's an affirmation of growth, resilience, and mutual support in love.

3. Incantation for Self-Love and Confidence

"From within, my light shines bright,
In self-love, I find my might.
With confidence, I stand in light,
Whole and strong, in my own right."

This incantation emphasizes the importance of self-love and personal confidence. It's about recognizing one's worth and the inner strength that comes from self-acceptance and self-care.

4. Incantation for Healing a Broken Heart

"Wounds of heart, now heal and mend,
Let the hurt and sorrow end.
From this pain, I now ascend,
Towards new joys and love's amend."

This chant is aimed at healing from heartbreak, focusing on recovery, emotional healing, and moving forward towards new opportunities for love and happiness.

5. Incantation for Rekindling Passion

"Flame of passion, rise once more,
In our hearts, let love's fire roar.
With renewed desire, let our spirits soar,
In love's dance, forevermore."

6. Incantation for Finding a Soulmate

"Soulmate of mine, in time we'll meet,
Two paths entwine, in love complete.
Drawn by the stars, in harmony sweet,
In each other's eyes, our fates shall greet."

This incantation is for those seeking to find their soulmate. It's about attracting a deep, meaningful connection destined by the stars.

7. Incantation for Trust and Honesty in a Relationship

"Trust be woven, honest and true,
In our words and actions through.
In our bond, let these virtues renew,
Building a love that's forever anew."

This chant is aimed at fostering trust and honesty in a relationship, vital components for a healthy and lasting partnership.

8. Incantation for Overcoming Relationship Obstacles

"Obstacles ahead, now we face,
With strength and love, we embrace.
Together we conquer, with grace,
In unity, no challenge outplace."

Designed for couples facing challenges, this incantation invokes the strength and resilience needed to overcome obstacles together.

9. Incantation for Long-Distance Love

"Though miles apart, our hearts entwined,
By love's strong bond, we're aligned.

Across the distance, our souls bind,
In love's embrace, no space confined."

This chant addresses the challenges of long-distance relationships, focusing on maintaining a strong emotional and spiritual connection despite physical separation.

10. Incantation for Reconciling After a Fight

"After the storm, comes calm's embrace,
Let anger and hurt now be displaced.
With forgiveness, love we retrace,
In understanding, our hearts encased."

This incantation is crafted to rekindle passion and desire in a relationship where the initial spark may have dimmed. It's about reigniting the flame of love and desire, ensuring that the relationship remains vibrant and dynamic.

Each of these modern incantations is powerful in its right, offering practitioners specific words to channel their intentions and desires. Whether seeking new love, deepening existing bonds, fostering self-love, healing from heartache, or rekindling passion, these chants provide a focused and contemporary approach to love magic.

Integrating Chants into Love Spells

1. **Timing and Setting**: Choose the right time and setting for your ritual. Chants can be more powerful during certain lunar phases, such as a full moon for amplifying love or a new moon for new beginnings in love. Ensure your ritual space is quiet and undisturbed.

2. **Aligning with Intentions**: Select or create chants that align closely with your spell's intention. For a spell to attract new love, use chants that evoke openness and attraction. For deepening a relationship, choose chants that speak of bonding and understanding.
3. **Repetition for Energy Build-up**: Repeat the chant multiple times to build up energy. The repetition helps to deepen your focus and strengthens the spell's intent. It can also help to enter a trance-like state, making you more receptive to the energies you are working with.
4. **Visualization**: As you chant, visualize your intentions coming to fruition. Picture the love you wish to attract or the strengthening of a current relationship. Visualization during chanting can significantly amplify the effectiveness of your spell.

Practical Exercises for Chants in Love Magic

Incorporating chants into your love magic practice can be both powerful and fulfilling. To help you get started and refine your skills, here are some practical exercises and tips for recording and reflecting on your outcomes.

1. **Daily Recitation**: Start by reciting your chosen chant daily. Choose a time when you are least likely to be disturbed, such as early morning or late at night. This routine will help you memorize the chant and understand its rhythm and flow.
2. **Voice Modulation Exercise**: Practice modulating your voice as you chant. Try different tones and volumes to see how they affect your energy and the feel of the chant. Notice how changes in your voice impact the mood of the spell.

3. **Mirror Practice**: Chant in front of a mirror to observe your facial expressions and body language. Ensure your physical demeanor reflects the intent of the chant. This exercise helps in aligning your physical presence with your magical intentions.
4. **Nature Immersion**: If possible, practice your chants outdoors. The natural setting can enhance the energy of your spell and provide a more grounding experience. Pay attention to how the environment interacts with your chanting.
5. **Group Chanting**: Consider chanting with a group, if you are comfortable. The collective energy can significantly amplify the power of the chant. Notice how the energy changes with group dynamics and how your own energy contributes to the collective.

Recording and Reflecting on Outcomes

1. **Magical Journaling**: Keep a journal to record your experiences with different chants. Note down the date, time, moon phase, your emotional state, and the specific chant used. This record will be invaluable in tracking your progress and the effectiveness of different chants.
2. **Reflecting on Feelings**: After each chanting session, take some time to reflect on how you feel. Did the chant evoke strong emotions? Did you feel more connected to your intentions? Your emotional response can be a key indicator of the chant's resonance with you.
3. **Outcome Tracking**: Keep track of any noticeable outcomes or changes in your love life following your chanting practices.

This could be new opportunities, changes in existing relationships, or shifts in your emotional well-being.

4. **Review and Adjust**: Periodically review your journal entries to assess which chants seem most effective or meaningful to you. Don't hesitate to modify chants or try new ones based on your reflections. Remember, personalization can be a powerful tool in magic.
5. **Sharing Experiences**: If you are part of a magical community, consider sharing your experiences with chanting. Discussions with fellow practitioners can provide new insights, feedback, and suggestions to enhance your practice.

By actively practicing and reflecting on your chanting experiences, you can hone your skills in this magical art. The key is to remain open, observant, and responsive to both the subtle and significant shifts that chanting brings into your love magic practices.

The Vibrational Science Behind Chants

Understanding the vibrational science behind chants in love magic is essential for tapping into their full potential. Sound is not merely a medium of communication but a powerful tool that interacts with the energy fields around us, influencing emotions, thoughts, and even physical realities.

The scientific basis for the efficacy of chants lies in the principles of sound vibration and its interaction with human consciousness and the surrounding environment. At a fundamental level, everything in the universe, including human thoughts and emotions, is composed of vibrations. Sound, particularly the human voice, generates vibrations that can influence these subtle energies.

The Science of Sound in Magic

Every sound, including the human voice, emits vibrations. In love magic, these vibrations are harnessed through chants, crafted to resonate with specific frequencies associated with love and desire. The words and tones used in a chant are meticulously chosen to align with the caster's intentions, thereby amplifying the energy directed towards the desired outcome. For instance, a chant spoken in a soft, melodious tone creates vibrations that align with the gentle, nurturing energy of love.

When a chant is recited, especially with intention and focus, it creates sound waves that propagate through the air. These waves are not just auditory experiences but also vibrational energies that interact with the energy fields or auras surrounding individuals and objects. According to quantum physics, the observer's consciousness can influence the outcome of events at a quantum level. In this context, the focused intention behind a chant, coupled with the vibrational energy of the sound, can influence the probability of desired outcomes in the area of love and relationships. This aligns with the concept of the observer effect, where the act of observation itself can alter the outcome of an event.

These chants go beyond the practitioner, potentially influencing the energy fields of the subject of the spell. The rhythmic repetition of words and sounds can harmonize and balance these fields, making them more receptive to the energies of love, connection, and healing.

Harmonizing with Natural Frequencies

Harmonizing chants with the natural frequencies and rhythms of the universe can significantly enhance their effectiveness. This harmony can be achieved in several ways:

- **Aligning with Lunar and Solar Cycles**: Utilizing the natural energies of lunar and solar cycles can boost the power of chants. For example, performing a love chant during the full moon leverages the moon's powerful energy for enhancing emotions and desires.
- **Rhythmic Alignment**: The rhythm of a chant should ideally be in sync with natural rhythms like the heartbeat or the ebb and flow of breathing. This alignment creates a natural flow of energy that resonates deeply with the life force present in all things.
- **Seasonal Energies**: Each season imparts its unique energy to the environment. Aligning chants with these seasonal vibrations can be very effective. For instance, springtime chants might focus on new beginnings in love, while winter chants might concentrate on deepening and nurturing existing bonds.

By tapping into the vibrational science behind chants, practitioners of love magic can significantly enhance their spellwork. This method involves more than just reciting words; it's about consciously syncing with the universe's vibrational frequencies to maximize the power and effectiveness of your magical practices.

The Art of Incantation

The art of incantation in love magic is a profound practice that goes beyond mere recitation of words. It is an intricate blend of art, emotion, and intent, deeply rooted in the understanding that our voices can connect us to the most fundamental energies of the universe. Chants and incantations in love magic are not just tools for manifesting desires; they are expressions of our deepest yearnings, harmonizing our personal vibrations with the universal energies of love and connection.

At its core, incantation is a form of magic that harnesses the power of spoken words to influence the fabric of reality. The rhythmic and intentional use of language, combined with the powerful vibrational qualities of the human voice, creates a unique form of energy. This energy, when directed with clarity and purpose, can open channels of communication with the universe, inviting the energies of love and affection into our lives.

In practice, the art of incantation requires more than just speaking; it necessitates a deep, heartfelt connection to the words being spoken. Each syllable, each vibration, is imbued with the caster's desires, emotions, and intentions. This personal connection is what turns a simple phrase into a potent magical formula. It transforms the chant from a sequence of words into a living, breathing expression of the heart's deepest desires.

Furthermore, the practice of chanting in love magic is an exercise in aligning one's personal energy with the greater energies of the cosmos. It is a dance of frequencies where the individual's intentions meet the vast, boundless forces of love that permeate the universe. This alignment not only amplifies the power of the spell but also fosters a deeper sense of connection and unity with the world around us.

In conclusion, the art of incantation in love magic is a powerful and transformative practice. It is a journey of self-discovery, a way to tap into the deep reservoirs of personal power, and a means to harmonize our desires with the universal forces of love and connection. As practitioners of love magic, we engage in this art not only to shape our external realities but also to connect with the profound and mystical energies that govern our world.

CHAPTER 8.

MANIFESTING SELF-LOVE AND CONFIDENCE

In the magical journey of love, self-love stands as a pillar, fundamental and transformative. The introduction of self-love into magical practices is not just an act of self-care; it's a profound recognition of one's worth and a celebration of individuality. This chapter is an invitation to explore the depths of self-love and its manifestation in your magical practice. It's about empowering yourself to be the best version of you, not just in romance but in all areas of life.

The Importance of Self-Love

Self-love in magic is more than a concept; it's a vital practice. It forms the bedrock upon which all other forms of love are built. When we cultivate love within ourselves, it radiates outward, affecting every aspect of our lives. This internal reservoir of love empowers us to attract and nurture healthier relationships, make choices that align with our true selves, and engage with the world from a place of strength and authenticity. In love magic, self-love acts as a catalyst, amplifying the power and effectiveness of spells and rituals. It invites a deeper connection with the energies around us and within us, creating a harmonious balance that enhances every magical endeavor.

Self-Love vs. Selfishness

Understanding the difference between self-love and selfishness is crucial. Self-love is an act of kindness towards oneself. It's recognizing and honoring your needs, setting healthy boundaries, and treating yourself with the same compassion and understanding that you offer to others. It's a nurturing force, encouraging growth and fostering a sense of inner peace.

Conversely, selfishness stems from a place of fear and insecurity. It's an excessive focus on oneself to the detriment of others, often driven by unmet needs or a lack of fulfillment. Self-love, in contrast, is about fulfillment from within, creating a wellspring of love that naturally extends to others.

Principles of Self-Love Magic

Self-love magic is a journey inward, a path to understanding and embracing your intrinsic worth. It's about recognizing the unique magic within you and using it to enhance your life. Here, we explore the foundational principles that guide this transformative practice.

Understanding Personal Worth

At the heart of self-love magic is the recognition of your inherent value. This understanding is crucial, as it sets the stage for all the magical work you do for yourself. It's about seeing and accepting who you are—flaws and all—and understanding that your worth is not determined by external validation or achievements. Your worth is a given; it's non-negotiable and independent of any conditions.

To cultivate this understanding, begin by reflecting on your qualities and accomplishments, no matter how small they may seem. Practice self-affirmation, acknowledging your strengths, talents, and the unique qualities that make you who you are. Remember, acknowledging your worth doesn't mean you're flawless. It means accepting yourself as a beautifully complex individual who is deserving of love and respect.

Aligning Intentions for Self-Love

Intention-setting is a powerful tool in self-love magic. It involves directing your focus and energy towards specific aspects of self-compassion, acceptance, and confidence-building. When setting intentions for self-love, it's important to be specific and authentic. Instead of vague desires, pinpoint exactly what aspect of self-love you wish to enhance. Is it self-acceptance, self-esteem, body positivity, or emotional resilience?

As you set these intentions, visualize them taking root within you and manifesting in your daily life. Use affirmations to reinforce these intentions, repeating them daily to embed them into your subconscious. For instance, if your intention is to cultivate self-acceptance, an affirmation could be, "I am whole and complete just as I am."

Remember, the power of intention in self-love magic lies in its consistency and your belief in it. Aligning your intentions with self-love means committing to a practice that honors and nurtures your inner self. This practice isn't a one-time event but an ongoing process of growth and self-discovery. As you continue on this path, you'll find that self-love becomes not just a part of your magical practice but a way of life.

Self-Love Rituals and Spells

The practice of self-love in magic is enriched through specific rituals and spells that focus on affirming one's value and fostering a deep sense of personal acceptance. Here we will explore some effective rituals and spells that can be easily incorporated into your daily routine to strengthen self-love.

Daily Affirmations and Mantras

These affirmations for self-worth and mantras for inner peace can be repeated to yourself in the mirror, during meditations or at quiet moments throughout the day.

10 Affirmations for Self-Worth:

1. "I am deserving of love, happiness, and success."
2. "My worth is inherent and immeasurable."
3. "I am a unique and valuable presence in this world."
4. "I respect my boundaries and honor my soul's needs."
5. "I am worthy of my dreams and ambitions."
6. "My contributions to the world are valuable and significant."
7. "I am capable of overcoming any challenges that come my way."
8. "I am deserving of respect and kindness from myself and others."
9. "My value is not defined by external achievements or validations."
10. "I embrace my strengths and accept my vulnerabilities."

10 Mantras for Inner Peace:

1. "Peace begins within me; I choose serenity."
2. "With each breath, I release anxiety and welcome calmness."
3. "I am centered, peaceful, and grounded."
4. "In this moment, I choose to let go of worry and embrace tranquility."
5. "Harmony is my natural state; I return to it effortlessly."
6. "I trust the journey of life and find peace in its flow."
7. "I am a beacon of peace and calm in a chaotic world."
8. "My heart is a sanctuary of peace; I dwell in its calm."
9. "I release thoughts that do not serve me and embrace peacefulness."
10. "I am connected to the tranquil rhythm of the universe."

Incorporate these affirmations and mantras into your daily routine. Repeat them during your morning ritual, while commuting, or before going to sleep. The key is consistency - the more frequently you affirm these positive messages, the more deeply they are ingrained.

The Mirror Gazing Ritual

The mirror gazing ritual is a simple yet profound practice for fostering self-acceptance and love. This ritual involves more than just looking at your reflection; it's an opportunity for deep self-connection and healing.

1. **Setting the Scene**: Choose a time and place where you won't be disturbed. Ensure the lighting is soft and conducive to a relaxed atmosphere. You might want to light a candle or have some gentle music playing in the background to create a soothing environment.
2. **Commencing the Ritual**: Stand or sit comfortably in front of a mirror. Begin by taking several deep breaths to center yourself. Let go of any tension in your body and clear your mind of the day's worries.
3. **Eye Contact**: Gently bring your gaze to your eyes in the mirror. Maintain eye contact with yourself. It may feel awkward or challenging at first, but allow yourself to really see and be seen by your own gaze.
4. **Offering Words of Love and Acceptance**: As you look into your eyes, start to speak words of love and acceptance to yourself. These can be affirmations you've prepared, or simply what comes to your heart in the moment. Phrases like "I love and accept you exactly as you are" or "You are worthy

of love and joy" can be powerful. You might say, "I love and accept my body as it is" or "My strength is in my uniqueness."

5. **Deepening the Connection**: With each affirmation, allow the meaning of the words to sink in deeply. Notice any emotional responses that arise. It's common to feel a range of emotions during this practice, from discomfort to profound love and acceptance.
6. **Ending the Ritual**: Spend as long as you feel necessary in this practice. When you're ready to finish, take a few deep breaths, and express gratitude to yourself for taking this time for self-connection. Gently close the ritual by blowing out the candle or simply stepping away from the mirror with a sense of closure.

Regular practice of the mirror gazing ritual can lead to significant shifts in how you see and treat yourself. This practice helps in breaking down negative self-perceptions and building a more loving and accepting relationship with yourself. It's a journey towards embracing your true reflection—beyond the physical appearance—to the beautiful soul that resides within.

Self-Acceptance and Self-Love Spell

This simple spell is designed to enhance self-acceptance and foster a deeper sense of self-love. It uses basic elements and can be performed easily, making it perfect for beginners or those new to the practice of self-love magic.

You Will Need:

- A small mirror
- Rose quartz crystal (for love and self-compassion)

- Lavender or rose oil (for calming and heart-opening properties)
- Pink candle (symbolizing love and affection)
- Paper and pen

The Spell:

1. **Preparation**: Find a quiet space where you won't be disturbed. Cleanse the area, yourself, and your tools with sage or simply by visualizing a bright light removing any negative energy.
2. **Anointing the Candle**: Take the lavender or rose oil and anoint the pink candle, starting from the base to the wick, while focusing on your intention for self-love and acceptance.
3. **Crystal and Mirror Placement**: Place the rose quartz on or near the mirror. This arrangement will help to reflect and amplify the loving energy of the crystal.
4. **Lighting the Candle**: Light the pink candle, focusing on your intention to open your heart to self-love and acceptance.
5. **Writing Affirmations**: On the paper, write down affirmations of self-love and acceptance. These could be statements like "I am worthy of love and happiness" or "I accept myself unconditionally."
6. **Mirror Gazing**: Hold the mirror in your hands and gaze into your eyes. Recite the affirmations aloud, really feeling the truth of the words as you say them. Allow yourself to feel the love and acceptance flowing through you.
7. **Meditation with Rose Quartz**: Hold the rose quartz in your hands, close your eyes, and meditate on the feeling of love and acceptance. Visualize a pink light emanating from the stone, surrounding you with warmth and affection.

8. **Concluding the Spell**: Once you feel the ritual is complete, blow out the candle. You can carry the rose quartz with you or place it in a special area to remind you of the love you hold for yourself.
9. **Storing the Affirmations**: Fold the paper with your affirmations and keep it in a safe place, such as under your pillow or in a drawer, as a reminder of your commitment to self-love.

Through these rituals and spells, you can deepen your connection with yourself, fostering a sense of love and acceptance that radiates from within. Remember, the journey of self-love is ongoing. It's about making a conscious choice every day to honor and cherish yourself. By integrating these practices into your life, you're not just performing a spell; you're weaving a tapestry of self-love that supports and enriches every aspect of your being.

Spells for Confidence and Courage

Boosting confidence and courage through magic can help you overcome fears, take on new challenges, and embrace your true potential. Here are three spells specifically crafted to enhance these qualities.

1. Lionheart Courage Spell

You Will Need:

- A red candle (for strength and courage)
- Bay leaves (for victory and protection)
- A small piece of carnelian or tiger's eye (for confidence)
- A piece of paper and a pen

The Spell:

1. **Candle Preparation**: Carve your name and the word "courage" onto the red candle.
2. **Crystal Charging**: Hold the carnelian or tiger's eye in your hand, envisioning it filling with bright, empowering light. Place it in front of the candle.
3. **Writing Intentions**: On the paper, write down the areas in which you seek courage and confidence.
4. **Bay Leaves Placement**: Place the bay leaves around the candle.
5. **Lighting the Candle**: Light the candle, focusing on your intention to be filled with bravery and self-assurance.
6. **Chant for Courage**: Repeat a simple chant like, "With strength of lion, heart so bold, I claim the power that I hold."
7. **Candle Meditation**: Meditate on the flame, visualizing yourself facing and overcoming your fears confidently.
8. **Closing the Spell**: Let the candle burn out safely. Carry the crystal with you for an added boost of confidence.

2. Warrior's Confidence Amulet

You Will Need:

- A small cloth pouch
- Basil leaves (for courage and protection)
- A small piece of sunstone (for personal power)
- Lavender (for calmness and clarity)

The Spell:

1. **Amulet Creation**: Place the basil leaves, sunstone, and lavender in the cloth pouch.

2. **Charging the Amulet**: Hold the pouch in your hands, envisioning it glowing with a bright, empowering light.
3. **Affirmation of Power**: Say aloud, "I am strong, I am brave, I am powerful and wise."
4. **Sealing the Amulet**: Tie the pouch securely.
5. **Carrying the Amulet**: Keep this amulet with you, especially in situations where you need an extra boost of confidence.

3. Solar Plexus Chakra Spell

You Will Need:

- A yellow candle (for personal power)
- Lemon essential oil (for clarity and focus)
- A piece of citrine (for self-esteem and empowerment)

The Spell:

1. **Anointing the Candle**: Anoint the yellow candle with lemon oil.
2. **Crystal Placement**: Place the citrine in front of the candle.
3. **Candle Lighting**: Light the candle, focusing on activating your solar plexus chakra, the center of personal power.
4. **Visualization**: Visualize a bright yellow light at your solar plexus, expanding and filling you with confidence and strength.
5. **Affirmation**: Repeat the affirmation, "I am powerful, I am worthy, I am confident in all I do."
6. **Candle Meditation**: Spend a few minutes meditating on the flame, feeling the energy of the citrine and the candle empowering your solar plexus chakra.

7. **Closing the Spell**: Let the candle burn out safely. Keep the citrine with you or place it in a space where you spend a lot of time.

These spells, when performed with intention and belief, will significantly boost your confidence and courage, empowering you to face life's challenges with a strong and assured heart.

Confidence-Boosting Oil Recipes

Creating magical oils specifically designed to boost confidence can be a rewarding and effective practice. Each recipe below is tailored to enhance self-assurance, courage, and strength in various aspects.

1. Empowerment Oil

Ingredients:

- 1/2 cup base oil (like almond or jojoba)
- 10 drops bergamot oil (for confidence and positivity)
- 5 drops ginger oil (for courage and success)
- 3 drops black pepper oil (for protection and strength)
- Small citrine or tiger's eye crystal (optional, for added empowerment)

Instructions:

1. **Blend the Oils**: In a clean bottle, combine the base oil with bergamot, ginger, and black pepper oils.
2. **Crystal Infusion**: If using, add a cleansed citrine or tiger's eye crystal to the bottle.
3. **Charge the Oil**: Hold the bottle and envision a bright light surrounding it, charging the oil with empowering energy.
4. **Resting Period**: Let the oil sit for at least 24 hours before use.

2. Self-Confidence Anointing Oil

Ingredients:

- 1/2 cup base oil (like olive or coconut)
- 8 drops cedarwood oil (for grounding and stability)
- 6 drops rosemary oil (for mental clarity and self-esteem)
- 4 drops lemon oil (for freshness and clarity)
- Small piece of clear quartz (for amplification)

Instructions:

1. **Combine Ingredients**: Mix the base oil with cedarwood, rosemary, and lemon oils in a glass bottle.
2. **Add Clear Quartz**: Place a small clear quartz in the bottle.
3. **Energize the Oil**: Visualize golden energy charging the oil with confidence and clarity.
4. **Mature the Oil**: Allow the oil to mature for a few days for the ingredients to synergize fully.

3. Boldness Boosting Oil

Ingredients:

- 1/2 cup grapeseed oil (for lightness and adaptability)
- 7 drops cinnamon oil (for warmth and stimulation)
- 5 drops ylang-ylang oil (for inner harmony and charisma)
- 3 drops peppermint oil (for energy and alertness)
- Small amethyst or lapis lazuli (for intuition and inner strength)

Instructions:

1. **Oil Mixture**: Mix grapeseed oil with cinnamon, ylang-ylang, and peppermint oils in a bottle.

2. **Crystal Enhancement**: Add an amethyst or lapis lazuli crystal for extra support.
3. **Activate the Oil**: Focus on infusing the mixture with intentions of boldness and bravery.
4. **Let It Blend**: Store in a cool, dark place for several days to blend the energies.

Using the Oils: These oils can be used to anoint yourself, especially on the wrists, behind the ears, and over the heart. They can also be used to anoint objects like amulets or talismans for continuous confidence support. Remember, the key to their effectiveness lies in your intention and belief in their power.

Overcoming Negative Self-Talk

Our internal dialogue significantly influences our emotional well-being and how we interact with the world. Thus, transforming negative patterns and healing past emotional wounds becomes an essential part of our magical practice.

Identifying and Transforming Negative Patterns

The first step in overcoming negative self-talk is to become aware of it. This often-subconscious dialogue can be a persistent echo of past criticisms or negative experiences. Start by paying attention to your thoughts. When you catch yourself engaging in negative self-talk, pause and examine the thought. Ask yourself, is this really true? More often than not, you'll find these thoughts are based on outdated beliefs or fears, not reality.

Transforming these patterns involves rewriting your internal narrative. One effective method is to use affirmations. For every negative thought, counteract it with a positive affirmation. For instance, if you find yourself thinking, "I am not good enough," immediately replace it with, "I am worthy and capable." It's also helpful to perform a daily ritual where you write down negative thoughts and then physically destroy the paper as a symbol of releasing these limiting beliefs.

Healing Rituals for Past Hurts

Past emotional wounds can be a significant source of negative self-talk. To heal these wounds, engage in rituals that promote emotional release and healing. A simple but powerful ritual is the 'Candle Release Ritual.' Light a blue candle (for healing) and write down the hurtful experiences or feelings on a piece of paper. As you burn the paper in the candle's flame, visualize the pain and hurt dissolving away with the smoke. Then, meditate on the flame, allowing its soothing light to fill the voids left by past hurts with love and peace.

Another healing ritual involves using rose quartz, known for its heart-healing properties. Create a sacred space, hold a rose quartz crystal, and visualize its gentle, pink energy washing over you, healing your emotional wounds. As you do this, recite affirmations of healing and self-love.

The Role of Self-Care in Magic

Self-care is not just a wellness trend; it's a vital practice that intertwines the care of the physical body with the nurturing of the soul. By incorporating magical elements into self-care routines, you create a holistic approach that enhances your overall well-being and strengthens your magical practice.

Magical Self-Care Practices

Self-care in magic involves rituals and routines that bring peace, balance, and rejuvenation to both your physical and spiritual self.

A popular magical self-care practice is the ritual bath. Infuse your bathwater with salts, herbs, and essential oils that correspond with love and self-acceptance, such as rose petals for love, lavender for relaxation, and chamomile for inner peace. As you soak, visualize the water cleansing away any negative energy and filling you with self-love and confidence.

Another practice is anointing yourself with oils specifically crafted for self-love. Use oils infused with herbs like rose, jasmine, or vanilla. As you apply the oil, focus on affirming your worth and loving yourself unconditionally.

Creating a sacred space solely for yourself is also a form of magical self-care. Dedicate a corner of your home for meditation, reflection, or journaling. Adorn it with items that bring you joy and peace, like crystals, candles, and images that represent love and happiness.

Nurturing the Body and Soul

In the journey towards self-love, it's important to remember that taking care of your physical body is as crucial as nurturing your soul. This holistic approach ensures that your magical practices are grounded in a well-cared-for physical vessel. Engage in activities that nourish your body, like gentle exercise, eating nourishing foods, and getting enough rest. Treat these activities as rituals; for example, as you prepare a meal, infuse it with intentions of health and self-care.

On a soul level, engage in practices that fill you with joy and peace. This could be spending time in nature, practicing yoga, meditating, or engaging in creative activities like painting or writing. These practices help to align your energy and keep you connected to your inner self.

By integrating these magical self-care practices into your daily life, you not only enhance your physical and emotional well-being but also deepen your connection to the magic within you. This approach to self-care reinforces the belief that taking care of yourself is a fundamental act of self-love, which in turn, strengthens your overall magical practice. Remember, the magic you wield starts with the love and care you give to yourself.

Self-Love in Relationships

The journey towards self-love significantly impacts the quality and nature of our relationships. By cultivating a sense of wholeness within ourselves, we not only attract healthier partnerships but also foster a loving environment where personal boundaries are respected and cherished.

Attracting Love from a Place of Wholeness

The first step in attracting love is to become a source of love for yourself. When you nurture self-love, you create a foundation of confidence and self-respect, which radiates outward. This inner wholeness becomes a magnet for relationships that mirror these qualities. Magic focused on self-love can help reinforce these energies, making you more attractive to potential partners who value and respect your sense of self.

Incorporating self-love rituals, affirmations, and spells into your daily practice can shift your energy from seeking love to attract love. These practices help to break patterns of attracting relationships based on neediness or a sense of incompleteness, paving the way for connections that arise from a place of mutual respect and admiration.

Setting Boundaries with Love

Setting boundaries is an essential aspect of self-love and is crucial for maintaining healthy relationships. In the practice of love magic, setting boundaries is not just about saying 'no' or keeping others at a distance; it's about defining your personal space and what you are comfortable with, allowing relationships to flourish within these healthy parameters.

A magical approach to setting boundaries might involve rituals that affirm your personal space and protect your energy. For instance, a simple boundary-setting spell could involve visualizing a protective circle around you, affirming that only love and positivity may enter this space. You could also create an amulet or talisman charged with the intention of maintaining your boundaries.

Regularly practicing these rituals strengthens your resolve to maintain healthy boundaries, ensuring that your relationships are respectful, nurturing, and supportive. It's important to remember that boundaries are not barriers to love; instead, they are the framework within which genuine love and respect can grow.

By focusing on self-love and the magic of setting healthy boundaries, you empower yourself to attract and nurture relationships that reflect your inner wholeness. This approach to love magic underscores the idea that the most potent spell for attracting love starts with loving yourself.

CHAPTER 9.

BALANCING LOVE ENERGIES

In the intricate tapestry of love magic, the balance of energies plays a pivotal role. This chapter delves into the art of maintaining harmony within relationships through magical practices, offering insights into the subtle yet profound ways energy influences our connections with others.

The essence of balance in love magic cannot be overstated. It's the equilibrium that allows relationships to flourish, ensuring that love, like a dance, is a mutual exchange of give and take. This balance is not just a concept but a living, breathing aspect of our interactions. It manifests in the way we give and receive love, the respect we show for each other's space and individuality, and in the deep, unspoken understanding that forms the foundation of any lasting relationship.

The role of energy balance in love magic is to harmonize these dynamics. It's about aligning our own energies with those of our partners or desired relationships in a way that promotes mutual growth and understanding. Spells and rituals centered around love are most effective when they are crafted with this sense of balance in mind. They become not just tools for attraction or affection but for nurturing a profound and enduring connection.

Understanding Energetic Exchange

At the heart of every relationship is the concept of energetic exchange. This exchange is the invisible yet powerful force that binds people together. It's the warmth you feel in a loved one's embrace, the comfort in their presence, and the unspoken understanding that you are in a safe space. In love magic, acknowledging and respecting this exchange is crucial.

A balanced energetic exchange ensures that both parties in a relationship are not just taking but also giving back. It's about creating a cycle of positive energy that flows seamlessly between individuals. In a magical context, this means crafting spells and conducting rituals that consider the needs and well-being of all involved. It's about sending out energies that attract love in a way that is healthy, respectful, and harmonious.

As we delve deeper into this chapter, we will explore various practices and considerations for maintaining a healthy balance of energies in love magic. From understanding the subtle nuances of energetic interactions to creating spells that foster equilibrium, this chapter will guide you in harnessing the power of balance to enhance your love-related practices. Remember, in the dance of love, harmony in energies is the music that guides our steps.

Techniques for Balancing Energies

The harmony of energy is essential for fostering fulfilling relationships. This section focuses on techniques like meditation and chakra work, which are powerful tools in achieving and maintaining this balance.

Meditations for Harmony

Meditation is a deeply effective practice for attaining a state of inner balance, and when it comes to relationships, it can help align your energies with those of your partner or desired love.

Heart-Centered Meditation

1. **Finding a Quiet Space**: Choose a quiet, comfortable spot where you won't be disturbed. Sit or lie down in a relaxed position.

2. **Breathing and Centering**: Start with deep, slow breaths. Inhale tranquility and exhale any tension or stress.
3. **Focusing on the Heart Chakra**: Place your hand over your heart to connect physically with your heart chakra. This chakra is the epicenter of love, compassion, and understanding.
4. **Visualizing the Energy**: Close your eyes and visualize a radiant light in the color of soft green or pink emanating from your heart center. With each inhale, see this light grow brighter and more vibrant.
5. **Expanding the Energy**: Imagine this light expanding beyond your body, creating a warm, loving aura around you. Feel it radiating love, empathy, and compassion.
6. **Setting Intentions**: Silently or aloud, affirm your intentions of unconditional love and empathy for yourself and others. Repeat affirmations like, "I am love, I receive love, I give love unconditionally."
7. **Closing the Meditation**: Gradually bring your focus back to your breath. Gently open your eyes, carrying the warmth and love of the meditation with you.

Harmonizing Meditation

1. **Creating a Calm Environment**: Find a peaceful area where you can meditate without interruption. Sit in a comfortable position and take a few deep breaths to relax.
2. **Visualizing Harmonious Energy**: Picture yourself and your partner or intended love in a serene setting, bathed in a soft, harmonious light.
3. **Intertwining Energies**: Envision both of your energies, represented by gentle glows, slowly reaching out to each

other. See them intertwining gracefully, symbolizing a balanced exchange of love, understanding, and respect.

4. **Feeling the Connection**: Focus on the sensation of your energies mingling. Feel the harmony, balance, and mutual understanding growing between you.
5. **Affirming the Harmonious Bond**: Use affirmations to reinforce this connection. You might say, "Our energies harmonize and strengthen our bond, bringing mutual understanding and respect."
6. **Gently Concluding the Meditation**: Slowly draw back your energy, visualizing it returning to you, enriched by the harmonious exchange. Take a deep breath, open your eyes, and carry this sense of balanced connection into your day.

Chakra Work for Relationship Balance

Chakras, the energy centers in our body, play a significant role in how we connect with others. Balancing these can lead to healthier and more harmonious relationships.

Heart Chakra Alignment

1. **Selecting the Right Crystals**: Choose crystals like rose quartz for unconditional love or green aventurine for emotional healing. These crystals resonate strongly with the heart chakra.
2. **Preparing for Meditation**: Find a peaceful space where you won't be disturbed. Lie down comfortably and place the chosen crystal over your heart center.
3. **Activating the Heart Chakra**: Close your eyes and focus on your breath. Visualize a soft green or pink light emanating

from the crystal, seeping into your heart chakra. This light represents love, healing, and compassion.

4. **Chakra Balancing Visualization**: Imagine this light spreading throughout your chest, balancing and healing your heart chakra. Feel any emotional blockages dissolving, making way for love and understanding.
5. **Heart Chakra Affirmations**: Silently recite affirmations such as, "My heart is open to giving and receiving love," or "I am deserving of healthy, balanced love."
6. **Concluding the Session**: After spending several minutes in this meditative state, gently remove the crystal. Take a few deep breaths, open your eyes, and sit up slowly. Carry the sense of love and balance with you throughout your day.

Sacral Chakra Healing

1. **Choosing Sacral Crystals**: Opt for crystals like orange calcite for emotional balance or carnelian for passion and intimacy. These resonate with the sacral chakra's energy.
2. **Setting Up the Meditation Area**: Create a calm environment, ideally in a place where you feel comfortable and relaxed. Lie down and place your chosen crystal just below your navel.
3. **Activating the Sacral Chakra**: Focus on your breathing, and as you inhale, visualize an orange light emanating from the crystal, energizing your sacral chakra.
4. **Emotional Connection Visualization**: Picture this warm orange light expanding, filling your lower abdomen with a sense of balance, creativity, and emotional connection.
5. **Sacral Chakra Affirmations**: Use affirmations like, "I embrace my emotions and form healthy relationships," or

"My emotions are balanced and in harmony with my well-being."

6. **Ending the Meditation**: Spend a few more minutes absorbing the crystal's energy. Then, gently remove the crystal, take deep breaths, and open your eyes. Feel refreshed and emotionally balanced as you rise.

By incorporating these meditations and chakra work into your regular practice, you can significantly enhance the balance of energies in your relationships. Remember, the goal is not to control or alter the other person's energy but to harmonize your own, creating a resonant and mutually fulfilling connection.

Spellwork for Energy Equilibrium

The spells and rituals in this section are designed with the specific intention of harmonizing and balancing the energies within relationships. They cater to different aspects of a relationship's energetic dynamics, from enhancing mutual understanding and cooperation to releasing excess emotional energies that might be hindering the natural flow of love and communication.

Approach these spells with an open heart and a clear intention, and let the magic guide you towards a more balanced and harmonious state of being in your relationships.

Spells for Harmonizing Relationships

1. **Dual Candle Harmony Spell**:
   - **Purpose**: To balance and harmonize the energy within a relationship.

- **Materials**: Two candles (one representing you and the other your partner), lavender oil, and a small piece of rose quartz.
- **Method**: Anoint both candles with lavender oil. Place them side by side and put the rose quartz between them. As you light the candles, visualize a harmonious balance of energy flowing between you and your partner. Chant, "Balance and harmony, flow in unity, as these candles burn, so our energies turn towards peace and understanding."
- **Closing**: Let the candles burn out safely. Carry the rose quartz as a reminder of the harmony you seek.

2. **Harmony Knot Spell**:
    - **Purpose**: To strengthen understanding and cooperation in a relationship.
    - **Materials**: A length of ribbon or cord.
    - **Method**: As you tie nine knots in the ribbon, with each knot, state an aspect of your relationship you wish to harmonize, like communication, love, or respect.
    - **Closing**: Place the knotted ribbon in a safe space or carry it with you to maintain harmonious energy.

3. **Equilibrium Water Spell**:
    - **Purpose**: To cleanse and balance the emotional energies in a relationship.
    - **Materials**: A bowl of water, sea salt, and two rose petals.
    - **Method**: Dissolve sea salt in water. Place a rose petal representing each partner in the bowl. Gently stir the

water while visualizing any imbalances in your relationship dissolving away.

- **Closing**: Pour the water and petals outside, returning the energy to nature in a balanced state.

Rituals for Releasing Excess Energy

1. **Emotional Release Stone Ritual**:
   - **Purpose**: To release overwhelming emotions and restore balance.
   - **Materials**: A stone or crystal, like hematite or black tourmaline.
   - **Method**: Hold the stone in your hand, pouring all excess emotional energy into it. Visualize the stone absorbing this energy, leaving you feeling balanced.
   - **Closing**: Place the stone under the moonlight overnight to cleanse it.

2. **Soothing Wind Ritual**:
   - **Purpose**: To release and transform excessive emotional energies.
   - **Materials**: A feather, an open space, and a small bell.
   - **Method**: Hold the feather and bell, and as you walk around your space, gently ring the bell, imagining the sound waves carrying away excess energy. Use the feather to guide the energy out.
   - **Closing**: Place the feather outside to let the wind carry away the residual energies.

3. **Cleansing Fire Ritual**:
   - **Purpose**: To burn away overwhelming emotions and restore calm.
   - **Materials**: A fire-safe bowl, a piece of paper, and a lighter or matches.
   - **Method**: Write down the emotions you wish to release on the paper. Carefully burn the paper in the bowl, visualizing the flames transforming your emotional energy into smoke and releasing it.
   - **Closing**: Dispose of the ashes outside, symbolizing the release of these emotions into the universe.

Practicing these spells and rituals can significantly contribute to maintaining a balanced emotional state, both within yourself and in your relationships. Remember, the key is to approach these practices with a clear intention and a calm mind, allowing the magic to work towards restoring equilibrium in your energies.

Balancing Individuality with Togetherness

In the dance of love and relationships, striking the right balance between togetherness and individuality is key. It's essential to cherish the shared moments while also respecting and nurturing each partner's need for personal space and individuality. This balance prevents the relationship from becoming stifling or codependent.

To support this delicate balance, certain spells and rituals can be particularly effective. For example, a simple boundary-setting spell could involve creating a personal talisman charged with the intent of maintaining one's individuality while fostering mutual respect and understanding. Another approach could be a ritual to reinforce personal energy fields, ensuring that both partners can enjoy shared spaces without losing their sense of self.

Handling Energy Vampirism

An important aspect of energy balance in relationships is recognizing and protecting oneself from energy vampirism. This term refers to dynamics where one partner consistently drains the energy of the other, leaving them feeling depleted.

Identifying such patterns is the first step towards addressing them. Once recognized, protective spells and the use of amulets can be effective. For instance, creating a protective amulet with crystals like black tourmaline or hematite can help shield you from energy-draining dynamics. Rituals that cleanse your aura and reinforce your energetic boundaries can also be instrumental in dealing with such situations.

Maintaining Long-Term Balance

In long-term relationships, maintaining an energetic balance is an ongoing process. As partners grow and evolve, so do the dynamics of the relationship. Regular rituals that focus on harmonizing energies can be immensely beneficial. These rituals might involve periodic energy cleansing of shared spaces, reaffirming intentions and goals together, or even meditations focused on deepening mutual understanding and empathy.

Adapting to the evolving nature of a relationship is also crucial. This might mean altering your rituals and spells to align with new phases in your life together. The key is to stay attuned to each other's energies and needs, adapting your magical practices to support the growth and deepening of your bond.

The Continual Practice of Balancing Energies

As we conclude our exploration of balancing love energies, it's vital to recognize that this is not a one-time task, but an ongoing journey integral to nurturing healthy and fulfilling relationships. The equilibrium of energies in love is a delicate dance, one that requires continuous attention, understanding, and effort.

Relationships are dynamic and ever-evolving, shaped by the energies we and our partners bring into them. As such, the practice of balancing these energies should be seen as a fundamental aspect of a healthy relationship. It's about constantly tuning into each other's needs, adapting to changes, and being mindful of how energies flow between you. Whether through meditative practices, spellwork, or simple daily gestures, maintaining this balance is key to a relationship's longevity and happiness.

Remember, the goal of balancing energies isn't to achieve a static state of harmony but to cultivate a relationship where there is a mutual give and take, a place where both partners feel heard, understood, and valued. It's about creating a space where individual energies complement and enhance each other, leading to a deeper, more meaningful connection.

Incorporate the practices and insights from this chapter into your relationship, and let them guide you towards a more balanced and fulfilling partnership. With every spell cast, every ritual performed, and every moment of understanding and empathy shared, you strengthen the bonds of love and harmony. Embrace this journey with an open heart, and let the magic of balanced energies enrich your love and your life.

CHAPTER 10.

NAVIGATING LOVE CHALLENGES WITH MAGIC

In the journey of love, encountering challenges is as inevitable as the changing tides. Every relationship, no matter how strong, faces its share of obstacles and complexities. These challenges, ranging from communication breakdowns to the fading of passion, or the interference of external factors, are not just hurdles to be overcome; they are opportunities for growth and deepening bonds.

This chapter delves into the role that magic can play in navigating these challenges. The ancient art of love magic isn't just about attracting love or weaving spells of affection; it's also a powerful tool for addressing and resolving the issues that arise in the course of a relationship. When used wisely and ethically, love magic offers a unique pathway to understanding, healing, and strengthening the bonds of love.

As we explore the various aspects of relationship challenges, we'll learn how to apply specific spells, rituals, and meditations tailored to each situation. Whether it's a spell to enhance communication, a ritual to rekindle passion, or a protective charm against external negativity, the magical practices outlined here are designed to align with your intentions and the needs of your relationship.

However, it's crucial to approach these challenges with not just magical solutions but also with a heart open to understanding and empathy. The true essence of love magic in navigating relationship challenges lies in its ability to foster a deeper, more empathetic connection between partners. It's about using magic not as a quick fix but as a means to facilitate genuine understanding, healing, and emotional growth.

In this chapter, we'll guide you through using love magic responsibly and effectively to turn the challenges in your relationship into stepping stones towards a stronger, more harmonious bond.

Common Relationship Challenges

Relationships, in their essence, are complex and multifaceted, often presenting a variety of challenges that can test the strength and resilience of the bond between partners. Understanding these common issues is the first step in addressing them effectively, both magically and practically.

1. **Communication Issues**: Perhaps the most prevalent challenge in relationships is a breakdown in communication. Misunderstandings, assumptions, and unexpressed feelings can create barriers, leading to conflicts and a feeling of disconnect. Recognizing these patterns is crucial for finding ways to open and improve dialogue.
2. **Loss of Spark**: Over time, many relationships experience a diminishing of the initial passion and excitement. This 'loss of spark' can manifest as a sense of routine, boredom, or emotional distance. Reigniting this flame often involves exploring new avenues of connection and rediscovering each other in different contexts.
3. **Jealousy**: Jealousy in relationships often stems from insecurities, past traumas, or a lack of trust. It can lead to controlling behaviors, resentment, and a toxic cycle of accusations and guilt. Addressing the root causes of jealousy is essential for overcoming this challenge.
4. **External Interference**: Relationships do not exist in a vacuum; they are often influenced by external factors.

These could include family opinions, societal pressures, work stress, or even friendships that encroach on the relationship's boundaries. Navigating these external influences requires a balance of assertiveness and understanding.

5. **Incompatibility Issues**: Differences in values, goals, or lifestyles can sometimes lead to feelings of incompatibility. While diversity in a relationship can be enriching, stark contrasts might create friction. Finding common ground or mutual respect for differences is key to managing these issues.
6. **Emotional Disconnect**: An emotional disconnect can occur when partners feel emotionally unfulfilled or neglected. This might stem from not spending enough quality time together or not being emotionally available and supportive.

Each of these challenges, while potentially daunting, also presents an opportunity for growth and deepening the relationship. By identifying the specific issues you face, you can begin to apply targeted strategies, both magical and mundane, to address them effectively. The subsequent sections of this chapter will explore how specific spells and rituals can be aligned with these common relationship challenges to foster understanding, healing, and a stronger bond.

Communication Enhancement Spells

Communication is the lifeline of any relationship. It's the medium through which partners express their needs, desires, and concerns, and how they connect and understand each other on a deeper level. However, maintaining effective communication isn't always easy. Misunderstandings, unexpressed emotions, and barriers to open dialogue can often create gaps in a relationship. This is where the magic of communication enhancement spells comes into play.

In this section, we will introduce three carefully selected spells and rituals that are crafted to open lines of communication and foster understanding between partners. These spells are not just about compelling words to be spoken; they are about opening hearts, aligning energies, and creating a space where true listening and understanding can occur.

Each spell is designed to address different aspects of communication in a relationship. Whether you're facing difficulties in expressing your true feelings, finding yourself in a pattern of misunderstandings, or struggling with a partner who has closed off, these spells offer a magical helping hand. They work by energetically aligning both partners to a state of openness and empathy, paving the way for honest and heartfelt dialogue.

1. **"Speak from the Heart" Candle Ritual**:
    - **Purpose**: To encourage open and honest communication.
    - **Materials**: Blue candles (for truth), lavender oil (for calm communication), paper and pen.
    - **Method**: Anoint the candles with lavender oil and light them. Both partners write down what they wish to express. Fold the papers and place them under the candles. Visualize a calm, blue light enveloping both partners, fostering a space of truth and understanding.
    - **Conclusion**: After the candles burn down, discuss the contents of the papers openly and calmly.

2. **"Hear My True Intent" Herbal Sachet**:
    - **Purpose**: To promote understanding and clear up misunderstandings.
    - **Materials**: Dried lavender (for clarity), chamomile (for understanding), small sachet bags.
    - **Method**: Mix the herbs and fill the sachets. Each partner keeps a sachet with them, especially during conversations. The herbs work to clear the air and promote a deeper understanding of each other's words and intentions.
    - **Conclusion**: Regularly meditate with the sachet, focusing on understanding your partner's perspective.

3. **"Align Our Voices" Crystal Grid**:
    - **Purpose**: To harmonize communication energies between partners.
    - **Materials**: Aquamarine (for clear communication), rose quartz (for loving communication), clear quartz (to amplify intentions), a sacred space for the grid.
    - **Method**: Arrange the crystals in a grid that represents both partners and their shared communication path. Activate the grid with the intention of harmonizing your communication channels.
    - **Conclusion**: Meditate near the grid, visualizing both partners engaging in open, honest, and loving communication.

These spells are a blend of intention, natural elements, and the power of visualization. They are designed to be performed with respect, love, and the genuine desire for improved understanding and connection. Remember, the goal is not to force communication but to create a supportive environment where it can naturally flourish.

Rekindling Passion Rituals

Passion is the spark that ignites the fire in a relationship, but over time, this spark can sometimes dim, making way for routine or complacency. Rekindling the flame of passion and intimacy is not just about reigniting physical attraction; it's about reconnecting with the vibrant, emotional, and spiritual energies that initially brought two people together. In this section, we explore three powerful rituals designed to reignite these vital aspects of your relationship, fostering a renewed sense of passion and closeness.

1. **Candlelit Desire Ritual**
   - **Purpose**: To awaken the dormant flames of desire and intimacy.
   - **Materials**: Red candles (for passion), rose petals (for romance), ylang-ylang oil (for sensuality), a private, comfortable space.
   - **Method**: Create a circle with rose petals and place the red candles within it. Anoint the candles with ylang-ylang oil, invoking sensuality. Both partners sit within the circle, holding hands, and gaze into each other's eyes. Light the candles and take turns expressing desires and appreciations for each other.
   - **Conclusion**: Let the candles burn down safely. Conclude the ritual with a shared activity that both partners find connecting and intimate, like a slow dance or sharing a glass of wine.

2. **Sensual Bathing Ceremony**
   - **Purpose**: To create a space of relaxation and openness, fostering deeper emotional and physical connection.

- **Materials**: Warm bathwater, essential oils like jasmine or sandalwood (for sensuality), Epsom salts (for relaxation), soft music, and dim lighting.
- **Method**: Prepare the bath with the essential oils and Epsom salts. Both partners should enter the bath together, focusing on relaxing and letting go of daily stresses. Use this time to communicate openly, sharing feelings and thoughts that often go unspoken.
- **Conclusion**: After the bath, continue the night with activities that both partners find romantic and intimate, reinforcing the connection established during the ceremony.

3. **Passion Igniting Crystal Grid**
   - **Purpose**: To energetically align both partners to the frequency of passion and intimacy.
   - **Materials**: Crystals like garnet (for passion), tiger's eye (for sensuality), and rose quartz (for emotional connection), a sacred space for the grid.
   - **Method**: Arrange the crystals in a heart-shaped grid. As both partners work on the grid, focus on setting intentions for reigniting passion. Once the grid is complete, meditate together near it, visualizing a glowing energy of passion enveloping the relationship.
   - **Conclusion**: Keep the grid intact in a shared space to continually radiate its passionate energy. Regularly spend time near the grid, reiterating your intentions and nurturing the rekindled energy.

These rituals are designed to create an atmosphere where passion can flourish anew. They combine the magical properties of natural elements with the power of intention and shared experiences, creating a fertile ground for renewed intimacy and connection. Remember, the most important part of these rituals is the genuine desire and effort from both partners to rekindle their passion and deepen their bond.

Healing from Emotional Wounds

Every relationship is a tapestry woven from the threads of both partners' pasts. At times, this past includes emotional wounds and baggage that, if left unaddressed, can impact the present relationship. Healing from these past hurts is not only crucial for personal well-being but also for the health of the relationship. In this section, we focus on three spells and meditations designed to facilitate this healing process, helping individuals and couples to release emotional baggage and move forward with a renewed sense of clarity and connection.

1. **Heart Chakra Healing Meditation**
    - **Purpose**: To open and heal the heart chakra, the center of emotional processing and healing.
    - **Method**: Find a quiet, comfortable space for meditation. Visualize a bright, healing green light at the center of your chest, growing with each breath. As you focus on this light, allow it to gently dissolve any pain or hurt residing in your heart. Envision these negative emotions leaving your body and being replaced with love and healing energy.

- **Materials**: Green aventurine or rose quartz crystals, soothing background music, and a comfortable sitting position.
- **Conclusion**: Conclude the meditation by journaling your feelings and experiences. Acknowledge the emotional release and affirm your journey towards emotional healing and openness.

2. **Cleansing Ritual for Emotional Baggage**
   - **Purpose**: To symbolically and energetically cleanse past emotional wounds.
   - **Materials**: White candles (for purification), sage or palo santo (for cleansing), a bowl of water (for emotional release), and a quiet, private space.
   - **Method**: Light the candles and sage or palo santo. Pass the bowl of water over the smoke, charging it with cleansing energy. Hold the bowl and reflect on past hurts, allowing yourself to feel and acknowledge them. Then, gently pour the water onto the ground outside, symbolizing the release of these emotions.
   - **Conclusion**: Spend a few moments in quiet reflection or meditation, feeling the lightness and relief from releasing emotional baggage. Affirm your commitment to moving forward with a healed and open heart.

3. **Forgiveness Spell for Self and Others**
   - **Purpose**: To foster forgiveness, both for oneself and others, as a crucial step in emotional healing.
   - **Materials**: Lavender (for peace), a small piece of paper, a pen, and a fire-safe bowl or cauldron.

- **Method**: Write down the names or situations that require forgiveness on the paper. Light the lavender and use its smoke to bathe the paper, infusing it with energies of peace and forgiveness. Carefully burn the paper in the bowl or cauldron, visualizing the act of burning as a release of the burden of these past hurts.
- **Conclusion**: As the paper turns to ash, feel the weight of past grievances lifting. Conclude with a personal affirmation of forgiveness and a commitment to emotional freedom and healing.

These spells and meditations are crafted to assist in the delicate process of emotional healing. By addressing past wounds and working to release them, individuals and couples can create a stronger, more resilient foundation for their relationship, one that is based on mutual understanding, compassion, and a shared journey towards healing and growth.

Overcoming Jealousy and Insecurity

Jealousy and insecurity, while common emotions, can create significant challenges in relationships. They often stem from deep-seated fears and past experiences and can lead to destructive behaviors if not managed healthily. Addressing these feelings requires a combination of self-reflection, open communication, and magical practices. This section presents three techniques and three spells specifically designed to help individuals deal with jealousy and insecurity constructively and transform these emotions into opportunities for personal growth and relationship strengthening.

Techniques to Manage Jealousy and Insecurity

1. **Mindful Reflection**: Regularly practice mindfulness to become aware of when jealousy and insecurity arise. Reflect on the root causes of these feelings. Are they based on current relationship dynamics, or do they stem from past experiences or personal fears?
2. **Open Communication**: Foster an environment where you can openly discuss feelings of jealousy or insecurity with your partner. Expressing these feelings in a safe space can prevent misunderstandings and help both partners understand and support each other better.
3. **Affirmation and Visualization**: Use affirmations and visualization techniques to reinforce self-worth and trust in the relationship. Visualize a scenario where you feel secure and loved, and regularly affirm your value and the strength of your relationship.

Spells to Overcome Jealousy and Insecurity

1. **"Shield of Trust" Visualization Spell**
    - **Purpose**: To create a protective shield around the relationship, fostering trust and security.
    - **Materials**: Blue candles (for trust), a small mirror (to reflect back negative emotions), and lavender oil (for peace).
    - **Method**: Anoint the candles with lavender oil and light them. Hold the mirror and visualize a blue light emanating from it, forming a protective shield around you and your relationship. As you do this, chant, "With trust and love, we are secure, jealousy and fear, we endure and cure."

- **Conclusion**: Extinguish the candles and place the mirror in a shared space as a reminder of the protective shield.

2. **"Root of Confidence" Grounding Ritual**
   - **Purpose**: To ground yourself and strengthen inner confidence, reducing feelings of insecurity.
   - **Materials**: Red jasper or hematite stones (for grounding), earthy incense (like patchouli), and a quiet space for meditation.
   - **Method**: Hold the grounding stones and sit comfortably, focusing on your root chakra. Light the incense and meditate, visualizing roots growing from your base, anchoring you to the earth. As you meditate, repeat the affirmation, "I am grounded, I am secure, I am confident in my love pure."
   - **Conclusion**: Conclude the meditation feeling centered and secure. Keep the stones with you as a reminder of your inner strength and stability.

3. **"Balm of Harmony" Herbal Bath**
   - **Purpose**: To soothe feelings of jealousy and promote emotional balance.
   - **Materials**: Chamomile (for calm), rose petals (for love), and a warm bath.
   - **Method**: Prepare a bath and infuse it with chamomile and rose petals. As you soak, focus on the warm, comforting sensations, allowing them to wash away feelings of jealousy or insecurity. Visualize harmony and trust filling your heart.

- **Conclusion**: After the bath, feel refreshed and emotionally balanced. Affirm your commitment to nurturing a relationship based on trust and mutual respect.

These techniques and spells are designed to be part of a holistic approach to managing jealousy and insecurity. By combining practical self-reflection and communication strategies with the supportive power of magic, individuals can foster healthier emotional dynamics in their relationships, turning challenges into opportunities for deeper connection and understanding.

Dealing with External Influences

Relationships often exist within a complex web of external influences, ranging from family dynamics and societal pressures to external admirers and past connections. These influences, if not managed properly, can impose stress and negativity on a relationship. It's vital to establish protective boundaries to shield your relationship from these external factors. This section will guide you through three strategies, coupled with three spells, to safeguard your relationship from negative external influences, ensuring that it remains strong, healthy, and insulated from outside interference.

Strategies for Protecting Your Relationship

1. **Open and Honest Communication**: Establish a habit of open dialogue with your partner about external pressures. Whether it's family issues, social expectations, or past relationships, discussing these openly can preempt misunderstandings and strengthen mutual trust.
2. **United Front Approach**: Present a united front when dealing with external pressures. Make decisions together and support

each other in upholding these decisions, reinforcing the bond and commitment you share.

3. **Mindful Awareness of Influence**: Cultivate an awareness of how external factors are influencing your relationship. Acknowledge and address them consciously instead of allowing them to subtly erode the relationship's foundations.

Spells for Shielding and Boundary Setting

1. **"Circle of Protection" Ritual**
   - **Purpose**: To create a protective barrier around your relationship.
   - **Materials**: White candles (for protection), a circle of salt (for purity and boundaries), and a small item representing your relationship (like a photo or a shared keepsake).
   - **Method**: Arrange the candles in a circle around the item representing your relationship. Light the candles and pour a circle of salt around them, visualizing a protective barrier forming. Chant, "Around us now, a shield of light, protect our love, day and night."
   - **Conclusion**: Let the candles burn down safely within the circle. Keep the item in a safe place as a symbol of your protected relationship.

2. **"Boundary Stone" Setting Spell**
   - **Purpose**: To set clear energetic boundaries against negative external influences.
   - **Materials**: Black tourmaline or obsidian stones (for protective energy), paper to write down external influences, and a small bag or pouch.

- **Method**: Write down the external influences you wish to protect your relationship from on the paper. Place the paper and protective stones in the bag. Hold the bag and visualize these influences being absorbed and neutralized by the stones. Bury the bag outside your home as a symbol of setting boundaries.
- **Conclusion**: Feel the sense of security and peace as you set clear boundaries. Regularly cleanse and recharge the stones as needed.

3. **"Harmony Shield" Amulet Creation**
    - **Purpose**: To create an amulet that guards against discord and maintains harmony.
    - **Materials**: Blue lace agate or amethyst (for harmony and peace), small cloth pouches, and lavender oil (for calming).
    - **Method**: Anoint the stones with lavender oil and place them in the pouches. Hold the pouches and focus on your desire for a harmonious relationship, free from external turmoil. Keep the pouch with you, especially in situations where external influences are present.
    - **Conclusion**: The amulet serves as a constant reminder and source of protection against outside negativity, helping to maintain harmony in your relationship.

These strategies and spells are designed to fortify your relationship against external influences. By proactively addressing and protecting against these factors, you create a nurturing environment where your relationship can thrive, unaffected by external negativity and interference.

Self-Reflection and Inner Work

A healthy relationship is often a reflection of the health and harmony within each individual. Self-reflection and inner work are crucial for personal growth and self-awareness, which in turn can significantly strengthen a relationship. This section will focus on encouraging this personal journey, offering three spells designed to aid in introspection, self-love, and personal growth, all of which contribute to a stronger, more meaningful relationship.

Spells for Introspection and Self-Love

1. **"Mirror of the Soul" Reflection Spell**
    - **Purpose**: To enhance self-awareness and encourage honest self-reflection.
    - **Materials**: A mirror, a white candle (for clarity), and sage (for cleansing negative self-perceptions).
    - **Method**: Light the candle and sage, and sit before the mirror. Gaze into your reflection, allowing yourself to see beyond the physical. As you look into your own eyes, ask yourself questions about your desires, fears, and dreams. Use this time to confront truths about yourself, your past, and your aspirations.
    - **Conclusion**: Extinguish the candle and close the ritual with an affirmation of self-acceptance and commitment to personal growth.

2. **"Heart's Embrace" Self-Love Ritual**
    - **Purpose**: To cultivate self-love and acceptance.
    - **Materials**: Rose quartz (for self-love), lavender oil (for calming), and a piece of paper to write down affirmations of self-love.

- **Method**: Anoint the rose quartz with lavender oil. Write down affirmations of self-love and acceptance on the paper. Hold the rose quartz and recite these affirmations, allowing their energy to resonate within your heart. Visualize a loving, pink light enveloping you, emanating from the stone.
- **Conclusion**: Keep the stone and the affirmations in a place where you will see them daily as a reminder of your inherent worth and self-love.

3. **"Path of Growth" Introspection Ritual**
   - **Purpose**: To facilitate personal growth and understanding of one's journey.
   - **Materials**: A green candle (for growth), a journal, and a quiet space for contemplation.
   - **Method**: Light the green candle and sit in a reflective state. Consider the path you've walked, the lessons you've learned, and how they have shaped you. Write in your journal the insights and realizations that come to you during this introspection.
   - **Conclusion**: After you finish writing, read through your entries, acknowledging your journey and growth. Extinguish the candle with gratitude for the journey thus far and excitement for the path ahead.

These spells and rituals are designed not just to provide temporary insights but to foster a continuous process of self-discovery and growth. By engaging in regular self-reflection and inner work, you can develop a deeper understanding of yourself, which will, in turn, enrich and strengthen your relationships. Remember, the journey towards personal growth is ongoing, and each step forward enriches not just yourself but your connections with others.

Rituals for Relationship Longevity

A lasting relationship requires more than just initial chemistry and shared interests. It demands ongoing effort, mutual growth, and continuous nurturing. This section introduces three long-term rituals and three practices designed to maintain the health and longevity of a relationship. These rituals and practices focus on reinforcing the bonds of love, ensuring that the relationship continues to thrive and evolve over time.

Long-Term Relationship Rituals

1. **“Eternal Flame” Renewal Ritual**
   - **Purpose**: To periodically renew commitment and love in the relationship.
   - **Materials**: Two intertwined candles (representing partnership), rose oil (for love), and a piece of paper to write renewed vows or affirmations.
   - **Method**: Annually, on a significant date (like an anniversary), light the intertwined candles. Anoint them with rose oil, symbolizing the continuous nourishment of love. Write down renewed vows or affirmations for each other, focusing on your commitment and aspirations for the coming year.
   - **Conclusion**: Read your vows or affirmations aloud to each other, then let the candles burn down completely, symbolizing the enduring nature of your love.

2. **"Harvest of Happiness" Gratitude Jar**
    - **Purpose**: To cultivate and acknowledge the joy and happiness in the relationship.
    - **Materials**: A jar, small pieces of paper, and a pen.
    - **Method**: Throughout the year, both partners should write down moments of happiness, gratitude, and love experienced together on the pieces of paper, placing them in the jar. These can be small moments like a shared joke, a supportive gesture, or a special occasion.
    - **Conclusion**: At the end of the year, open the jar and read these moments together, celebrating the love and joy shared throughout the year.

3. **"Circle of Growth" Annual Ritual**
    - **Purpose**: To reflect on and celebrate the growth both partners have experienced over the year.
    - **Materials**: A green candle (for growth), a shared journal, and a quiet, comfortable space.
    - **Method**: Once a year, light the green candle, and take turns sharing how each partner has grown, both individually and together. Record these reflections in the shared journal, acknowledging challenges overcome and milestones achieved.
    - **Conclusion**: Conclude the ritual with a toast or a shared activity that holds significance to both partners, celebrating another year of growth and love.

Practices for Relationship Maintenance

1. **Regular Relationship Check-ins**: Schedule regular, intentional conversations to check in with each other. Discuss

any current issues, future plans, and feelings about the relationship.

2. **Shared Goals and Projects**: Work on setting and achieving goals together, whether they're short-term projects or long-term aspirations. This practice fosters teamwork and a shared sense of purpose.
3. **Traditions and Shared Rituals**: Establish your own traditions and rituals, whether it's a weekly date night, an annual vacation, or a simple nightly routine. These create shared experiences and memories that strengthen the bond.

These rituals and practices are designed to ensure that the relationship remains vibrant, strong, and deeply connected through the years. They acknowledge that love is a living, evolving entity that requires care, attention, and dedication. By regularly engaging in these rituals and practices, couples can create a foundation of love and mutual respect that stands the test of time.

Transforming Challenges into Growth

Transforming challenges in a relationship into opportunities for growth is an essential skill that can significantly strengthen the bond between partners. In any relationship, challenges are inevitable. They can range from minor disagreements to major conflicts, differing life goals, or external stressors. However, rather than viewing these challenges as roadblocks, they can be seen as catalysts for personal and mutual growth. This transformation requires a shift in perspective, open communication, and a commitment to learning and evolving together.

Firstly, understanding that challenges are a natural part of any relationship is crucial. They are not necessarily indicators of incompatibility or failure. Instead, they present a unique opportunity to deepen understanding, empathy, and connection. When faced with a challenge, it's important to approach it with a mindset of curiosity and openness, rather than defensiveness or blame. This approach allows both partners to explore the underlying issues, express their feelings and needs, and understand each other's perspectives.

Open and honest communication is the cornerstone of transforming relationship challenges into growth. It involves actively listening to each other, expressing thoughts and feelings without judgment, and seeking to understand before being understood. Effective communication also means discussing expectations, fears, and desires openly. It's about creating a safe space where both partners feel heard, valued, and understood.

Another key aspect is the willingness to self-reflect and take responsibility for one's contributions to the challenges. This means acknowledging personal flaws, triggers, and past experiences that may influence current behaviors and reactions. It involves a continuous process of self-awareness and self-improvement. By working on oneself, an individual not only enhances their own life but also brings a healthier self to the relationship.

Moreover, viewing challenges as a joint venture can foster a stronger partnership. It's about working together to find solutions, compromises, and ways to support each other. This collaborative approach reinforces the idea that both partners are on the same team, with common goals and shared commitments. It also involves recognizing and respecting differences, understanding that each partner brings unique strengths and perspectives to the relationship.

Adopting a growth mindset in a relationship means embracing change and being open to learning and evolving both individually and as a couple. It's about seeing challenges as opportunities to learn more about each other, develop new skills, and grow stronger together. This mindset encourages resilience, flexibility, and a willingness to adapt.

Furthermore, it's important to celebrate progress and growth. Acknowledging and appreciating how challenges have been navigated and what has been learned can be incredibly affirming and motivating. It reinforces the bond and provides a sense of achievement and optimism for the future.

In addition, seeking external support when needed can be invaluable in transforming challenges into growth. This may involve consulting with relationship counselors, therapists, or trusted mentors who can provide guidance, mediate conflicts, and offer new perspectives. They can also teach effective communication and problem-solving strategies that can be applied in the relationship.

Finally, fostering a sense of gratitude and focusing on the positive aspects of the relationship can help in weathering challenges. It's about appreciating each other's efforts, celebrating the love shared, and reminding oneself of the reasons why the relationship is valued. This positive focus can provide the strength and motivation needed to navigate difficult times together.

Transforming challenges into growth opportunities in a relationship is a multifaceted process that requires communication, self-reflection, collaboration, and a growth mindset. It involves seeing challenges not as threats but as chances to deepen understanding, strengthen the bond, and evolve as individuals and as a couple. By embracing this approach, partners can build a resilient, fulfilling, and enduring relationship that thrives on mutual growth and shared journeys.

Navigating the Complexities of Love

In summarizing this chapter, it's clear that magic, when approached with wisdom, respect, and ethical consideration, can be an incredibly supportive tool in navigating the complexities of love. It provides a unique lens through which we can view and enhance our relationships, allowing us to delve deeper into the realms of emotional connection and mutual understanding. The spells and rituals outlined in this chapter are not just tools for immediate solutions but are pathways to greater self-awareness, enhanced communication, and a strengthened bond with our partners.

The journey of love is multifaceted, often filled with as many challenges as there are moments of joy. Magic serves as a guide and companion on this journey, offering ways to harmonize energies, resolve conflicts, and celebrate the beauty of love in all its forms. It encourages us to see beyond the superficial and to understand the profound energetic interplay that underlies our relationships. By aligning our intentions with actions, words with emotions, and desires with ethical considerations, we can create a love that is not only magical in its essence but grounded in mutual respect and understanding.

The power of love magic lies in its ability to transform, heal, and elevate. From simple spells to elaborate rituals, each practice is a step towards understanding the deeper facets of love and the role we play in nurturing it. Whether it's through enhancing communication, reigniting passion, or fostering self-love, each magical practice offers a valuable lesson in the art of love. These lessons, when internalized and practiced with care, can lead to profound personal growth and a more fulfilling love life.

Moreover, this chapter reminds us that the true magic of love lies within us. It's in our ability to give and receive love, to grow and learn from our relationships, and to face challenges with courage and grace. The spells and rituals are simply tools to help us tap into this innate magic, guiding us towards a more harmonious and fulfilling experience of love.

As we close this chapter, it's important to remember that love magic is a journey, not a destination. It's an ongoing process of discovery, learning, and growth. With each spell cast and ritual performed, we open ourselves up to new possibilities of love and connection. We learn to navigate love's challenges not just with magical tools but with wisdom, empathy, and a deep respect for the sacred bond we share with others. In this way, magic becomes more than a practice; it becomes a transformative force in our journey of love.

CHAPTER 11.

REFLECTIONS AND FUTURE PATHWAYS IN LOVE MAGIC

As we reach the conclusion of this book, it's the moment to reflect on the journey we've embarked upon together. Through the pages of this book, we've traversed a path rich with ancient wisdom, practical spells, and transformative insights, all dedicated to the art of love magic. This journey, though unique for each reader, has been a shared adventure in discovering the profound ways in which magic can influence and enhance our experience of love.

From the foundational principles of love magic to the detailed rituals and spells, we've delved into the very heart of what it means to weave magic into our romantic lives. We've learned about the importance of self-love as the bedrock of any magical practice, understanding that the love we nurture within ourselves sets the tone for the love we attract and radiate. Our exploration has also guided us through the ethical considerations essential to any practice, ensuring that our magical workings are not only effective but also respectful and harmonious.

We've ventured through a diverse range of spells and rituals, each designed to tap into different aspects of love – from attracting new love and rekindling romance to deepening existing relationships and fostering self-acceptance. Alongside these spells, we've discussed the magical properties of various ingredients, tools, and techniques, equipping you with the knowledge to craft your own love-enhancing potions, elixirs, and rituals.

Throughout this journey, we've emphasized the importance of intention, energy, and balance in our practices. We've explored how the energy we emit and the intentions we set play a crucial role in shaping our experiences in love and relationships. By maintaining a balance between giving and receiving love, and between our individuality and our connections with others, we've learned to create harmonious and fulfilling relationships.

This book has also invited you to reflect on your personal journey with love magic. Through real-life stories, testimonials, and case studies, we've seen the transformative power of love magic in action – how it can heal, empower, and bring joy. These stories have served as both inspiration and affirmation of the profound impact that love magic can have on our lives.

It's important to remember that the journey with love magic doesn't end here. The pages within this book are just the beginning. Love magic is a lifelong exploration, an ever-evolving practice that grows and changes with you. The future of your journey with love magic is a canvas awaiting your creative touch, filled with endless possibilities and opportunities for growth, discovery, and magical experiences.

This journey through love magic has been an invitation to open your heart to the many ways love can manifest in your life. It's been a journey of empowerment, healing, and deep connection – not just with others, but with the magic contained within you. As you continue to walk your path, may you carry with you the wisdom, insights, and spells you've gathered, weaving them into your life with love, intention, and magic.

Success Stories and Testimonials

Reflecting on the transformative power of love magic, I am reminded of the many individuals I've encountered who have shared their success stories and testimonials. These narratives not only testify to the effectiveness of love magic but also offer inspiration and hope.

Let me share with you a few stories that stand out in my memory, each a testament to the profound impact that love magic can have.

Marian's Rekindled Romance: Marian was a woman in her late thirties who felt the spark in her marriage fading. Despite her deep love for her husband, their connection had grown stale over the years. Desperate to rekindle the passion, Marian turned to love magic. She performed a simple candle ritual, focusing her intentions on reigniting the flame of love and passion in her relationship. Over the following weeks, she noticed a gradual but unmistakable change. Conversations flowed more freely, laughter returned, and the intimacy they once shared reemerged stronger than before. Marian's story is a beautiful reminder of how love magic can breathe new life into relationships.

Leo's Journey to Self-Love: Leo's story is particularly close to my heart. He struggled with self-esteem issues and found it hard to believe that he was worthy of love. After attending one of my workshops, he started incorporating self-love affirmations and mirror work into his daily routine. Gradually, Leo began to see himself in a new light. He grew more confident and started attracting positive relationships into his life. His transformation was a powerful example of how love magic can start from within and radiate outwards.

Ava's Long-Awaited Love: Ava had been single for many years and longed to find a meaningful relationship. She decided to try a love attraction spell, aligning her energies with the universe to draw love into her life. She crafted a personal sigil and carried it with her, believing deeply in its power. To her delight, within a few months, she met someone who resonated with her on every level. They shared interests, values, and a deep emotional connection. Ava's story is a testament to the power of love magic in attracting the right person at the right time.

Ethan and Mia's Harmonized Relationship: Ethan and Mia's relationship was plagued with misunderstandings and disagreements. They turned to love magic as a last resort, performing a harmony spell together. The ritual involved meditations and chanting, focusing on balancing their energies and enhancing communication. To their amazement, their relationship transformed. They learned to listen to each other and resolve conflicts with understanding and love. Their story is a beautiful example of how love magic can harmonize and strengthen a relationship.

Each of these stories shares a common thread – the power of love magic to bring about positive change. Whether it's reigniting lost passion, fostering self-love, attracting new love, or harmonizing existing relationships, the magic of love is a potent force. These testimonials affirm the transformative power of the practices and rituals shared in this book. As a practitioner and teacher of love magic, witnessing these transformations has been incredibly rewarding. It reinforces my belief in the power of intention, energy, and the magic of love. These stories are just a few examples of the many lives touched and changed by love magic, and I hope they inspire you to explore and experience its wonders in your own life.

Lessons Learned and Insights Gained

Through my years of delving into this magical world, I've learned lessons that are both profound and practical, shaping my understanding of love, magic, and the intertwining of the two.

One of the most crucial lessons I've learned is the importance of patience. Love magic is not about instant gratification or quick fixes. It's a subtle art that works in harmony with the natural rhythms of the universe. Just as a gardener plants seeds and patiently waits for them to grow, so must we plant our intentions and give them time to manifest. This patience is not passive; it's an active engagement with our intentions, nurturing them with hope and belief.

Another key insight is the power of intention. Our intentions are the heart of our magic – they are the seeds from which our magical practices grow. I've seen how focused, clear intentions create more potent and effective spells, while scattered or uncertain intentions lead to less satisfactory outcomes. Intention is the soul's true voice, and in love magic, it's imperative to align our spells and rituals with the truest desires of our heart.

Ethical considerations are paramount in love magic. Over the years, I've witnessed how spells cast with pure intentions and respect for free will lead to the most positive and harm-free outcomes. Conversely, attempts to manipulate or control often backfire, causing more harm than good. Love magic taught me that the most powerful magic is that which honors the autonomy and spirit of all involved.

The journey with love magic is a path of continuous learning. There is always more to discover, more to explore. I encourage you, as a reader and practitioner, to view love magic as an endless horizon of growth and exploration. Expand your knowledge through books, courses, and workshops. Engage with communities of fellow practitioners to share experiences and learn from each other. Experiment with different spells and rituals, and observe how they resonate with you.

Remember, love magic evolves as you do. As your understanding deepens, so will your practice. Embrace the changes in your magical journey just as you embrace changes in life and love. Allow your practice to reflect your growing wisdom, your expanding heart, and your deepening connection with the magic that surrounds us.

The Future of Love Magic

In my journey with love magic, I've witnessed a fascinating evolution, a blending of age-old rituals with the pulse of modern life. This fusion promises a future where love magic continues to grow, adapt, and thrive, embracing new trends, techniques, and even technology.

One emerging trend in love magic is the integration of modern psychological insights with traditional spellcasting. As our understanding of the human psyche deepens, so does our ability to craft spells and rituals that not only attract love but also foster emotional healing and growth. This integration offers a more holistic approach to love magic, one that addresses the complexities of modern relationships and personal well-being.

Another exciting development is the use of technology in love magic. While this may seem like a departure from traditional practices, it's simply another tool in our magical toolbox. From online rituals connecting practitioners across the globe to digital grimoires and apps that help track moon phases and planetary alignments, technology is opening up new possibilities for connection, learning, and practice.

In addition to technology, there's a growing interest in incorporating eco-friendly and sustainable practices into love magic. As we become more conscious of our impact on the planet, this awareness is reflected in our magical practices. Using locally sourced, ethical ingredients in spells and potions, and focusing on rituals that honor and protect nature, are ways love magic can contribute to the wellbeing of our planet.

The future of love magic also lies in its continued diversification and inclusivity. Love in all its forms – across different cultures, identities, and expressions – is finding a place in modern love magic practices. This inclusivity not only enriches the tapestry of love magic but also makes it more accessible and relevant to a wider range of people.

Emerging techniques in love magic are also incorporating elements from other spiritual practices. For instance, the use of mindfulness and meditation in spellcasting, or integrating concepts from Reiki and energy healing into love rituals, are ways practitioners are expanding the boundaries of traditional love magic.

As we look to the future, it's clear that love magic is not a static art; it's a living, breathing practice that grows and changes with time. It adapts to the needs and understanding of each generation, yet retains its core essence – the harnessing of magical energies to enrich our experience of love.

In this continuous evolution, one thing remains constant – the power of love as the driving force behind our magical endeavors. Whether through ancient rituals or modern adaptations, the future of love magic holds limitless possibilities. It invites us to be creative, to be open-minded, and to continue exploring the depths and heights of magical love.

Fostering a Community of Love Magicians

As a practitioner who has walked this path for years, I have come to realize the immense value of connecting with fellow practitioners. Through vibrant online communities, local groups, workshops and festivals these connections serve not just as a source of knowledge and inspiration, but also as a reminder that we are part of a larger, magical tapestry.

The digital age has blessed us with the ability to connect with like-minded individuals from across the globe. Online forums, social media groups, and virtual workshops have created a thriving network of love magicians, each sharing their unique insights, experiences, and practices. These platforms offer a space to exchange ideas, seek advice, and find support. They allow us to share our love spells, successes, challenges, and learnings, fostering a sense of belonging and mutual growth.

Local communities and groups provide a more tangible connection. Here, in the warmth of physical presence, love magicians can engage in rituals, celebrate festivals, and participate in workshops together. Such gatherings are a profound way to experience the collective energy of love magic. They offer a space for personal interaction, mentorship, and the kind of magic that arises from shared experiences and rituals.

Participating in workshops, whether online or in person, is another enriching way to deepen our practice. Workshops led by experienced practitioners offer valuable insights into the nuances of love magic. They provide a structured learning environment where one can acquire new skills, understand different perspectives, and refine their practice. Furthermore, they often serve as a catalyst for personal transformation, as they encourage introspection, experimentation, and the exploration of new magical frontiers.

The beauty of fostering a community in love magic lies in its diversity. Each practitioner brings their own experiences, cultural backgrounds, and personal energies to the group. This diversity enriches the community, offering a mosaic of magical practices and perspectives. It reminds us that love magic, in all its forms, is a universal language, transcending boundaries and uniting us in our common pursuit of understanding, harnessing, and celebrating love.

These communities, both virtual and physical, also play a crucial role in preserving the traditions of love magic while nurturing its evolution. They act as custodians of ancient wisdom and incubators for new ideas. In these gatherings, the old and the new, the traditional and the innovative, come together, weaving a rich tapestry of magical practice.

As we conclude this journey, I ask you to explore and seek out these communities. Engage with fellow practitioners, share your stories, learn from others, and contribute your own wisdom. Remember, while the practice of love magic is deeply personal, it also thrives in shared experiences and collective energies.

Fostering a community of love magicians is more than just forming connections; it's about building a supportive network that celebrates love in all its forms. It's about contributing to a collective repository of knowledge and experience that enriches not just our individual practices, but the entire field of love magic.

Intentions for the Future

In my years of embracing the mystical path of love magic, I've learned that the intentions we set are not just mere wishes; they are powerful declarations that shape our magical journey and influence the energies we attract.

In setting intentions for your future in love magic, I encourage you to dream big. Let your heart and soul speak their deepest desires. Whether it's finding a soulmate, nurturing existing relationships, or embarking on a journey of self-love, allow your intentions to be as boundless as your dreams. Remember, we are limited only by the breadth of our imagination and the strength of our belief.

Begin by reflecting on what you truly seek in your journey of love magic. Is it deeper connections, a more profound understanding of love, or the discovery of uncharted magical territories? Whatever it may be, hold these aspirations at the center of your heart as you set your intentions. Visualize your future in love magic as a vibrant tapestry, woven with the threads of your deepest desires and aspirations.

Stay open to the possibilities that love magic can bring. The path of magic is ever-evolving, full of surprises and transformative experiences. Embrace the unknown with an open heart, trusting that the universe will guide you toward experiences that foster growth, wisdom, and fulfillment in love.

As you set your intentions, infuse them with positivity and clarity. Be specific about what you wish to attract or achieve, but also remain flexible, allowing the magic to unfold in its unique way. The journey of love magic is as much about the destination as it is about the journey itself – a journey of discovery, learning, and evolution.

Incorporate rituals or practices that resonate with you as you set these intentions. It could be a simple candle ritual under the moonlight, crafting a vision board adorned with symbols of love, or writing your intentions in a journal to solidify them. These acts of magic serve as powerful affirmations, sending your desires into the universe and attracting the energies that align with them.

As you venture forward, nurture your intentions with regular reflection and reevaluation. Love magic is dynamic, and as you grow and evolve, so might your desires and goals. Allow your intentions to evolve with you, adapting to the changing landscapes of your heart and life.

Final Thoughts

As we now bring our journey through the pages of this book to a close, I find myself reflecting on the transformative power of love magic and the incredible journey it has been for each one of us. Love, in all its forms, is a force that shapes our lives, our dreams, and our very existence. Through love magic, we have explored the depths of our hearts, uncovered hidden strengths, and tapped into a wellspring of hope and possibility.

I want to leave you with some words of encouragement and inspiration, for your journey with love magic is just beginning. Remember, the path of magic is as unique as the individual who walks it. It is a path of discovery, growth, and profound transformation. As you continue to explore love magic, let your heart be your guide, let your intuition light your way, and let your passion for love and life fuel your individual journey.

You possess an inner strength, a magical essence that is only yours. Embrace it. Nurture it. Let it shine brightly as you weave your spells and craft your rituals. The magic within you is powerful and boundless; it can move mountains, cross seas, and reach the farthest stars. It can also heal wounds, bridge gaps, and create enduring bonds of love and affection.

As you journey forward, do so with hope and courage. Hope for the love you desire and deserve, and the courage to pursue it with an open heart. The road may sometimes be uncertain, and challenges may arise, but remember, it is through these experiences that we grow the most. Each step you take is a step toward becoming the most authentic and empowered version of yourself.

Never lose sight of the magic within you. It is the spark that ignites your spells, the intuition that guides your rituals, and the love that fills your heart. It is your connection to the ancient and timeless art of magic, a lineage that spans centuries and cultures, connecting us all in the universal pursuit of love and connection.

In closing, I offer you these final words of encouragement: Continue your journey with an open heart and an open mind. Embark on a journey of joy, wonder, and profound transformation. Believe in love, for it is the most potent force in the universe. As you walk the path of love magic, you are not alone. You are part of a community of seekers, dreamers, and magicians, each on their own journey, but all united in the pursuit of love's infinite magic.

May your journey be filled with bright blessings, deep fulfillment, and endless discovery. May it bring you closer to the true essence of love, in all its forms, and may it empower you to live a life filled with love, joy, and happiness. Go forward with hope, courage, and a deep sense of purpose, for the magic of love is within you, around you, and always with you.

Blessed be.

Resources

Books and Literature

1. **"The Book of Shadows" by Gerald Gardner** - Often considered the foundational text for modern Wicca, this book contains a collection of magical practices, spells, and rituals. Gardner's work is seminal in the neo-pagan and witchcraft communities, providing insights into the rituals and beliefs that form the basis of many contemporary magical practices.
2. **"Arbatel: Concerning the Magic of Ancients"** - This mysterious grimoire, first published in 1575, is a significant work in the history of Western occultism. It focuses on the positive and spiritual aspects of magic, with a particular emphasis on the personal relationship between the practitioner and the divine. Despite its age, the wisdom within "Arbatel" remains influential in modern magical traditions.
3. **"The Magus, or Celestial Intelligencer" by Francis Barrett** - First published in 1801, this comprehensive handbook on occult and magical theory and practice was influential in 19th-century magical circles. Barrett compiles an extensive range of esoteric material, including information on natural magic, alchemy, talismanic magic, and the Kabbalah, making it a treasure trove for practitioners interested in exploring the depths of historical magical practices.

Online Platforms and Websites

1. The Lost Book Project (www.TheLostBookProject.com) – A bookstore specialising in rare, out-of-print books on esoteric subjects.

2. The Hoodwitch (www.thehoodwitch.com) – Modern witchcraft advice, focusing on self-care and spirituality.
3. Llewellyn Worldwide (www.llewellyn.com) – A leading publisher of books on witchcraft and magic, with a vast online resource section.

Podcasts and Audio Resources

1. "Magic and the Law of Attraction" – Delving into various aspects of magic, including love spells.
2. "The Witch Wave" – Hosted by Pam Grossman, exploring magical practices and contemporary practitioners.

Video Channels

1. Harmony Nice – Discusses various aspects of Wicca, witchcraft, and spellcasting.
2. The Witch of Wonderlust – Tutorials and discussions on magical practices including love magic.

Apps and Digital Tools

1. Labyrinthos Academy – Teaches tarot reading, essential for love divination.
2. Moon Calendar – Tracks moon phases, essential for timing love spells and rituals.

Workshops and Courses

1. Local Witchcraft Workshops – Check for local workshops or gatherings for practical learning.
2. Online Platforms like Udemy or Coursera – Often host courses on witchcraft and related subjects.

Communities and Forums

1. Reddit Witchcraft Community (r/witchcraft) – A forum for discussing witchcraft, including love magic.
2. The Magicka School (www.magickaschool.com) – Offers courses and a community forum for practitioners.

About This Author

Hazel Evermore, a name that has become synonymous with the mystical and the magical, is more than just an author; she is a guardian of ancient wisdom and a beacon for those seeking to connect with the deeper mysteries of love magic. Hailing from the picturesque landscapes of the United Kingdom, Hazel's journey into the realm of witchcraft began over two decades ago, rooted in a profound fascination with the natural world and its hidden energies.

Her path has been one of continuous exploration and discovery, marked by a deep commitment to understanding the intricate tapestries of magic and its harmonious dance with nature. Hazel's expertise is not just academic; it is a lived experience, a journey that has taken her from the misty shores of her homeland to the sacred sites of ancient magic around the world.

A prolific writer, Hazel's works are a reflection of her passion for the craft and her desire to share this love with a broader audience. Her writings are not just collections of spells and rituals; they are invitations to embark on a transformative journey, to explore the depths of one's soul and the boundless possibilities of the heart.

Hazel's approach to magic is deeply rooted in ethics and a profound respect for the free will of all beings. Her teachings emphasize the importance of personal growth, self-discovery, and the ethical considerations that come with wielding magical power. This approach has not only earned her respect within the witchcraft community but has also made her a beloved figure among those new to the path.

Her accolades include numerous awards and features in prestigious publications, but perhaps her most significant achievement is the impact she has had on the lives of her readers and fellow practitioners. Through her work, Hazel has created a legacy that transcends the written word, one that inspires and empowers, guiding many to find their own magic within.

As you delve into the pages of her latest work, "101 Powerful Love Spells That Work," you are not just reading a book; you are entering Hazel Evermore's world, a place where magic is real, love is boundless, and every spell is a step closer to the true essence of your heart.

Printed in Dunstable, United Kingdom

79444679R00268